Praise for

ıntegral
cıty
ınquıry & actıon

Integral City Inquiry and Action continues Marilyn Hamilton's (and her colleagues') rather unique exploration into the application and extension of Integral Metatheory (and related disciplines) into the entire urban landscape and all of its dimensions, aspects, functions, and qualities. The modern city is the most complex social structure that exists, as far as we know, anywhere in the universe, and as such it is made to order for an Integral approach. This is exactly what Marilyn and her team do. The results are illuminating, novel, insightful, extremely useful and urgently needed. What *Integral City* tells us, among numerous important specific insights, is that any approach that is less comprehensive or less integral is doomed to failure, because only an integrally pluralistic theory and practice will cover all the truly important bases. These important bases are carefully elucidated in 16 chapters, each one covering a significant ingredient of a genuinely integral approach to city planning, living, exploring, discovering, applying. My congratulations to the authors for another profound, timely, and superb work!

— **Ken Wilber**, Philosopher, Integral Theorist, Author: *The Integral Vision, Sex Ecology & Spirituality, Integral Psychology, A Brief History of Everything*

The unusual and captivating hero of this book is the city. Not an inert mass of buildings, but a collective, a hive, a holarchy that brings people and processes of inquiry together in action. This human centered approach to systems of a city offers well chosen "sticky" concepts, grounded in practice and expressed with a simplicity that belies their complexity. What's more, the book offers tons of great questions and grounded frameworks that help us articulate *Gaia's reflective capacity*. It's a resource for action researchers in the field of urban planning and perhaps for all whole systems/integration oriented professionals.

— **Hilary Bradbury**, PhD, Professor (OHSU), Editor Handb̶o̶o̶k̶ ̶o̶f̶ Re search & Action Research Journa̶l̶

After urban planning, what's plan B? Given the scale, complexity and interdependencies of our global crises, 20th century urban plans and solutions are simply inadequate. This leading edge and thoroughly practical contribution to inquiry and impact on the crucial dilemmas faced by cities today, is a gift to next generation urban change workers. It's elegant and accessible structure, fresh models and integrating tools are the product of iterative testing over many years in contexts of place-based yet globally shared challenges faced by 21st century architects, planners, city managers, developers, designers, communities, investors and activists.

— **Lisa Norton**, Professor of Design Leadership and Associate Dean, School of Design Strategies, Parsons School of Design, New York, NY

Integral City Inquiry and Action is a complex compendium of ideas and processes to bring about a new vision of the city. This approach is not about having one singular vision of our city win out, but, rather, the on-the-ground methods for achieving the illusive integration of many voices today's cities seek. It's about measuring and monitoring the performance of cities, yes—and also about the emerging form and order cities will take as expressions of designing them for our human experiences and expressing our collective values. The methods here tell us how to move beyond participatory design, how to transcend the gridlock of competitive pluralism, and how to evolve the collective urban consciousness to create the city we want. That city will manifest and take shape to solve climate change, to nurture our collective welfare, to connect us to nature and beauty, and to be a crucible for individuals' potentials.

— **Prof. Mark DeKay**, author of *Integral Sustainable Design: Transformative perspectives*, Professor of Architecture, Director of Graduate Studies, College of Architecture and Design, University of Tennessee, Knoxville.

Integral practitioners will benefit from this book by seeing concrete practices they can do to transform integral theory into integral action. City specialists will benefit from finally having a comprehensive map and set of methodologies that can engage the many crucial dimensions of the city in an integrative way.

— **Sean Esbjörn-Hargens** PhD, Author *Integral Ecology: Uniting Multiple Perspectives on the Natural World*, Coauthor *Metatheory for the Twenty-First Century*, Founder and Chief Design Officer MetaIntegral Associates

We are living in a fast-paced mode toward uncertain futures. Dr. Marilyn Hamilton, and her colleagues teach us how to converge the city's four voices +1 toward a common superordinate goal to evolve in an integral and harmonious way. This book is what we were expecting in Mexico and Latin America, as a very comprehensive practitioner's handbook, to inquire about current realities and to design and build better futures for our highly diverse cities. I consider this research as a bright awakening call for measurable actions. It shows us the map of how to activate local intelligence and resources in an ongoing change needed for any human hive (aka city).

— **Roberto Bonilla,** Organization Co-pilot and Social Innovator at Novarum Innovation Lab, Leon, Mexico

In the process of lifelong learning, sharing and caring we need "evolutionary intelligences for the human hive" in the integral city. This book gives us not only the 'top down' view but also from the 'bottom up' practical point of view and easy to understand examples about real life by city activators.

— **Cees Donkers**, Urban Designer (Retired), City of Eindhoven, Netherlands

This is a 'how to' book for practitioners. From preparing yourself spiritually and attaining a state of integrated connectedness with fellow practitioners to practical on-the-ground community projects, this is a book about making a difference. It covers all the elements necessary not only for sustainable development of the city but also to give it enhanced life and nurture its well-being.

— **Keith E Rice** – Sociopsychologist, Master Practitioner, Professional Guild of NLP, York, UK

This book is truly a feast of insight, innovation and simplicity on the other side of urban complexity.... The bottom line is that if you feel in over your head regarding catalyzing cities to thrive, then upgrade not only your head but also your heart and skills by reading and using this book.

— **Barrett C. Brown**, PhD, Executive Coach and Author of *The Future of Leadership for Conscious Capitalism*

The poetry in this book is palpable and invisible. Maybe this is how Rumi writes when reborn as a designer, architect, or metaphorical bee herder … through, this workbook on creating happy, healthy cities, there is a fragrance woven of joy, service, promise, affirmation, love…. This is truly a masterful intellectual, how-to mapping, of the greatest experiment human collectives have ever attempted. And, I finished the book… with that rising tide in my heart that says, "Maybe we really can be as great as this."

— **Tom Christensen**, Broker, Realtor, ABR, GRI, CRS, SRES, RECS, Editor, *Innovative Development, Developmental Innovations*

In what could only be described as an official desk reference for the design of the future of cites, Dr. Hamilton and her colleagues have penned, what I consider the most authoritative work on the subject…. Essential to this model of sustainable cities, is the placement of the community back at the center of all actions that empower family, personal development and human relationships to produce resilient institutions that can handle humanity's increasing challenges…and creates a system of distributed intelligence that empowers each one of us to have a voice in shaping the future of humanity.

— **Said E. Dawlabani**, Author, MEME*nomics, the Next Generation Economic System*

This is a comprehensive hands-on guide that connects up the dots so you can take as much of the city into account as possible—in your research, decision-making and interventions. A must for all those working in the cities of today's world.

— **Peter Merry**, Chief Innovation Officer, Ubiquity University

integral
city
inquiry & action

Designing Impact for the Human Hive

MARILYN HAMILTON

CONTRIBUTORS

Diana Claire Douglas, Beth Sanders, Alia Aurami, Cherie Beck, Joan Arnott, Linda Shore, Anne-Marie Voorhoeve, Alicia Stammer, Ellen van Dongen

This book is dedicated to the evolution of the Human Hive Mind,
Gaia's Reflective Organ.

CONTENTS

INTRODUCTION

INQUIRE. ACT. IMPACT.

When I am called to action for a city change project, I want to achieve impact that makes a difference to the well-being of generations to come. Like, how do we change the headline in my own city of Abbotsford, BC from the shocking declaration of, "Murder Capital of Canada" to "Youth Leadership Capital of Canada"? (Bolan, 2009)

Perhaps your interests are not quite as dramatic—but you want to re-energize your city center, inspire a thriving economy, eliminate homelessness, green the supply chain, or overcome gridlock?

I am a student of how human systems change, develop, and evolve. My career has taken me through the study and practices of developing individual adults (how to operate computer systems), leaders (how to manage global insurance brokers), teams (how to construct auto testing sites), organizations (how to supply an international hotel chain), sectors (how to merge regional credit unions), communities (how to engage multi-community support for walking-biking trails), and most recently, cities (how to craft visions and implement strategies for sustainability and resilience).

Not surprisingly, with this history of relationships and interactions, the filters I bring to look at the city arise from this spectrum of human systems development which has taught me that the patterns I observed at the individual scale, were repeating at the larger scales. Teams, who unfolded through the stages of "form, storm, norm, perform" (Tuckman & Jensen, 1977) were mirroring a similar process of developmental stages that the individuals who made them up undergo (D. Beck & Cowan, 1996; Graves, 2005; Kegan, 1994; Wilber, 2000a). Likewise, organizations cycled through lifecycle stages that reflected human system life patterns of "start-up, growth, go-go, maturity, prime, old age" (Adizes, 1999).

On an even larger (and more universal scale), I have learned that living systems of all species—including cities—seem to adapt to their environment by cycling through stages of "exploitation, conservation, breakdown, and redistribution" (Gunderson & Holling, 2002). As these cycles of development and adaptation continue, the systems tend to become more complex in their structure and relationships. A natural hierarchy of organizational complexity emerges that embodies and supports the purpose of the living systems. When we are trying to understand a city where murder happens or how leadership emerges, we can look around us in the city and see family hearths, kinship circles, power gangs, ordered bureaucracies, results-based companies, social safety enterprises, flexible biomimicry systems, and global networks, all designed to serve different purposes and functioning, like organs in a human being.

So I look at the city not just as a single living human system but a system that is made up of multiple human systems—individuals, families, clans, groups, workplaces, neighborhoods/communities. As such, the city is a special class of living system—it is a social system—where all the subsystems coexist and influence one another all the time as they function within an ecology of human systems.

Perhaps because my grandfather was a beekeeper, I visualize this whole system with a metaphor that seems easier to grasp; namely, that the city is the social habitat for humans just like the beehive is for bees. That's why I call the city "the human hive." The hive and the humans it holds are adapting and evolving together so that the city is as much in me and you (as an internal mental model we are usually not aware of), as we are in the city (as an external environment we inhabit every day). As a social system, we have a reciprocal relationship with each other and with the city as a whole. It both cares for us and makes us as we care for it and make it together.

A basic definition of a city then, is that it is a place that cares for us and a place that makes us as we care for it and make it.

However, you choose to care and make what matters to you in the city, in order to achieve impact that is deep, wide, clear, and high, you need to start with a question. Finding the right question is a more powerful guide for city change than an immediate answer. Asking the right question, with the right people in the room can set up the conditions to enable action that even transforms a habitat for murder into a habitat for youth leadership—sometimes remarkably quickly.

If you are an action-oriented problem solver like me, framing the right question can seem like a waste of time. But when I began to see the city as the human life "writ large," then I realized the city is a dynamic, integrally interconnected living system that functions because of how I (and all others in the city) think, act, relate, and create. Asking the right questions can help us discover the mental models that lie behind the assumptions that cause the problems we wish to solve—whether that be how to prevent murder or promote leadership.

My inquiry into what makes human systems develop capacities to care has been informed by my growing fascination for the beehive. What started as a useful metaphor to describe the human hive, has become a series of lessons in biomimicry from another species—the honey bee. For example, I have learned that somehow the honey bees have figured out how to care for themselves and their habitat (hive) in a way that not only sustains them (by producing 40 pounds of honey per year), but through their acts of pollination, impacts their eco-region to provide a renewable energy supply for the hive year after year. (Read more about this in *Chapter 4: Spiritual Communities to Serve Evolution of the Human Hive.*) On learning this story of resilience, Alexander Laszlo, a colleague of mine has asked, "The Earth knows what bees have to contribute to the Planet's well-being—what is it that humans contribute?" I reframed this startling question into a line of inquiry that relates to human purpose: What is the purpose of humans and their cities?

Then I heard James Lovelock, author of the Gaia Hypothesis (that the Earth herself is a living system) postulate that the contribution that humans make to Earth's well-being is as "Gaia's Reflective Organ." That amazing proposition caused me to speculate that the purpose of human hives (aka cities) might be to act as the planet's reflective organs, while individual humans and their variety of organizations are like cells and organelles (the subsystems that enable organs to function). A "Planet of Cities" then, might act as Earth's Reflective Organ System.

Therefore, one of my deepest inquiries regarding the capacity of cities to serve the planet's well-being has become, "what is the equivalent metric for the human hive (aka city) of the 40 pounds of honey for the beehive?" How can we create a double sustainability loop that ensures city survival at the same time that the city contributes to eco-regional survival—and even planetary survival?

As corollaries to these questions related to city purpose and metrics, I wonder if we can pose questions that help us to understand how the nest of city subsystems from individual and family through organizations and communities can sustain murder or leadership?

WHAT IS AN INTEGRAL CITY?

In pursuing these inquiries, over the last decade, I have found ways to experiment with designing and delivering a series of methods for my own and other cities, with an emerging community of practice and local core teams.

This book looks at the city as a human system. Its practical design guidance draws on the Integral City Systems that have evolved as we have tested this approach in the world. These inquiry systems attempt to know the city not just as a third-person object but also as a first-person experience and second-person relationship. Through the multiple "twists" of the quadrants where these persons can be located (see below) we push beyond inquiring "about" or acting "on" the city to inquiring and acting "with" and "as" the city. Such an approach is only possible when our inquiry is designed to enact our roles as Gaia's Reflective Organs, organelles, and cells (as discussed in *Chapter* 4).

An Integral City[1] brings together first, second, and third persons as the 4 Voices of the city—Citizens, Civil Society, Civic Managers, and Business—and

---

1   Book 1 in this series, ***Integral City: Evolutionary Intelligences for the Human Hive*** explains in detail the 12 Intelligences of an Integral City and the 4 maps we use in this Book 2. Map 5 is explained in the article by (Hamilton, 2012a) and in Chapter 1 of Book 3, forthcoming. All five maps are presented in this Book 2 in *Appendix B: Integral City Maps (1–5)*.

builds on their intrinsic qualities to create optimal conditions for human innovation, emergence, and eco-regional resilience. Together with the 4 Voices, we have developed 5 maps of the Integral City (see *Appendix* B) each of which shapeshifts to reveal key aspects of the city. At the risk of boring the reader with the technicalities of Map 1, we offer this explanation (in the shaded inset below) as a basic foundation for understanding what an Integral City is.

FOUNDATIONS FOR UNDERSTANDING INTEGRAL CITY

Map 1 (in Figure 1 and *Appendix* A: *Integral Quadrants*) uses 4 quadrants and 8 levels[2] to capture the archetypal roots of the Integral City and its 4 Voices:

1. Upper Left (UL): **individual first person "I"** represents the interior/internal/subjective/intangible qualities.

2. Lower Left (LL): **collective second person "We/You"** represents the interior/internal/intersubjective/intangible qualities.

3. Upper Right (UR): **individual third person "It"** represents the exterior/ external/objective/tangible qualities.

4. Lower Right (LR): **collective third person "Its"** represents the exterior/ external/interobjective/tangible qualities.

Map 1 reveals how the interplay of diverse qualities in the city naturally creates energies that arise from the tensions between them. The sets of opposites align along vectors we call Perspectives, Realities, and Worldviews.

Perspectives (on the vertical vector) include:

- I vs WE
- IT vs ITS

Realities (on the horizontal vector) include:

- Intentional vs Bio-physical
- Cultural vs Social

---

2   This framework is adapted from the extensive work of Beck and Wilber (D. Beck & Cowan, 1996; Wilber, 1995, 1996, 2000a, 2000b, 2007).

Worldviews/Values Systems (on the diagonal vector in 8 Levels) include:

- Two levels each of "I and We" for Worldviews at increasing levels of complexity: Traditional, Modern, Post-Modern, Integral

Map 1 has both a center (symbolized as the spiral of evolutionary impulse) and a boundary that captures the concentration of the energy of individual humans and the diffusion of this energy across the many groups of humans in the city such as families, workplaces, and neighbourhoods.

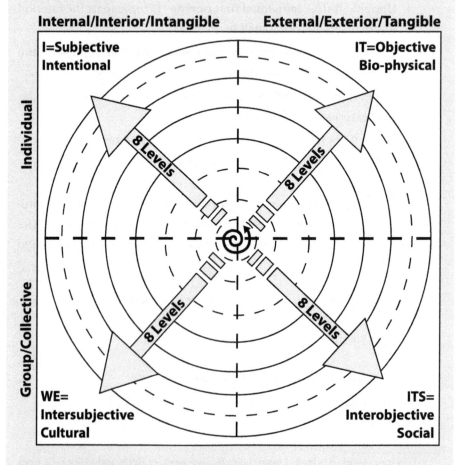

Figure 1: Integral City Map 1– 4 Quadrants, 8 Levels

Map 1 appears very ordered and stable, but it actually embeds competitive tensions that exist between and along all these vectors. Clare Graves had the insight that the human species has evolved a survival strategy, that keeps it alternately swinging between the individuated "Express Self" poles of the vectors (where innovation often occurs) and the collective "Sacrifice Self" poles (where shared governance can emerge).

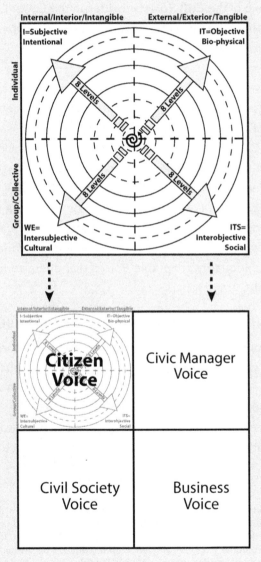

Figure 2: 4 City Voices in the City as a Whole

While Map 1 locates the vectors for any individual in the city, this map is a fractal pattern of reality (one that applies at many scales) that can be applied to each of the 4 Voices and can also locate the 4 Voices as a fractal pattern in the city as a whole (see Figure 2).

- The Voice of the **Citizen** resides in the upper left.
- The Voice of the **Civil Society** resides in the Lower Left.
- The Voice of the **Civic Manager** resides in the Upper Right.
- The Voice of **Business** resides in the Lower Right.

Map 1 reveals a richly polarized system where Voices both require one another to strengthen their own anchor of expression and also constantly change one another in order for the whole city system to survive (for example, Citizen revolts in cities in the Middle East and United States at time of writing are challenging the roles of Civic Managers in city hall, police, and justice systems; Civil Society is defying Business practices in the banking sector; Business appears to be exporting Citizen jobs to other global locations; and Civic Managers struggle with a multiplicity of Citizen expectations deriving from different cultural worldviews). Map 1 shows the evolutionarily adaptable Voices that energize human systems at the city scale.

PLACECARING ENABLES PLACEMAKING AND WELL-BEING

The 4 Voices of the city have inspired the frameworks and templates we share, in this book's 16 chapters, structured into a 4-quadrant process that explores Placecaring as the left-hand quadrants (and Voices) and Placemaking as the right-hand quadrants (and Voices).[3]

It should be noted that, at the same time as this framework has evolved, a number of other city specialists have focused on "Place" in a wholistic

---

3   Our exploration of Placecaring and Placemaking serendipitously echo the proposition of Patrick Geddes and Victor Branford (originators of the whole field of sociology). They considered that society had Spiritual Hemispheres for cultural powers and expressions of subjectivity and emotionality (analogous to our left-hand quadrants) and Temporal Hemispheres for economic and political powers (analogous to our right-hand quadrants). (Scott & Bromley, 2013, pp. 87–88)

way.[4] Some may object to my parsing apart Placecaring from Placemaking. But I have found that people only care to make what they have capacity to care about. Ironically, in this intensely ever-connecting world (re)learning to care is a basic building block for all 4 Voices to cogenerate well-being in the making of place and all of the city's systems and subsystems.

It is through the caring, inquiry, valuing, and meshworking of the 4 Voices in the *Food for Thought Project* (Hamilton, 2010a) that the City of Abbotsford changed its headline from "Murder Capital of Canada" to a "City of [Youth] Character" and now on an annual basis celebrates when the Youth Commission presents UROC awards (Abbotsford Youth Commission, 2016). By contrast, consider the misalignment of the 4 Voices in the newscasts of Aleppo in the Syrian conflict 2016, or Kathmandu after the earthquake in 2015, or New Orleans during Hurricane Katrina in 2005.

PRACTICE THE MASTER CODE

Fundamentally, I consider that Placecaring and Placemaking are inextricably interlinked into a whole. But, the way that I have learned to hold that whole, is through keeping in mind what I have come to call the Master Code of the Integral City. The Master Code simply says:

- Care for Yourself.
- Care for Each Other.
- Care for this Place.
- Care for this Planet.

---

4 Particularly Ian Wight and Mark DeKay have explored place, Place, PLACE from intimate and advanced integral perspectives revealing Modern, Post-Modern and Integral definitions (Wight, 2016a, 2016b, 2016c). Wight says: "consider a place/Place/PLACE differentiation similar to [DeKay's] nature/Nature/NATURE elucidation. [Move beyond] locating 'place' in just the physiosphere and/or the biosphere... locating 'Place' as–additionally–in the noosphere... thinking of PLACE as all quadrants, all levels (including the theosphere? (see p. 327 in DeKay's ISD).... similarly situate/differentiate your sense of city/City/CITY... there are other integral interpretations of place and placemaking for folks who might want to explore these, if/when their integral appetites have been whetted.... these interpretations strive for even greater, more expansive, notions of wholeness... city/City/CITY wholeness in your case [the whole-making, at the core of both placemaking and well-being for myself, is the terrain around which we both might eventually find common ground]."

In this Master Code context, I am using the word "Place" to represent the city and "Planet" to represent the Planet of Cities (see Figure 3 below). When we can care like this simultaneously with all 4 Voices, in all situations in the city, then we will have mastered and integrated the wholeness that is Place and the functions that enable the well-being of Gaia's Reflective Organ.

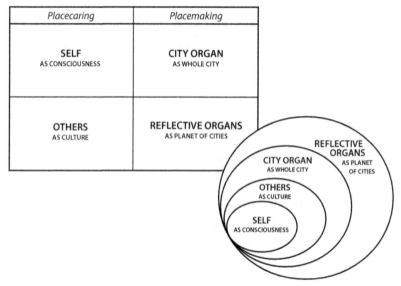

Figure 3: Master Code of Placecaring & Placemaking

In the process of learning how to do this, I associate the consciousness and culture in the left-hand quadrants with Placecaring and the behaviors and systems/infrastructures in the right-hand quadrants with Placemaking. Like all other phenomena in the city the Placecaring and Placemaking quadrants are fractal (similar to Figure 2), holographic, and all are co-arising—happening simultaneously—a characteristic of the Integral City Paradigm which will become more widely held as time moves on (even as Geddes hoped a century ago—see footnote[4]).

At this point in time, in order to move our thinking in the direction of considering the city as a whole system (and in the process evolve a view of the Integral City) I propose that one consider Placecaring separately from Placemaking. This gives us opportunities to develop our Place-relevant capacities through the many nuances and distinctions of development (often called lines and levels) that make up each of the Voices with greater focus.

HAPPINESS INDICATES THE CARING ROAD TO WELL-BEING

One way that I develop my capacities for caring is to review my practice of the Master Code, something I do at the beginning and end of each day (see *Chapter 3: Amplify Caring Capacity with Master Code*). It seems to give me comfort, inspires me, and makes me happy!

Mastering the Master Code as a practice makes me simultaneously aware of caring for the 4 Voices of the city through Self, Other(s), Place, and Planet. My research indicates that this practice may generate a metric all city Voices can use to notice our success at Placecaring and Placemaking. A growing number of studies and faith practices point to happiness as a fundamentally desirable state of being for humans. (Perhaps that is why our consumer driven culture is addicted to seek the shallow ego-centered happiness that comes from rewarding ourselves with the purchase of all manner of trivial goods?)

Happiness studies have produced early evidence that the sense of well-being of individuals, cities, cultures, and nations is both desirable and attainable ("Gross National Happiness Index," n.d.;(anon; Cummins et al., 2004; Haidt, 2006; Lama & Cutler, 1998; Montgomery, 2014; Wills, Hamilton, & Islam, 2007a, 2007b). This kind of happiness is not merely ego or self-centered, nor is it ethno- or regional-centred, nor even merely place or planet-centred. Instead, this indicator integrates all the scales of possible happiness that arise when our decision sets for well-being are aligned. This happens when we live the Master Code—choosing to take care of our Selves, each Other, our Cities/Places, and the Planet all at once—SIMULTANEOUSLY—an opportunity we have never before experienced in history.

When we consider the practices of the beehive (explained in greater detail in *Chapter 4: Inspire Spiritual Communities to Serve Evolution of the Human Hive*) we might do well to consider how the bees use pheromones (as their equivalent metric for happiness) to motivate right action that helps them achieve the production of their 40 pounds of honey (and thereby sustain themselves and their eco-region). When bee pheromones decline below a given level (because energy supplies are withheld when they do not perform as needed for hive survival) bees become "depressed" and are motivated to change behaviors to seek new energy sources.

In the human being, happiness may be the measure of success that tells us that our practices of the Master Code are balancing well-being for all 4 Voices and all circles of care—Individuals, Others, Place, and Planet. This happiness is not the inconsequential good-feeling of shallow pleasure seeking, but the deep sense of well-being that arises from investing in and expanding the circles of care—and as a result, growing Placecaring and Placemaking in the process.

If we want to learn more about how our relationships with happiness, well-being, and the Master Code are contributing to our capacities to become an Integral City and act as Gaia's Reflective Organ (and Organelles and Cells), we need a methodology to inquire together.

ACTION CO-RESEARCHERS LEARN TOGETHER

I have been schooled deeply in the methodology of Action Research by teaching its principles to students of leadership who want to make a difference with leaders, organizations, and communities in many cities and nations.[5]

I have coached leaders to expand their capacity for caring as they have focused their passion in a purposeful way to research and make change in their organization, community, or city. As Action Researchers, these leaders (representing all the 4 Voices) became co-researchers with the people they engaged in their studies. As an indicator of growing reflective capacity, I have observed that inevitably at some mid-point in the conduct of the study, the leader-researcher exclaims, "This research is all about me!" At this juncture, they discover the focus of their study is a projection of their mental models and they wake up to the natural filters (and biases) they bring to their analysis, findings, conclusions, and recommendations of the systems involved in their research.

---

5   As a Royal Roads University, School of Leadership faculty member and an academic supervisor of 60+ theses and organization learning projects, largely grounded in Action Research. Also at Fielding University, California Institute of Integral Studies, Murdoch University, Adizes Graduate School and as an independent consultant.

Action Research is a powerful methodology to use for city change because it involves people inquiring together. It starts with an initiating researcher (I/We), a sponsor/client (Other), participants (Others/We/You)—who all inquire, act, and impact one another as co-researchers.

Like a musical ensemble, co-researchers shape a question for the inquiry. The question in turn shapes the inquiry by defining the scope, boundaries, assumptions, literature, methods, biases, and limitations that co-researchers bring.

Generally, as soon as we ask the question in Action Research, action and impact happen at the level of the individual and quickly spread to spheres of influence touched by everyone in the study. Following the first cycle of inquiry, action, and impact with another such cycle, charges the study with a spirit of reflection that leads us to deepen the understanding of the question we ask and opens the door to a never ending quest of continuous learning (surely a quality required of Gaia's Reflective Organs, Organelles, and Cells).

Continuous learning becomes the path that enables our living system of 4 Voices to survive, connect to our environment, and regenerate. Ultimately this is the *life-giving pattern that drives our intention for this book—to learn at the city scale how to inquire, act, and achieve impact, and whether that cycle will motivate murder[6] or lead to well-being.*

INTEGRAL CITY ACTIVATES PRACTITIONERS, CATALYSTS, MESHWORKERS

Over the years, a core group of Integral City specialists has emerged from the projects we have undertaken to produce online webinars, conferences, articles, chapters, web pages, and approaches to city challenges. As an evolving community of practice, we have noticed that users (including ourselves) are attracted to Integral City practices who have different levels of experience, skills, and capacities. We have recognized that these capabilities are rarely learned in a linear fashion, are often discoveries

---

6 I retain the harshness of the word "murder" because it is not simply criminal behavior (a Western framing), but murder, in defined circumstances, is a cultural expression that the jihadis and wahabis, from their worldviews prefer to life and well-being. When cultures who value the taking of life are at war with cultures who value the sustaining of life, cities are trapped in a set of wicked problems that can only be resolved through engaging the power, authority, and influence of all 4 Voices on a long term, multi-generational, evolutionary basis.

from "hybridized cross-pollinations" of knowledge domains, and are rarely being delivered in institutionalized curricula. However, using a frame of prior learning assessment to review prior learner accomplishments and an attitude and core willingness to combine reflection on inquiry, action, and impact, we propose a natural progression of activating Integral City practice that we call: **Practitioner, Catalyst,** and **Meshworker.**

A **Practitioner** tends to work on their own with one organization and/or one voice of the city, providing individual support with a focus on well-being.

A **Catalyst** tends to work with other team members (including Practitioners) connecting two or more organizations, sectors, or voices with a focus on change, transformation, and/or sustainability.

A **Meshworker** works with multiple sectors, voices, cities, and organizations, not just connecting, but aligning these entities into coherent value and impact chains for resilience.

It should be noted that the qualities of the Catalyst transcend and include the qualities of the Practitioner and the qualities of the Meshworker transcend and include the qualities of the Catalyst.

In other words, each of these profiles demonstrates discernable qualities whose capacity for practice expands with the level of complexity of the profile. However, we readily point out that in order for an Integral City to emerge and be sustained all three profiles need to be active. People will tend to select the level of complexity and focus that amplifies their own purpose (and therefore joy and energy). We recommend that this nexus of energy—the crossroads—where the practice profile and the city's greatest needs cause Integral City energy to expand—be used as the "sweet spot" to notice when, where, how, and who to assemble and activate a team for optimum Integral City results.

We define the Integral City Activator Profile qualities as follows: (see summary of the profiles in Table 1).

- **Passion/Energy for the Work**: the natural energy and joy the worker and work cogenerate
- **Practice Area**: geographical situation of city voices, organizations, sectors, regions
- **Education**: formal institutionalized educational attainment of profile

- **Knowledge**: informal, on-the-job (OTJ), practice studies, and knowledge network of profile
- **Experience Scale**: scale of actual experience working with human systems, related to profile, increasing in scale as related to Practice Area(s) (see above)
- **Strengths**: Tendency for profile to be strongly weighted in functional, process, and design capacities
- **Focus**: the focus complexifies as it progresses across the profiles through: Purpose, Profit, People, Principles, Processes, Praxis[7]
- **Decision Horizon Scale & Measurement Dimensions**: this is a measurement of the leadership decision expanse horizon that embraces time, space and morality[8]
- **Boundaries**: a measure of the city boundary frame in relation to the Planet of Cities—city, eco-region, global
- **Paradigms**: a way of framing the metrics of Gross (x) Happiness vs Gross Community Product, Gross Regional Product or Gross National Product. (It is proposed that Happiness is a critical metric for measuring the outcome of living the Integral City Master Code (discussed in *Chapter 3*).
- **Integral City Intelligence Source**: the target population (i.e., number of cities) the profile has direct access to for observing the 12 Integral City Intelligences.
- **Integral City Learning**: sources and processes of direct Integral City learning

---

7   derived from the Integral City Book 1 Chapter 7 on Building Intelligence, (Hamilton, 2008a, pp. 174–175)

8   ibid

Table 1: Profiles of Integral City Activators: Practitioner, Catalyst, Meshworker
++ *Note: Meshworker Profile transcends and includes Catalyst; Catalyst transcends and includes Practitioner.*

Quality	Practitioner	+Catalyst	++Meshworker
Passion/Energy	Health, Well-being, Positive Change in the City Local Community	Change, Transformation, Sustainability, Bridge Builder, Climate Change, Eco-Region	Human Hive, Gaia's Reflective Organ, Resilience, Emergence Glocal/Global
Practice Areas	1. Civil Society & Activists - the Human Hive and living systems 2. Civic Leaders / Bureaucrats (from City Hall, Education, Health) - story of Abbotsford Values Map and how to apply it; The Map, Mesh & Human Hive 3. Elected Officials (all levels of Govt with a city-related portfolio but mainly city) 4. Private Sector - CSR - resilience and sustainability 5. Professionals/ Academics like Urban Planners, architects, engineers, accountants - living whole systems, sustainability, KSF/ KPI	Connecting two or more organizations, sectors, voices	Aligning, creating coherence, meshworking, connecting the dots in the city; and or between city/cities/ eco-region

Quality	Practitioner	+Catalyst	++Meshworker
Education	Undergraduate Degree or 5 years OTJ Experience	Graduate Degree &/or 10 years OTJ Experience	Graduate Degree &/or 15+ years OTJ Experience
Knowledge	Integral Framework, Spiral Dynamics. Living Systems, Complexity, Integral City, Personal Management, Integral Life Practice or Integral Transformative Practice or Equivalent	Leadership Development, Team Development, Art of Hosting, Inquiry, Conflict Resolution, Social Artistry, Polarity Management, Eco-Footprint, The Natural Step, Balanced Scorecard, Values Tools, Appreciative Integral Inquiry, Holacracy	» Facilitating, Learning Design » Thinking & Learning Communities » Calculating Carrying Capacity for: Social, Cultural, Environmental, Economic
Experience Scale (Human Systems)	Two or more: Profession(s) Organization Association, Activism	Two or more: Community, City, Eco-Region, Integral Activism, OD, Energy, Governance	Two or more: Community, City, Eco-Region, Federal, International
Strengths	Operations, Implementation, Project Management, Spiritual Practice, Speaker	Dialogue, Collaboration, Cooperation, Process Management, Group Leader	Design, Co-Design, Flow, Energy Work, Non-Linear Creativity, System Nudger, Influencer, Teacher/Professor, Meshworker, Mentor
Focus	» Purpose » Profit » People	» Principles » Processes	» Praxis
Decision Horizon Scale & Measurement Dimensions	» 10 yr. » time/space/ morality	» 20 yr. » time/space/ morality	» 50 yr. » time/space/ morality
Boundaries	» Boundaries – integral city	» Boundaries – Eco-Regional	» Boundaries – Shifting and/or multi Eco-Regional and/or global

Quality	Practitioner	+Catalyst	++Meshworker
Paradigms	GCommunityP vs Gross Community Happiness	GRegionalP vs Gross Regional Happiness	GNP vs Gross National Happiness
Integral City Intelligence Source	2–4 Integral City Intelligences	3–6 Integral City Intelligences from 2 or more sets	6+ Integral City Intelligences from 3 or more sets
Integral City Learning	» Integral City Books » Map, Mesh, Human Hive » Livable Cities » Generations, Saecula, Cities	» Resilient City Leadership » RRU Sustainable Community Development Grad Certificate » Integral Vital Signs Monitors » Assessing City/ Community Values » Integral Node Developer » The Natural Step » RRU MA	» Learning Event Designer/Co-Designer » Designing City Scale Meshworks

The Integral City Team is continuously refining our practices and recalibrating our own capacities as Practitioners, Catalysts, and Meshworkers. This book is a meta-framework of key processes that have helped us to learn by doing. We are honored to be companions on your design journey for developing and evolving capacities for impact in the human hive and invite you to share your learning and doing with us.

Integral City started with one person, expanded to 10 Integrators of the Human Hive, and now nurtures a growing number of city-based communities of practice. Through sharing our processes, we hope that we can multiply Integral City activators from all the 4 Voices, into hundreds and thousands in service to a Planet of Integral Cities. (Contact information for joining us is located at the end of the book in PROFILES: AUTHORS & CONTRIBUTORS.)

DESIGN GUIDELINES
FOR NAVIGATING THE BOOK

PLACECARERS AND PLACEMAKERS WILL BENEFIT FROM THIS BOOK

When the student of the city is ready the teacher will appear. This book acts as a teacher to all 4 Voices—particularly to two populations. The first set of Voices tends to be the city specialists who speak as the Civic Managers and Business Voices. The second set of Voices tends to be the users of integral frameworks who speak with the Voices of Citizens and Civil Society. For city specialists this book guides you to understand the vital role of consciousness and culture in relation to the behaviors and systems/infrastructures you manage and develop in the city. For students of integral frameworks, this book reveals how behaviors and systems/infrastructures in the city impact consciousness and culture. And because of these natural biases in city specialists and integrally informed developmentalists, each potential audience will probably want to start with a different line of inquiry.

By parsing the inquiry into Placemaking separate from Placecaring, I want to offer a variety of starting points for inquiry, action, and impact. Just as my city-discovery path has involved very non-linear jumps from studies of human systems to curiosities about beehives to the overview of Gaia's Reflective Organ, I have tried to design this book so that it could be both a non-linear and linear experience.

Find the question that fits your curiosity. Find the action that precipitates your engagement. Find the impact that you intend to happen. Reflect on the questions that lead you to grasp the power of the Master Code that unifies all caring efforts in the city. Any of these offerings in the following pages might ignite the starting point on your path for change. I hope the rest of it may become a larger map to guide a lifetime of inquiry, action, and impact in an orderly, unfolding (even non-linear) way.

SEQUENCE OF CHAPTERS: PART 1 AND PART 2

The sequence of the chapters in Integral City Inquiry & Action: Designing Impact for the Human Hive is set out in two parts. Part I addresses Placecaring and Part 2 addresses Placemaking.

The sequence once again reflects the fractal pattern that is embedded in practicing the Master Code and provides a consistent design for composing each chapter.

As Figure 3 demonstrates, the Master Code (which addresses caring for Self, Others, Place, and Planet) can be situated in the Integral Quadrants where Caring emerges through the left-hand quadrants of Self and Culture and where Making emerges through the right-hand quadrants for realizing tangible artefacts, through the Systems and Infrastructures for the whole city and Planet of Cities (keeping in mind that each quadrant represents a whole that has its own quadrants).[9]

METHODOLOGY CLUSTERS

Practicing the Master Code of Caring and Making provides a kind of blueprint for integral inquiry, action, and impact. It also helps provide guidance to select Methodologies appropriate to the quadrant(s) of study and an evaluation framework for measuring impact.

---

9   The design of Part 1 and Part 2 may also be viewed by some as following a Theory U pattern (down the left-hand quadrants and up the right-hand quadrants) (see Glossary for fuller explanation).

Figure 4 demonstrates how the quadrants provide a meta-framework to locate key Methods used in Integral City—Inquiry, Interpretation, Monitoring, and Prototyping. This also provides a logical sequence for the pattern of the overall Methodology and the Clusters of Methods in each quadrant within Parts 1 and 2. Each Cluster forms a Section in the respective Part.

Part 1: Placecaring

Inquire

- Activate Inquiry in the Knowing Field
- Embrace the Master Code

Interpret

- Assess the 12 Intelligences of the Integral City
- Discover and Map City Values & Vital Signs

Part 2: Placemaking

Monitor

- Engage the 4 Voices of the City
- Prototype Design for Learning Lhabitats, Pop-ups, and Sustainable Community Development

Prototype

- Meshwork Purpose, People, Place, and Planet
- Evaluate Impact

CHAPTER DESIGN

I have located the sections of each chapter in quadrants as WHO, WHY, WHAT, and HOW (as in Figure 5).

WHO (UL): is represented by the inquiry designer and also the participants in the inquiry.

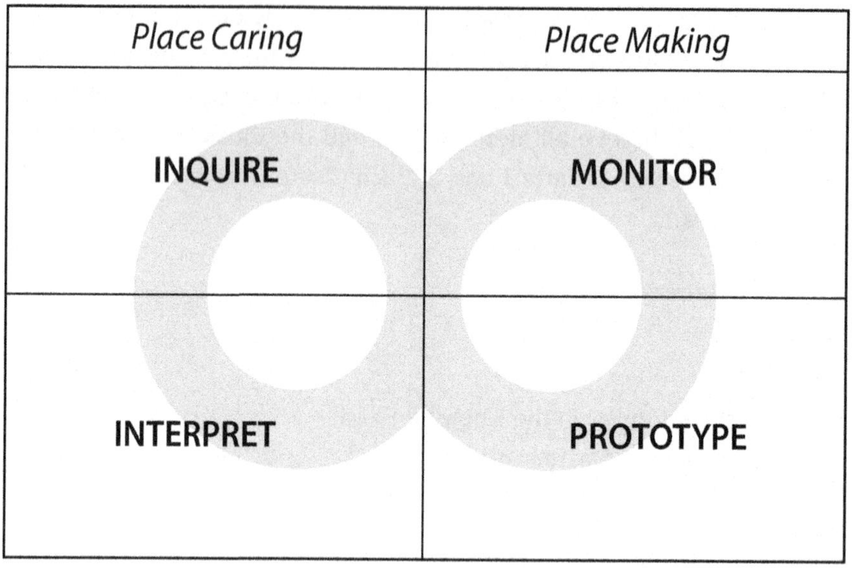

Place Caring	*Place Making*
INQUIRE	**MONITOR**
INTERPRET	**PROTOTYPE**

Figure 4: Integral City Methods

WHY (LL): is represented by the meaning that emerges from the inter-subjective relationships of the people in the design. WHY1 addresses the meaning before the inquiry. WHY2 addresses the meaning that emerges as a result of the inquiry.

WHAT (UR): is represented by the Inquiry Question and/or the object of inquiry.

HOW (LR): is represented by the design methodology itself.

INTEGRATED REFLECTIVE-ACTION PRACTICES & QUESTIONS

Together with the Integral City Community of Practice, I have positioned this design guide in the "never-ending quest" of inquiry and learning inspired by Clare Graves (Graves, 1974, 2003, 2005), with a consider-able measure of gratitude to the communities of Action Inquiry, Action Research, Action Learning, Appreciative Inquiry, and Integral Research (see *Appendix F*).

Every practice we share involves and/or has been inspired by one or more of these grand mixed method methodologies (that combine qualita-tive and quantitative epistemologies).

WHO	**WHAT**
WHY 1 **WHY 2**	**HOW**

Figure 5: Inquiry, Action, Impact Chapter Design

At the same time, we recognize that a new paradigm calls us to use new language. To help in gaining fluency with key terms that may be unfamiliar to readers, we offer a Glossary at the end of the book. Appendices provide easy access to resources such as maps, templates, and worksheets.

Furthermore, every chapter concludes with an Action Plan for Practitioners and Impact Questions addressing the dynamic change process embedded in the 4 quadrants. The Action Plan focuses readers on their own learnings through the body, mind, heart, and soul, based on a powerful field-tested appreciative Leadership-Learning method (Bushe, 2001). The Impact Questions are drawn from the Integral Research process developed by MetaIntegral Foundation (S. Esbjörn-Hargens, 2015a). Thus every inquiry and action pairing spring-boards (and hopefully pays forward) further inquiry into the impacts of future pools of 4-quadrant learning that are deep, wide, clear, and high (as shown in Figure 6).

Upper Left DEEP—How will my **mindsets** about the city change?

Lower Left WIDE—In what ways will our city **relationships** change?

Upper Right CLEAR—How do my city **behaviors** change?

Lower Right HIGH—How do our city **systems** change?

DEEP	CLEAR
How will my mindsets about the city change?	How do my city behaviors change?
WIDE	HIGH
In what ways will our city relationships change?	How do our city systems change?

Figure 6: Activator Impact Questions

CONSISTENT CHAPTER FORMAT

While each chapter addresses a different template or case study with their own unique revelations, we have cross-referenced each chapter, figure, table, section, and appendix to enable non-linear access. Furthermore, each chapter is formatted in a consistent structure. We hope this will make the design guide easy to follow and also address our criteria for sharing designs that are replicable, iterative (within and/or across stages), and locatable within a grand cycle for enacting change at the city scale. As a result, this is what you will find for each chapter:

- Inquiry Objectives
- Introduction to Inquiry, Action, and Impact
- Framing Inquiry: WHO, WHY1
- Inquiry Practice: WHAT / HOW
- Conclusion: WHY2
- Reiteration of Inquiry Objectives
- Action Plan for Practitioner, Catalyst, Meshworker

- Impact Questions: Deep, Wide, Clear, High
- Chapter Resources and/or Links
  - Integral City Maps
  - Integral City Intelligences
  - Integral City GPS

HOW TO ENGAGE WITH INQUIRY, ACTION, & IMPACT IN THIS BOOK

In the first book in the *Integral City Series* (Hamilton, 2008a) we asked, "How can cities open up the energy flow of human life so that we add value to the evolution of the planet?" In *Inquiry, Action & Impact*, we ask, **"How can we add value to the city through inquiry, action, and impact that changes us as we change the city?"** We offer designs, approaches, actions, and systems that enable energy to flow through the 4 Voices of cities, at every stage of their evolution.

Because of the Design Sequence and Chapter Structure (and cross-referencing), this book can be read in many orders to suit the reader (even starting with the last chapter first!). It has been our experience that the process described in each chapter changes your world, and in turn that world changes you. Each chapter offers indicators, hints, and suggestions for you to define and locate your intentions for inquiry, action, and impact. The Glossary and Appendices give you tools and guides to support you at each stage. So hopefully you can locate the place to start that is an appropriate and natural next step as you work with your city.

PART 1
Placecaring

Part 1 of the book starts with the left-hand quadrants of the Integral City model and explores how to enact Placecaring through inquiry and action. This is a vital sequence to recognize and respect because it completely underpins the effective practice we explore in Part 2—namely, inquiry and action for Placemaking. In Part 1 we explore the power of systemic constellation work and values creation in the Integral City which is foundational to the values realization that we explore in Part 2.

SECTION 1 — *Activate Inquiry in the Knowing Field*

These first 2 chapters introduce readers to a discovery that has profoundly impacted Integral City inquiry and practice—namely, inviting in the Knowing Field (which some, including this author, have compared to Rupert Sheldrake's morphic field; (Sheldrake, 1988, 2012)). This situates the Integral City work knowingly in the realm of consciousness. We have found this to be vital in making accessible the energetic qualities of the city at all scales of human systems within it. Working, playing, and recreating in the Knowing Field gives us insights into the invisible aspects of the city that we believe are continuously impacting it through stored energy, habits, lineages, traumas, and wisdom in the Knowing Field. We explain

1

also how the Knowing Field opens the Integral City practices from those engaged in by individuals to those embraced by a collective "We." It is our belief that our practices have uncovered the early stages of what we call the Human Hive Mind. By starting here, Integral City intends to open the doors to a unique inquiry and action practice that distinguishes its approach from other advanced but more technological or environmental frameworks (like Smart City and Resilient City).

Out beyond the Smart City, Out beyond the Resilient City
Lies a Field... We will meet you there.

— (with a nod and gratitude to Rumi)

ACTIVATE INQUIRY
FOR KNOWING CITIES

— by Marilyn Hamilton and Diana Claire Douglas

This chapter is extracted from an article by Diana Claire Douglas & Marilyn Hamilton, first published in Knowing Field, Issue 22, June 2013 as "Knowing Cities: The Knowing Field and the Emergence of Integral City Intelligence" (Douglas & Hamilton, 2013b). It also formed a presentation at the Infosyon Conference, Amsterdam, April, 2013.

INQUIRY OBJECTIVES

The Inquiry Objectives of this chapter are:

1. Discover why systemic constellation work (SCW) is a powerful method for waking up the city to her "knowing capacities" as a living system.

2. Experience how SCW offers a method to explore the outer edges of human consciousness, through creativity, spirituality, and self-organizing systems.

3. Learn how the Integral City paradigm situates the city in the context of a Planet of Cities, as a living human system, with consciousness and culture at its core and a morphic field as its evolutionary legacy.

INTRODUCTION TO INQUIRY, ACTION, AND IMPACT IN INTEGRAL CITY & THE KNOWING FIELD

Systemic constellation work (SCW) is a foundational form of Inquiry Methodology with a history in family and organizational systems inquiry. Because of this evolution from smaller (and historic) scales of human systems, it seems a natural methodology for inquiring into the complexity of the human system at city-scale.

SCW is particularly potent because it contexts (situates, and taps into) the invisible Knowing Field which flows from, to, and around an Integral City as consciousness and energy that others have called the morphic field. As we have written elsewhere (Hamilton et al., 2015; Hamilton, Douglas, Beck, Aurami, & Arnott, 2016), access to the Knowing Field gives us access to the greatest span and depth of context to understand the Integral City.

These chapters and the cases below do not attempt to train a Constellator on how to constellate an SCW. Like Action Inquiry or Appreciative Inquiry, SCW is now a specialized practice domain with multicultural roots and a world-wide community of practitioners (Diana's organization, *Knowing Field Designs* offers training in this methodology and links to other SCW resources. See *Appendix E*). However, describing the steps the SCW Constellator takes reveals how and why access to the Knowing Field opens up powerful territory for inquiry, action, and evolutionary development in the Integral City.

As noted in the Introduction Chapter:

[I]t *has become obvious in our* IC *community of practice that* SCW *opens the doors to our own development as an intersubjective* We-Space—*thus giving us direct experience of the development of a collective consciousness (which was raised in the Integral City Book 1's final chapter) as an anticipated outcome of Evolutionary Intelligence.*

Founder and Constellator of *Knowing Field Designs*, Diana Claire Douglas has developed SCW for application at the city scale working with Marilyn Hamilton, and the Integral City core team. The combination of these two paradigms (SCW and Integral) has allowed them to use the elements of each paradigm to co-create processes that work in service to city well-being. The method works both with participants located contiguously in the same room and/or with participants distributed around the world, connected by internet or telecommunication technology. (See *Appendix E* for explanation of process and technology.)

SCW offers a form of "grand inquiry" that can embrace the span of city-scale time/space/moral boundaries, and the depth of individual and family histories that span evolutionary time/space/morality (the Integral paradigm is uniquely suited to map the outcomes of such span and depth.)

FRAMING INQUIRY FOR KNOWING FIELD: WHO, WHY1

WHO: Inquiry Participants

The inquiry process (Hamilton et al., 2015), described in *Chapter* 2 or concisely in *Appendix* E requires the contribution of particular contributors:

- **Constellator**: guides the SCW process
- **Client (and/or Sponsor[10])**: initiates (or sponsors) **Inquiry Question**
- **Elements & Representatives**: participants who represent key elements of the inquiry question
- **Witnesses (optional)**: participants who witness the SCW process and may or may not be called on to comment on their observations

WHY: Understanding Integral City Paradigm

An Integral City integrates qualities that create optimal conditions for human innovation and emergence and eco-regional resilience. It has 12 Intelligences (as identified in the *Italicized* description below and in the fuller definitions in *Appendix* C1).

An Integral City:
- Builds capacity in the Individual (*Inner* and *Outer*)
- Builds capacity in the Collective (*Culture* and *Structures*)
- Develops *Inquiry* intelligences for generative exchanges
- Catalyzes *Meshworking*[11] strategies to bridge sectors, silos, stovepipes, & solitudes
- Designs feedback and feed forward loops for *Navigational* direction

---

10 Note sometimes Client and Sponsor are the same; sometimes they are different as in the case below.

11 Meshworking is a process derived from Meshworking Intelligence, which attracts the best of two operating systems—one that self-organizes, and the other that can replicate hierarchical structures—to create and align complex responsive structures and systems that flex and flow.

- Responds to critical Contexts: *Ecospherical, Emergent, Integral, Living*
- Expresses *Evolutionary Intelligence*

An Integral City meshworks evolutionary intelligences[12] to think about, act in, relate to, and work towards creating the *healthy city of the future* as the process of creating the *Human Hive*. We view an Integral City, with a *systems thinking* level of awareness, through 4 quadrants—which has become Map 1 of the Integral City (see Figure 7). In turn, we have anchored these quadrants into the 4 Voices of the city:

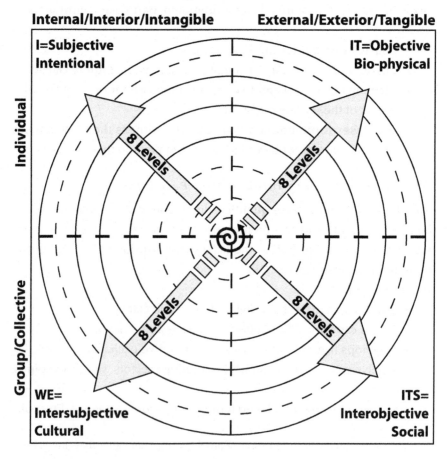

Figure 7: Integral City Map 1–4 Quadrants

---

12 Evolutionary Intelligence is the capacity to transcend and include the intelligences we currently demonstrate, in order to allow new intelligences to emerge.

UL: Citizen
LL: Civil Society

UR: City Manager
LR: Business

Diana and Marilyn have found that systemic constellation work (SCW) is a playground for sharing their mutual interests in maps and mapping, exploration and experimentation, seeing the previously invisible/unknown and finding its practical application for real-world issues.

Marilyn started participating in SCWs at differing scales (family, organization) in various roles (as a cosponsor, representative, and participant) with significant guidance from European constellators. Experimenting with the city work became possible through guidance from Diana. These early experiments addressed issues such as: how an electoral candidate could approach a city election; the role of organizations in the world; how four generations can relate to each other in the city; and how to design a visioning workshop for a multi-stakeholder city group (called a Citizen's Observatory).

The following Case illustrates how to use the elements and describes an example of a real outcome.

SCW CASE AS PRACTICE WHAT, HOW

WHAT: Inquiry Question

Marilyn, as Client, was invited by a Sponsor, the citizen observatory of a large Mexican city, to bring her Integral City work to their city. In preparation for her workshop in Mexico, the Client asked and received permission from her Mexican Sponsor for her to do a constellation process to learn about the city prior to her first visit. Working with Constellator at a distance (on Skype), the Client was asked to state her issue or sponsoring question: **"How can I catalyze the city's field of well-being?"**

HOW: SCW Process

The steps for practicing the SCW process were as follows.

Constellator: Consciously working in the Knowing Field, the Constellator suggested a number of elements as described next.

Elements: The Spirit of the City, historical traumas, well-being, Sponsor, angelic realms, and victim/tyrant shadows. Client also added some elements (informed by the Integral City 4-quadrant framework (as outlined above), from the 4 "Voices" of the City: Citizens, City Managers, Civil Society and Business, as well as the city's Purpose and Symbol.

SCW Sequence: Two sessions were needed for this process.

SCW1: In the first session, Client was outside the circle/Knowing Field and feeling pulled from behind by a force, away from the Spirit of the City. When Client stood as the force, it became clear that this was a resource for her work in this city. The movement was for Client to slowly walk towards the Spirit of the City (located in the Knowing Field at 12 o'clock). She was able to do so and hear from the Spirit of the City that she was welcomed and the City/Sponsor wanted to receive her gifts.

SCW2: For the continuation of the constellation two days later, the issue was to look at Client's relationship with the energies in the city itself and place these energies in the Knowing Field. So Client found the place in the field for representatives for victims, tyrants, Spirit of the City, well-being, the sponsor, Client, and Love. Guided by the Knowing Field, Constellator suggested that indigenous people and Devas from the earth realms be added.

In this first image, the victims were in the center of the field and "everyone else needed to go through the victims in order to connect." There was also a split in power between the earthly and spirit realms. To find a new image, the experiment was to see if there could be reconciliation between victims and tyrants which would create a field of well-being. Through both the use of Client's feedback and the webcam visuals, Constellator suggested Client experiment with re-aligning the representatives and the energies in the field. The Client did so by sensing how the elements wanted to realign. By the end of this self-organizing process, it was clear that the Client had discovered a new way to look at the Elements in the field because of the shift in their relationship to one another (and herself). She had lost her apprehension about serving the Spirit of the City and found that she had a message to bring to the city.

Commentary on the Constellation:

The Client had left the constellation set up in her home office while she travelled to Mexico. Both she and Constellator wonder whether this increased the field activity, its strength, and its impact on the outcome of her time in Mexico.

After the first session the Client felt that she was opened up to seeing herself and her role working with cities differently from what she had before. "It opened me up to seeing myself not just as a catalyst but as a 'City Intuitive.'"

The Client was surprised when the Constellator interjected other representatives, including indigenous peoples and the earth spirits. Client's greatest curiosity arose from the role of the indigenous peoples and the questions that came through Constellator's guidance. When Client travelled to the City on the day prior to the conference, the Devas turned up in the form of the first rain in several years. On a tour of the city, unexpectedly the indigenous people came forward, offered their gifts, and were invited to the conference. They energized their Symposium partners, identified their needs for translation and commerce and with their colorful baskets and lively presentations, became the turning point in the success of the conference. Their strong culture was a surprise to the Sponsor/Citizens' Observatory and a powerful wake-up call to the city.

In addition to the role of the indigenous peoples, the Spirit of the City manifested in the Lion statue on the gateway to the city center. Client used this as a symbol for the revival of the city's spirit and was invited by a city designer to work with her to engage and align multiple stakeholders to have this come alive. This work is still ongoing but it has fanned out to involve other stakeholders.

CONCLUSION: WHY2

We have learned from accessing the Knowing Field that it offers a powerful tool for glimpsing the invisible; for noticing the energies at play in the city; and for honoring key elements and their voices as Marilyn/Client stood as their representatives. Marilyn has come to respect and delight in the surprising outcomes that affirm what is revealed by the Knowing Field. Marilyn has learned that accessing the Knowing Field supports the clearing work that she does on a personal or team scale, by aligning with the forces within the city field and accessing the resources available to her. This has resulted in her expanding her courage to work in dangerous or threatening places because the field is able and willing to disclose threats and how to 'aikido' her work (or gracefully dance with the energies she encounters) to protect herself and others as they shift energies in the city field.

As initiator of the City Constellation questions, Marilyn has felt empowered by honoring the Knowing Field. It has given her confidence in trusting that the Knowing Field moves her from fear of the 'Unknown' to trusting the 'Knowable.' The identification of representatives reveals to her resources—partners and supporters—that she wouldn't otherwise have been aware of. Marilyn has been rewarded by the participation of team members in the constellation work, because they are also empowered by the engagement and continue to offer reminders and/or interpretations and/or revelations as the System of Inquiry unfolds in, with, and as them.

Starting from her Integral perspective, Marilyn has noticed the very subtle insights that come from standing as a representative for an element. Before she steps into the representative Field, the elements are just objects for her to contemplate. But when she steps into the Field as the representative, she finds her perspective shifts from objective to subjective. She becomes the "Representative Field" and experiences the energy and the Knowing as if she were that person or element. It is important for the Constellator to guide the disclosures as the subjective experience isn't always easy to articulate or convey. However, when debriefing the experience, Marilyn has learned to step back into the objective perspective with the benefit of having deeply experienced the subjective space, place, and/or grace of the representative. This gives her deep insights that would otherwise not be available to her.

In discussion, Diana and Marilyn have learned to differentiate between the typical uses of the terms "client" versus "sponsor." Marilyn was Diana's client and she was the initiator or sponsor of the question on behalf of the city or project sponsor.

In this case, as Constellator, Diana received affirmation (from the Knowing Field) that it was the personal/family work that was needed first so that Marilyn (the Client), by preparing and clearing her field, could allow herself to align with the elements and forces and become aware of and thus prepare for the shadows (potential problems).

For Marilyn, Diana's use of quadrants in her clock diagram (see *Appendix E*) for locating relationships aligned easily with Marilyn's use of quadrants from the Integral City model. For Diana, the quadrants had no meaning other than helping her to locate the representatives since they were using Skype. (In writing up this case, both Diana and Marilyn realized the quadrants served both as physical locators and IC meaning!)

Diana continues, like many in the constellations community, to try to understand, make meaning, and articulate the Knowing Field. She feels having a clear and direct relationship with the Knowing Field is one of the most important aspects of her work as a Constellator. When she is tuned into the Knowing Field, she is "in the flow," and in that flow, information is available from many dimensions. She has found that different information and energies show themselves with different clients; elements from what is often called "the invisible" make themselves known in these sessions! Also, the interplay of fields within fields can be strong in collaborations like this. While Marilyn conceptualized the Knowing Field as the field of the city or online conference, Diana understood she was holding a larger, essentially un-identified space.

Through her work with IC and others, Diana has developed a way of doing remote constellations via Skype and conference calls. She has found the multiple locations of SCW participants to be powerful and opens possibilities to enable this work around the world (especially as technology continues to improve synchronous communications).

WHY IS SYSTEMIC CONSTELLATION WORK IMPORTANT?

Systemic constellation work offers an energetically empowering technology that embraces the non-linear, ambiguous, invisible complexity of the Knowing Field for all those in service to the evolution of the city and Planet of Cities.

Cities are such complex human systems, that the normal tools of map-making, planning, and priority-setting cannot reveal all the dynamics that occur within it. All those Cultural Creatives and Integral Practitioners interested in city sustainability and resilience, can amplify their service to the city and the Planet of Cities by learning systemic constellation work. This will give them access to the invisible roots of culture that are embedded in the city's Knowing Field. The city is both a fractal of family systems and a holarchy of all human systems—thus it contains all the morphic resonance from human shadows and for the realization of human potential. SCW seems like the most powerful methodology to tap into the fractal, holarchic capacities of the Integral City.

REITERATION OF INQUIRY OBJECTIVES

The Inquiry Objectives of this chapter were:

1. Discover why systemic constellation work (SCW) is a powerful method for waking up the city to her "knowing capacities" as a living system.

2. Experience how SCW offers a method to explore the outer edges of human consciousness, through creativity, spirituality, and self-organizing systems.

3. Learn how the Integral City paradigm situates the city in the context of a Planet of Cities, as a living human system, with consciousness and culture at its core and a morphic field as its evolutionary legacy.

ACTION PLAN FOR PRACTITIONER, CATALYST, MESHWORKER

Review this chapter and make notes below of your impressions, insights, and questions. Locate yourself on the Integral City practice scaffolding. Notice what you have observed, thought, felt, and what you now want to do in any of the three possible practice configurations: as a Practitioner, as a Catalyst, as a Meshworker.

After you have made these notes, consider some of the Impact Questions (below). They also might help you reflect on how to generate impact through inquiry and action. Finally check out the Resources and Links suggested for this practice at the end of the chapter.

IMPACT QUESTIONS: DEEP, WIDE, CLEAR, HIGH

1. UL DEEP: As a coach, facilitator, catalyst, or meshworker with cities, how do I prepare myself to participate by using practices to clear my bio-psycho-cultural-social field? Consider: 1-2-3 Shadow work (Wilber, Patten, Leonard, & Morelli, 2008); Tonglen meditation;[13] embodied field clearing (a practice of "sweeping" the subtle energy field); and Huebl Presencing.[14] As a Client how do I come to the

---

13 Tonglen: http://en.wikipedia.org/wiki/Tonglen

14 Transparent Communication: http://www.thomashuebl.com/en/approach-methods/transparent-communication.html

systemic constellation with a "draft" question and remain open to the Constellator helping me to improve it for deeper access to the Knowing Field? How willing am I to let go of control and trust the Constellator to guide me in the gross realm and the subtle/Knowing Field realm?

2. LL WIDE: Are we open to the Constellator clearing the space before starting and how can we work with her/him to do so? Have we thought about what Elements we can propose and who our Representatives might be? Are we open to the Constellator suggesting others?

3. UR CLEAR: How comfortable am I—or what tensions do I carry (in my body) with my choice/need for the mode of constellation work: face-to-face; online; Skype; etc.? How have I prepared myself through contemplation, meditation, bio-psycho-active material (like reading, video, audio) to be in the Unknown?

4. LR HIGH: How can we hold the results of the systemic constellation with honor, but lightly? How do we remind ourselves that the effect of entering the Knowing Field continues after the constellation? Or, "It is not over until it is over"? How might we adjust our strategies formulated before the constellation to reflect any discoveries we make? How do we remember that our entry into the Knowing Field has already changed the Field, accepting that we don't need to do anything and Field effects will unfold on their own? How comfortable are we and how might we prepare to be surprised as the energies continue to play out (over days, weeks, months)?

CHAPTER RESOURCES AND/OR LINKS

Appendix B: Integral City Maps (1–5): 1, 5

Appendix C1: Definitions of 12 Intelligences: Integral, Inner, Outer, Structural, Cultural, Inquiry, Meshworking, Navigating, Evolutionary

Appendix C3: Integral City GPS Locator: Evolutionary, Integral, Smart, Resilient

Reflective Question for Whom /Where/ What I Could Use as:	Practitioner	Catalyst	Meshworker
What do I observe as I read?			
What do I think?			
What do I feel?			
What do I want to do next?			

CULTIVATE WE-SPACE INQUIRY FOR
HUMAN HIVE MIND

— by Marilyn Hamilton, Diana Claire Douglas Cherie Beck,
Alia Aurami, Joan Arnott, Linda Shore

This chapter is adapted from a chapter written by the contributors above, for the book "Cohering the We Space: Developing Theory and Practice for Engaging Collective Emergence, Wisdom and Healing in Groups." Editors: Michael Brabant, Olen Gunnlaugson, (Hamilton et al., 2016)

INQUIRY OBJECTIVES

The Inquiry Objectives of this chapter are:

1. Explore Systemic Constellation Work as prototyping methodology for We-space.
2. Prototype the Human Hive Mind as a We-space.
3. Recognize We-space as an outcome of inquiring into the Human Hive.
4. Understand the relationship between Human Hive Mind, Integral City, and Planet of Cities.
5. Learn how to tell the We-space story.

INTRODUCTION TO INQUIRY, ACTION AND IMPACT WITH SYSTEMIC CONSTELLATION WORK AND WE-SPACE AS THE HUMAN HIVE MIND

The process of SCW (placing representatives in the Knowing Field and watching their interaction) can be used in many ways. Originally, Bert Hellinger developed the process through a phenomenological (open, from the ground up, learn-through-experience) approach. The question or issue was placed in an "open field." But others have developed structural constellations where an already predetermined structure is placed in the field and the representatives interact with it and within it as well as with each other. Within our Integral City Community of Practice (ICCOP), we have used both types of constellations within our organizations and with cities.

The "Field"[15] in which we interact is a container for both individuals and collectives—a We-space with forces, energies, dynamics, and spheres of influence that are usually invisible to us. It is especially relevant for work with cities because when we look at the scale of life on this planet, we notice that cities as human systems are in the center of the space between self and planet.[16] As we look around the world it appears that higher-consciousness stages of We-space at various scales are increasingly active and prevalent as the next stage of evolution for human systems, including cities on the journey to becoming Integral Cities. As ICCOP, we attend to action in the world related to the integral evolution of cities, noticing where Second Tier[17] organizing principles are emerging in larger (communities and organizations) and smaller (teams and families) scales of human interaction. We are being invited to help individual cities evolve by working directly with a variety of emergent "We-fields."

In our ICCOP We-space an attractive force has emerged that is sensed by each individual and at the same time seems to have become the container

---

15   Our use of the word "Field" has more than one derivation. We embrace energetic AQAL state-structures as fields. We also use "Field" to mean the "Knowing Field"—a term created by Albrecht Mahr, a German physician, psychoanalyst and leader in Family Constellation Work. The "knowingfield" is the constellation energyfield, which informs the facilitator, representatives, client, and those observing the constellation of the underlying (often hidden) dynamics that are blocking or resourcing the flow of Life.

16   Hamilton (2008) represents these nested holarchy of human systems as Map 2, p. 62.

17   2nd Tier refers to levels of consciousness that embrace all six of the 1st Tier levels of consciousness; looking at reality through whole systems, and one world lenses.

in which we think, sense/act, relate and create. This force of attraction is neither simply the energy from inside the boundaries nor the energy from outside the boundaries of our container—rather it is a force that has a palpable energy of its own that we simply name the "Space Between." The fullness of the Space Between in our We-space may have implications for cities (which we may have discovered because the nature of this we is presently all women). Maybe that is why we sense that one of the important developmental tasks for cities is to create We-space as a womb/container that will birth what's next for cities. Is it possible that, because we see the city as a larger scale or fractal of our being mothers—or "I's" who have the capability of containing new life—capable of being life-givers for a new "we"? It is a question we pose and hold as we explore an outcome of this We-space experience that we call prototyping the Human Hive Mind.

As we progress through this inquiry, we notice we take 4 steps (as in Figure 8): crossing boundaries from individual I to we; presencing the Human Hive Mind; exploring the field; and discovering new stories.

Steps to Building our We-space Prototype
a. Crossing Boundaries: Individual transition
b. Noticing We-space as a presencing of the Human Hive Mind
c. Exploring space inside, space outside, space between, and expanding our boundaries to include the Mystery and the field of Human Hive Mind
d. Discovering new stories

Figure 8: Steps to Building We-Space Prototype

FRAMING INQUIRY FOR HUMAN HIVE MIND: WHO, WHY1

WHO

- SCW Facilitator
- Participants (IC Community of Practice)

Facilitators' Roles

In the Human Hive Mind prototyping work, two roles facilitate the process: The Lead Constellator (LC) and Integral City Facilitator (ICF).

The LC, through her work with IC (and other organizations), applies and evolves this experiential process as a natural emergence from the Knowing Field. She holds the palpable dimensions of SCW and through her embodiment of its philosophy and premises, she calls on the We's to reflect on and trust in We-space.

The ICF, as a cofacilitator, holds the dimensions of the city in the Field, and either sponsors or finds a sponsor of the question or issue that is constellated. The ICF also applies the information received from the Field in IC's work with cities.

Participants

Our prototype of the Human Hive Mind has gone through some noticeable stages in the Integral City Community of Practice. Each of us has noticed a form of individual transition from I to we and then to We-space. Then we became aware that our We-space had the qualities of a presencing field (discussed below) that we have come to call the Human Hive Mind (HHM). With a growing awareness of this emergent field, our boundaries began to dynamically shift, expand, and transform. New ideas emerged about how we could use our We-space presence for supporting the Integral City paradigm to emerge in the world by serving city leaders, city voices, and city roles in new ways. This Inquiry has been guided by the experiential process of Systemic Constellation Work that has helped us learn more about our We-space, the cities we are working with, and the designs we are using to make cities aware of "integral" framings and make integral communities aware of "city" scale impact.

WHY1

Recognize We-space as an outcome of inquiring into the Human Hive.

Practice within our We-space has shown us the paradox that within the city/Human Hive as a We-space, the individual "I's" don't disappear; rather they gain the capacities to come into coherence with the whole system of their We-space. Coherence arises from the internal alignment of all the elements of the Human Hive/city system/city We-space in pursuit of its Purpose, in such a way that energy is optimized. At the same time, "resonance" emerges when the Human Hive/city system/city We-space is aligned externally in the Purpose of service to its environment: as the human hive (like the beehive) literally resonates with its surroundings.

We are discovering an emergent fractal evolution from me to we, then through We-spaces such as our ICCOP group, and then through the fractals of We-spaces we find or catalyze within cities. Thus the leaps from me to we, to the city/Human Hive, and then to all of humanity, are becoming naturally bridged, with no part of the natural fractal growth sequence or scale skipped over.[18]

TEMPLATE TO CREATE WE-SPACE CONTAINER: WHAT, HOW

WHAT

The Research Question for the SCW is stated as an intention or question such as **"How can we develop a process for exploring Integral City insights at the Integral Theory Conference?"**[19]

HOW

Preparation:

We always begin with a silent meditation and check-in ritual. The purpose is to create and tend a sacred We-space container for all our work together. This ritual also prepares the team—collectively—to enter the Knowing Field.

The Process:

ICCOP uses these process steps when working in the Knowing Field:

Preparation

1. The Lead Constellator (LC) prepares herself by tuning into the Knowing Field (a sacred multidimensional space[20]) and receiving its guidance.

---

18 This is in contrast to some other groups where there appears to be an assumed grand leap from the group We-space to all of humanity.

19 Integral Theory Conference 2015, sponsored by MetaIntegral Foundation at Sonoma State University.

20 For example, both horizontal and vertical dimensions: past–future; above–below.

2. Each participant prepares themselves in their own way. Some meditate beforehand. They also prepare their own space – either desktop or floor space—by placing a clock chart in the center of the space. This represents the Knowing Field, the circle or field within which we work. Using computer paper or sticky notes as place-markers on the clock chart, each participant is able to map the process visually and then share with the others so we are all working from the same map.

Clarifying Intention & Placing Representatives

3. LC clarifies the intention or question to be constellated in conjunction with sponsor and ICCOP.

4. LC calls in the Knowing Field which holds us in our work together. It too is a "we" space.

5. The elements (unique to each constellation) to be represented in the field are named.

6. Representatives for each of the elements are chosen.

7. The representatives for each element are placed in the field. As the representatives stand in their place, they report back what they are experiencing (as images, body sensations, emotions, thoughts, or phrases) from the Knowing Field.

Observing Images

8. This first image (which is a visual and kinesthetic map of the question or issue) externalizes what the question-holder or team is carrying internally and perhaps unconsciously. We then explore this image—noticing how all the elements represented interact with each other. Hidden dynamics begin to reveal themselves.

9. Transition images: The first image begins to shift (this is the transition image) when representatives make slow movements—sometimes big, sometimes small—showing the direction for change. Most often the different elements dialogue with each other, which is one way we gather collective intelligence.

10. Resolution image: When everyone or thing represented feels strong and peaceful and in their rightful place. When that does not happen in the time allotted, we bring the process to completion, acknowledging there is more to do.

Release, Harvest, and Debrief

11. Representatives release themselves from the element they have been representing and come back into themselves.

12. Debrief: Although the SCW protocol is to not interpret or analyze the constellation process, we find that each member may interpret or give meaning to what we have heard or seen. We ask: What can we harvest?

13. LC tracks how the SCW process is informing and impacting us over time. It is as if a seed has been planted, and its fruits blossom in their own time!

14. We have found that we come together as a we who thinks and perceives together while each remains their own self (not thinking the same) having shifted our perspective through the greater knowing that is emerging from our SCW.

CONCLUSION: WHY2

Many benefits and insights have arisen from prototyping the HHM through exploring and experimenting in the Knowing Field. Here are a few outcomes with particular impact.

1. We practice our Inquiry Intelligence (see *Appendix C1: Definitions of 12 Intelligences*) by finding the clearest question or issue to bring to the field.

2. We give voice to all the elements related to an issue recognizing the Divine in all.

3. We hear from all elements, often at a level deeper than our conscious mind. For example, we listen to the Spirit of IC, the Spirit of the Planet of Cities, and other spiritual elements before

making decisions or taking actions. We hear the 4 Voices of the Human Hive.

4. By listening so deeply to each other, the Old Story, which is represented in the first SCW image, is opened into a new version—so that a New Story and a new stage of experience can emerge.

5. We can see the levels of change possible—an awareness of hidden dynamics; a shift in perspective; a movement either large or small that shifts direction; a resolution. The change may happen immediately or over time.

6. We allow and are conscious that the Mystery is present with us in the field.

7. We gather collective intelligence for the IC We-space and for the greater collective.

8. Every time we tap into our We-space through SCW we learn more about our own ways of making meaning.

9. We have come to trust in a Divine Order.

10. Such a deep exploration enables us to experiment with AQAL maps and structures and test ideas and solutions.

11. Through SCW, we have cared for our We-space. We have been and continue to be in the container with reverence.

REITERATION OF INQUIRY OBJECTIVES

The Inquiry Objectives of this chapter were:

1. Explore Systemic Constellation Work as prototyping methodology.

2. Prototype the Human Hive Mind as a We-space.

3. Recognize We-space as an outcome of inquiring into the Human Hive.

4. Understand the relationship between Human Hive Mind, Integral City, and Planet of Cities.

5. Learn how to tell the We-space story.

ACTION PLAN FOR PRACTITIONER, CATALYST, MESHWORKER

Review this chapter and make notes below of your impressions, insights, and questions. Locate yourself on the Integral City practice scaffolding. Notice what you have observed, thought, felt, and what you now want to do in any of the three possible practice configurations: as a Practitioner, as a Catalyst, as a Meshworker.

After you have made these notes, consider some of the Impact Questions (below). They also might help you reflect on how to generate impact through inquiry and action. Finally check out the Resources and Links suggested for this practice at the end of the chapter.

IMPACT QUESTIONS: DEEP, WIDE, CLEAR, HIGH

1. UL DEEP: How does my development as an "I" bootstrap development of others and together how do we bootstrap a "We-space"? How does developing "We-space" in turn bootstrap my own development?

2. LL WIDE: What feelings emerge when we contemplate moving beyond our individual "I," beyond participating as an aggregate of "I's" into a We-space where we share a consciousness as a Human Hive Mind? How do we tell the story about the "Space Between"? How does that story reflect the Human Hive Mind? How does the Human Hive Mind make possible deeper inquiry, action, and impact in the city?

3. UR CLEAR: What qualities attract me to a We-space as a container? What energy does it offer me? What energy do I offer the We-space container? What qualities do I notice about my personal boundaries? About group boundaries, where I am active in the city? How do I sense the "Space Between" myself and others; between myself and the group? How does this "Space Between" have its own energy?

4. LR HIGH: What other groups do we know in our city who are shifting from identification with the individual to a more collective sense of identity? How might we experiment together with inquiry, action, or impact for the well-being of our city (or other cities)? In what ways,

dimensions, or senses do we become aware of the energy in a "Space Between" that transcends individual and group boundaries?

CHAPTER RESOURCES AND/OR LINKS

Appendix B: Integral City Maps (1–5): 1, 2, 4, 5

Appendix C1: Definitions of 12 Intelligences: Integral, Inner, Outer, Cultural/Storytelling, Structural, Inquiry, Evolutionary

Appendix C3: Integral City GPS Locator: Evolutionary, Integral, Smart, Resilient

Reflective Question for Whom /Where/ What I Could Use as:	Practitioner	Catalyst	Meshworker
What do I observe as I read?			
What do I think?			
What do I feel?			
What do I want to do next?			

SECTION II — *Embrace the Master Code*

These two chapters explore the Master Code that is another hallmark of Integral City inquiry and action practice. Chapter 3 explains what it is and Chapter 4 gives a specific example how spiritual communities (as a Voice of the Civil Society) have a particular role to play in modeling, sharing, and practicing the Master Code with the other Voices of the city.

The Master Code is a whole systems meta-intelligence that coalesces the energies and intentions of all scales of human systems in the city.

AMPLIFY CARING CAPACITY WITH MASTER CODE

INQUIRY OBJECTIVES

The Inquiry Objectives of this chapter are:

1. Learn Integral City Master Code.

2. Learn importance of Master Code to city thriving.

3. Live Master Code to expand Circles of Care.

4. Link Master Code to Integral City Voices.

5. Explore simple practices for enacting the Master Code.

6. Consider how linking City Voices and Master Code amplifies Caring and Carrying Capacity.

INTRODUCTION TO INQUIRY, ACTION, AND IMPACT WITH INTEGRAL CITY MASTER CODE

Most Citizens ask "what can our cities do for us?" But Integral City asks "what can I and/or we do for our cities?" The driving purpose of Integral City practice is to discover and enable the well-being of the Human

Hive. The core methodology for nurturing well-being in the Human Hive is the focus of this whole book, but it all rests on the DNA of the Master Code that generates the blueprint for the Human Hive:

- Take Care of Self
- Take Care of Each Other
- Take Care of This Place
- Take Care of This Planet

FRAMING INQUIRY PRACTICE WITH THE MASTER CODE: WHO, WHY1

Some very mysterious, paradoxical, and powerful qualities attach to the IC Master Code that impact and are embedded in our Integral semiotics of WHO, WHAT, WHY, HOW.

Practice Daily Review: WHO, WHY

On the simplest level, you can use the IC Master Code as an object of meditation (see template below). It also forms a set of principles for daily practice and review. You can review your agenda for the day using the Master Code to inquire of your intentions and organize your actions. At the end of the day you can review your outcomes with an inquiry framed simply as:

How did I?... take care of Self... take care of Others... take care of this Place... take care of this Planet?

Expand Circles of Care & Well-being: WHO, WHY

On a second level, you might discover that a potent "mystery" underlies the Master Code. It turns out that when we practice each level of the Master Code it sets up the conditions to expand our Circles of Care. Each level is more complex than the one before. And as we learn to practice the basics of taking care of our Self then a surprising thing happens—we develop the capacity to take care of each Other.

When we learn well how to take care of each other—on different scales from family, to tribe, to organization, to sector, to community, to city and nation—then we develop even more capacity to take care of this Place.

And when we learn to take care of our Place—whether that is our home (apartment, house), our workplace, our neighborhood, our city, our eco-region, our planet—as the scale of the place increases, so do our Circles of Care.

Until finally we realize that the four elements of the Master Code: *Take care of Self. Take care of Others. Take care of this Place. Take care of this Planet.*—are not really separate from each other. They are not in conflict with one another. In fact, we can acknowledge each element as the same injunction for well-being at different levels of scale. Each of these elements of the Master Code surpasses and includes one another, in a kind of graceful developmental sequence.

Voices & Perspectives in the Master Code: WHO, WHY

When we discover how the Master Code expands our Circles of Care, we can start appreciating how this code offers us multiple perspectives of the city and connects us to the 4 Voices of the city, which give rise to the 12 intelligences in the city (as discussed in *Chapter 5* and *Appendix C1*).

4 Voices in the Integral City

In *Chapter 9: Attract the 4 Voices of the City* , we explore in depth the 4 Voices of the Integral City. Right now it is sufficient to acknowledge the 4 Voices as integral to the functioning, well-being, and thriving of every city and the roles they are continuously playing as we enact the Master Code in our daily lives. We each represent at least one voice—and in many cases multiple voices.

When you look at the list below, how do you see your voice in relation to the city? Which voice is the one you express most often in your life in the city? Maybe you express these voices for different purposes or different roles or in different locations? For now, think about the opportunities that you have to contribute to the intelligence of the city through any of these voices:

- Citizen
- Civil Society
- City Government/Institution
- Business/Organization

Multiple Perspectives in the Integral City

As you consider these 4 Voices, look around you as you enact your intentions or respond to others in your city environment. Become aware of: Which Voice the Self is speaking from? Which Voice is/are Other(s) using? What Voice arises from the Place and Planet? How does this awareness of multiple Voices and their relationship to one another naturally expand not only our Circles of Care, but also our capacity for multiple perspectives?

Ultimately, practice of the Master Code is a deeply Integral Practice that brings continuous awareness to the perspectives that arise from the 4 quadrants of existence that represent how we experience, act, relate to, and produce our reality (see Figure 9).

- The Self offers the subjective perspective of the city from the point of view of I.
- The Other offers the intersubjective perspective of the city from the point of view WE or YOU.
- The Place offers the objective perspective of the city from the point of view of IT.
- The Planet offers the interobjective perspective of the city from the point of view of ITS.

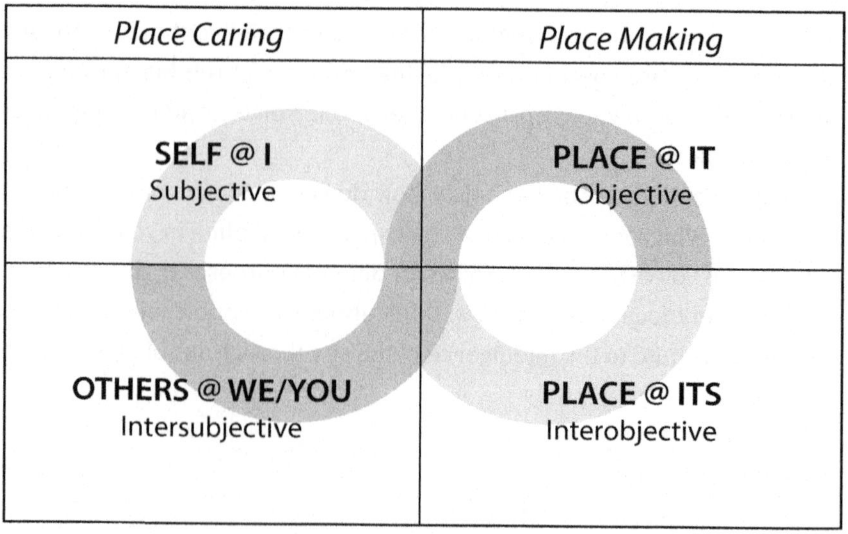

Place Caring	*Place Making*
SELF @ I Subjective	**PLACE @ IT** Objective
OTHERS @ WE/YOU Intersubjective	**PLACE @ ITS** Interobjective

Figure 9: Master Code: Perspectives in the Integral City

FRAMING PRACTICE OF THE MASTER CODE—5 TEMPLATES: WHAT, HOW

WHAT

The Research Question for practicing the Master Code is basically the same at every level of practice described below: **"How do I practice the Master Code?"**

HOW

Practicing the Master Code is deceptively simple because it can be done on your own or with others. The guidelines below take much longer to write out than to actually practice, so do not be discouraged by the apparent length of the explanation.

In whatever mode or for whatever time you practice "Taking Care," you will notice that living the Master Code pays dividends or rewards that will create and/or reinforce and amplify your daily practice. (However, if you practice the Master Code with others, be "warned" that it opens the doors to We-space and the Human Hive Mind, that we explored in *Chapter 2: Cultivate We-Space Inquiry for Human Hive Mind.*) That being said, here are guidelines for practicing the Master Code from all 4 perspectives.

I Perspective: Take Care of Self

Morning Practice: Self

- Take a deep breath and close your eyes. Listen to the Silence.
- Scan your reality through the 4 quadrants:
  - Scan your body physically from foot to head—ask: "How do I feel?"
  - Scan your awareness—ask: "What is my mood?"
  - Scan your relationship senses—ask: "Who (if anyone) is impacting my energy or space?"
  - Scan your environment sensitivity—ask: "How am I aware of life around me in this place/planet?"
- Connect to your spiritual source, your life's purpose, and your day's purpose—offer: "May my consciousness and my behavior serve all

beings in all worlds, liberating all into the suchness of this and every moment."[21] (Wilber et al., 2008, p. 149)

- Find joy and practice whatever kind of exercise sustains your health and picks up your energy (walking, weights, martial arts, dancing, yoga, swimming, etc.)
- Note if you do not yet know your life's purpose—ask: "What is my life's purpose?" [Sit, walk, dance or move in Silence with this question and notice what arises from within.]
- Record your discoveries: Use a journal, mind-map, sketchpad, flipchart, canvas, musical score, choreography, notation—whatever form of recording gives you energy and makes meaning of "Taking Care of Self."
- Live (or seek) your purpose; enjoy your day!!

Evening Practice: Self

- On retiring, close your eyes.
- Ask and answer for the day just past:
  ○ How did I care for myself?
  ○ How did I care for others?
  ○ How did I care for this place?
  ○ How did I care for this planet?
- Review your energy rewards for living the Master Code:[22]
  ○ What made me happy?
  ○ What gave me comfort?
  ○ What inspired me?
  ○ What am I grateful for?
- Sleep well and deeply.

---

21   Integral Dedication, from *Integral Life Practice* (Wilber et al., 2008, p. 149)

22   First 3 questions are from Buddhist Practice as cited by Shinoda in M. Schlitz et al. *Living Deeply* (Schlitz, Vieten, & Amorok, 2007)

We/You Perspective: Take Care of Others

Taking care of Others builds on the golden rule—to (not) do unto Others what you would (not) have done unto yourself. But it is more proactive, in that, by setting the intention to take care of Others, we actually and actively seek ways to take care of them.

Taking care of others embraces two dimensions: one relates to the span—or size and holarchic relationship—of the "Others" one serves; and the second relates to the depth or the level of complexity of care that one can offer.

Span of Care for Other(s): Nested Holarchy of Relationships

Integral City maps the holarchy of relationships in the city in Map 2 (see *Appendix* B)

This map discloses the span of care that the individual Self may offer. Effectively, the caregiver has many options for identifying the Other(s) to whom they choose to offer (or even target) care. Essentially Others come in a spectrum of social holons whose sizes and relationships unfold in this general direction: family/clan, group/tribe, organization (workplace, educational institution, healthcare agency), community, and city. Moreover, many of the Others we relate to will belong to more than one of these social holons.

Levels of Complexity of Care to Offer

In addition to our "target for care," the second element of the Master Code is informed by the developmental and evolutionary depth or level of care that we can offer. Being aware of these levels of complexity contributes to a positive, caring relationship in two ways: the care receiver values the care being offered and the caregiver offers care that will be valued. Locating this match is the basic work of practicing "meshworking intelligence" (see *Chapter* 13 and *Appendix* C1) and rests on the principles of effective selection of resources and efficient use or delivery of resources (in other words, care). Caring for others will generally be located in a "center of gravity" that spans one to three contiguous levels of complexity as described in Table 2.

Table 2: Levels of Complexity for Caring for Others

Levels of Complexity for Caring for Others
1. provide the basic necessities of life; e.g. food, shelter, clothing
2. offer safety and security and harmonize the values of kinship and familial traditions that bond people together most tightly
3. contribute to the pure unrestrained healthy expression of energy for and enjoyment in life
4. honor commitment and order to life and work, a sense of direction for a greater good, stability, and even recognition of duty to creating and sustaining it
5. strive towards achieving great things together with strategic and goal oriented plans
6. share those elements that are about care and sensitivity to others, with an egalitarian perspective that celebrates diversity
7. mesh flexibility, spontaneity, knowledge and systems thinking as a spur to integrating community development
8. contribute to community wholeness and global connections

Daily Practice: Others

Taking Care of Other(s) does not have to be an overwhelming practice but can be inspired by any of the following actions (note that the results of these actions are linked to the Daily Practice for *Taking Care of Place*, described below).

1. Starting at home provides little things, like taking time to pack a lunch or snack for your children.

2. Expanding the family circle, calling a family member who is in need of support (moral, physical, or financial), or remembering a favorite elder with a phone call.

3. Including your friendship group, wish someone a happy birthday, recognize their new accomplishment (school, work, sports), or invite an Other to celebrate a good time with you.

4. With commitment to Others who share your beliefs, offer volunteer time for a peer group, youth group, church, substance abuse support group, new neighbor, or language learning skills workshop.

5. Keeping a shared goal in mind, make plans with special interest groups you belong to, to accomplish specific results; for example, creating a community garden in an unused parking lot. Offer your skills to sell/persuade, strategize, implement, or evaluate.

6. Bring together two or more groups and help them collaborate to welcome diverse interests, share different perspectives, build bridges, and generate care in the community; for example, designing welcoming programs for new immigrants.

7. See the whole community as a system of many smaller systems and facilitate them to share stories, integrate their intentions and take action by helping to align purposes, priorities, people, and place; for example, facilitating discussions with city hall staff, developers, and investors.

8. On the largest scale possible, make connections between Others in your community or city, your eco-region and another part of the world; for example, connect scientists in local organizations with artists in the developing world to explore through art and science how climate change is showing up in different places.

It Perspective: Take Care of this Place

Taking Care of this Place differs from *Taking Care of Others* because it moves your focus from intersubjective people relationships to *Caring for your Place* as an object. In other words, care moves from the second person, *We/You* to the third person *It*. While *Taking Care of Others* is relationship oriented, *Taking Care of Place* is outcome oriented with a tangible result that can be apprehended through the senses. However, the Place-based results manifest in a similar spectrum of complexity as we observed in the *Taking Care of Others*, simply because they are the outcomes (nouns) of those caring actions (verbs) taken by Others—as can be seen in Table 3.

Table 3: Place-based Objects of Caring

Place-based Objects of Caring
1. basic necessities of life; e.g. food, shelter, clothing
2. places and practices of safety and security, bonding traditions
3. healthy expressions of energy for and enjoyment in life
4. practices for order, direction, stability, and duty of care
5. designs, results, strategic and goal oriented plans
6. caring and sensitive behaviors, tolerance, acceptance of diversity
7. flexible, evidence-based practices that integrate community life
8. connections that create community wholeness and global links

Daily Practice: Place

The review of *Caring for Place* can be done at the same time as the review of *Caring for Other(s)* by recognizing the outcome of any of the Other-Caring actions selected above (under You/We Voice).

- What outcome or result can I sense and witness: see, hear, feel, smell, taste?

Its Perspective: Take Care of this Planet

Taking Care of this Planet is an extension of *Taking Care of this Place*. It links the many Places and results at the global systems level. It calls for us to expand our attention for results from our local focus on Place to a global focus that ties our many places together in an interobjective way. *Taking Care of the Planet* invokes both the widest span of social holons and greatest depth of all complexity. We can use the same process of interobjective review as we did for the Place focus above and expand our objects of outcome to a planetary level. This gives us a kind of psycho-bio-cultural-social overview effect.[23]

Ultimately, my practice of *Taking Care of This Planet* evolves with the expansion of the scope of the place I consider my home: from my residence, to my neighborhood, to the town I live in, to our planet as a whole. Thus *Taking Care of Planet* aligns all the scales of caretaking into a global scale that transcends and includes Place, Others, and Self. Recognizing this impact, we have created a meditation practice for generating our *Caring for Planet* focus, that works equally well on your own or with a group of people (gathered for any purpose including a workshop).

---

23 The Overview Effect" is a phenomenon noticed by astronauts, looking back on planet Earth from space, realizing they were seeing the whole from an overview, that caused a psycho-active impact. We have the same opportunity to see our cities from "away"—not only as an aerospace voyager but also as a boat navigator, a train rider or an auto passenger.

Daily Practice: Planet[24]

Close your eyes and get present in this room. Take a deep breath and clear away as much of your mental chatter as you can. Find yourself in your body, feel the sensation of sitting in your chair (or standing on your feet). Look for and find the center of your being. When you feel centered, look around. Who else is here? Recognize this is a nested group within the larger collective of Others (other people, groups). Notice what you notice and let it go. See if you can connect with everyone in the room, by noticing them. Now see if you sense the center of this collective of individuals. Does it have a location in the room? Just notice what you notice quietly and let it go. Now bring your awareness to the room. Sense into the boundaries created by the walls. Locate yourself in relationship to the walls, including the ceiling, floor, and the doors. Then expand your awareness to the building itself. See the room inside of the building.... then imagine the building as it sits in its streetscape/landscape. Now practice expanding your awareness to the City. Imagine the street as it rises from land within boundaries which contains human habitat called the city [name]. It's time to pull your awareness higher, imagining the City as part of the County/Region and the County/Region as part of the Eco-region and the Eco-region as a node in the network of eco-regions across the planet where cities create hubs of human habitats in every nation and on six continents. Be aware that group includes Integral City practitioners who are present with us and working the space from nodes in other places [name them]. Today we serve the Spirit of a Planet of Cities, as potential from each of these cities. Calling forth "what is" by giving voice to the nested places where we are embedded, by interacting with others who are in this room with us, by caring about the experience we each have as we play with awareness of Self, Others, and Place and Planet, rest in the Care of the Planet as it cares for us.

Connect the 4 Perspectives to the 4 Voices to Amplify Care

Now that we have explored the Master Code through the 4 perspectives of I, We/You, It, and Its, we can return to the 4 Voices of the Integral City and suggest a voice dialogue that includes representatives from:

- Citizens
- Civil Society

---

24   This meditation was created by Cherie Beck for the Integral Theory Conference 2015 Pop-up Lunch (Hamilton et al., 2015)

- City Government/Institutions
- Business/Organizations

The structure for this practice is simple; the outcomes can be surprising. It starts by the Integral City facilitator inviting and convening the 4 Voices of the city (The size of the circle could be as small as 4 or as large as 40—but it is important that all 4 Voices be represented. It is also important to match the circle size to the time allowed for the sharing process. If you allow 1–2 minutes for each contribution in the cycle, that will give you an estimate of the time needed. Therefore, if you have a large attendance, you can create a variation of the dialogue circle by creating small dialogue groups where each of the 4 Voices is represented, and then reconvene the large circle of the whole for final sharing and checking out.) The invitation will advise participants which of the Master Code practices from the 4 perspectives that you will do together in voice dialogue.

The facilitator opens the circle, welcomes the 4 Voices (and invites introductions of Name/Voice/City location) and frames the Master Code in its simplest form: *In a healthy city I take care of my Self, so I can take care of Others, so we can take care of this Place and this Planet. Today we are going to share one of the practices for honoring the Master Code. We will start with completing this sentence: "One way I take care of myself is... ". For this round and the next two, each person will share in their small group and then we will harvest vital sharings with the large group.*

On a second round, we ask you to complete the sentence, "What I heard others say, and what this means to me for my Self care is... "

On a third and last round, we ask you to complete the sentence, "What I think (or feel) about Self care that could help me care for Other(s) is... "

On a check out round, we conclude by, "What I have learned about Self care today is... and what I want to do next is... "

At subsequent gatherings the same format can be used substituting the next object of care in the Master Code sequence: *Other(s), Place, Planet.*

The purpose of these voice dialogues is to reveal the interconnections of Self, Others, Place, and Planet that are embedded in our lives as individuals and the Voices of the Integral City. The dialogues identify, express, recognize, and amplify the ways that people care, in their relationship to each other in the city. This caring is of core importance to the well-being of the city, because there is a direct relationship between *Caring Capacity* and *Carrying Capacity*. In other words, *Placecaring* enables *Placemaking*. If we wish to grow the latter, we must nurture the former.

CONCLUSION: WHY2

To improve the well-being of the city, we must make practicing the Master Code a habit. It does not take long to do—minutes a day—but it aligns and brings into coherence your and our Integral City practice at all levels.

When/if you cannot practice all levels, practice the most basic—take care of your Self—because it is fundamental to all other caring and capacity building.

It turns out that cities who develop their caring capacity for self, others, and place/planet, are cities who develop their carrying capacity—their resilience for good times and bad.

Communities and cities who care have the capacity to rapidly respond and evolve into new ways of being and becoming together.

When we connect the 4 perspectives and the 4 Voices of the Integral City, the powerof the Master Code naturally enables the healthy flow of daily life and local and global well-being as you:

- Care for yourself
- Care for each other
- Care for this place
- Care for this planet

When we practice the Master Code we take the initiative and responsibility to replace the helpless plea of "What can our cities do for us?" with the enabling inquiry "What can I and/or we do for our cities?"
The rewards of practicing the Master Code are 4-fold:

1. You will create a new level of you as a caring individual.
2. You will augment your capacity to make a positive difference in the world as all us WE's work together.

3. You will become part of a vibrant community of mutually supportive relationships by connecting to People Who Care.

4. The Power of WE releases the DNA of our Master Code in your city as a contribution to the well-being of all the cities on our Planet of Cities.

REITERATION OF INQUIRY OBJECTIVES

The Inquiry Objectives of this chapter were:

1. Learn Integral City Master Code.
2. Learn importance of Master Code to city thriving.
3. Live Master Code to expand Circles of Care.
4. Link Master Code to Integral City Voices.
5. Explore simple practices for enacting the Master Code.
6. Consider how linking City Voices and Master Code amplifies Caring and Carrying Capacity.

ACTION PLAN FOR PRACTITIONER, CATALYST, MESHWORKER

Review this chapter and make notes below of your impressions, insights, and questions. Locate yourself on the Integral City practice scaffolding. Notice what you have observed, thought, felt, and what you now want to do in any of the three possible practice configurations: as a Practitioner, as a Catalyst, as a Meshworker.

After you have made these notes, consider some of the Impact Questions (below). They also might help you reflect on how to generate impact through inquiry and action. Finally check out the Resources and Links suggested for this practice at the end of the chapter.

IMPACT QUESTIONS: DEEP, WIDE, CLEAR, HIGH

1. UL DEEP: What personal development practices support my appreciation for the Master Code? How do I care for my Self?
2. LL WIDE: What family practices have modeled how we care for Others? Who and how in our families are good models for caring

for Others? Who has cared for us outside the family? How has that helped us learn how to care for Place and Planet?

3. UR CLEAR: In the next 3 months what will I do to live into the Master Code? What behaviors, actions, and service can I offer to learn and/or expand my practicing the Master Code? What is a stretch goal I set myself in the next 3 months to practice the Master Code?

4. LR HIGH: How could I boost the positive impact of taking care of this Place? What will it take to move from the current stage of taking care of my Self, taking care of Other(s) and taking care of this Place (home, street, community) to the next stage of caring for our City? Caring for our Eco-region? Caring for the Planet?

CHAPTER RESOURCES AND/OR LINKS

Appendix B: Integral City Maps (1–5): 1, 2, 3, 5

Appendix C1: Definitions of 12 Intelligences: Integral, Inner, Outer, Cultural, Structural, Inquiry, Evolutionary

Appendix C3: Integral City GPS Locator: Evolutionary, Integral

Reflective Question for Whom /Where/ What I Could Use as:	Practitioner	Catalyst	Meshworker
What do I observe as I read?			
What do I think?			
What do I feel?			
What do I want to do next?			

4

INSPIRE SPIRITUAL COMMUNITIES TO SERVE EVOLUTION OF THE HUMAN HIVE

INQUIRY OBJECTIVES

The Inquiry Objectives of this chapter are:

1. Learn the evolutionary lineage of Integral City.

2. Understand Human Hive goals and roles.

3. Connect Human Hive roles to city voices.

4. Connect Master Code to 4 city voices and 12 city intelligences.

5. Identify practices for 4 city roles.

6. Suggest opportunities for Integrator Role of Spiritual Communities.

INTRODUCTION TO INQUIRY, ACTION, AND IMPACT WITH SPIRITUAL COMMUNITIES

The book cover of *Integral City: Evolutionary Intelligences for the Human Hive* (Hamilton, 2008a) shows the evolutionary lineage from which we all come. You can see Gaia/Planet Earth in the context of our Solar System, Galaxy, and the Universe. She has birthed all geographies and life on earth—including our eco-regions and all its plants and animals—as well as us human beings. In turn, we have birthed our families, clans, kingdoms, nations, and states. We have co-created the cities—our Human Hives.

Predecessor work to Integral City focused on human systems at smaller scales, including study of the individual in families, teams, organizations, sectors, and communities. This trajectory of human scales leads inevitably to looking at cities as complex adaptive human systems that concentrate habitat for humans like a beehive does for bees.

Moreover, extrapolating from Lovelock's[25] (2009) proposition that humans are Gaia's Reflective Organ, we have come to consider that cities are Gaia's actual *organs,* and humans the *cells,* and organizations the *organelles* in that organ.

FRAMING INQUIRY FOR SPIRITUAL COMMUNITIES: WHO, WHY1

WHO

- Spiritual Community leaders
- Spiritual community members
- Facilitator

It is a distinctive human capacity to be reflective. Moreover, we have created institutions and communities with the specific function of reflection, namely Spiritual Communities. Because of their capacity for contemplative inquiry Spiritual Communities may be optimally situated to catalyze reflection in Gaia's Reflective Organs. Moreover, the reflective capacity of such communities may have an integrative function within the city to align other functions and roles so that we may all contribute to Gaia's very well-being.

This inquiry considers the role of Spiritual Communities as Integrators in the human hive.

---

25   I heard Lovelock interviewed by Anna-Marie Tremonti on CBC in 2009, who asked "Well I guess you don't have a very high opinion of humans with all the damage they have done to the Earth?" Lovelock countered with considerable vigor, "On the contrary, humans are Gaia's reflective organ!"

WHY1

We call cities Human Hives, because of what we have learned from another species—the honey bee. Apis Mellifera is the most intelligent species on the branch of the Tree of Life called the invertebrates. Homo Sapiens are supposed to be the most intelligent species on the branch called the vertebrates. Honey bees have populated every geography on Earth with their beehives. So, I have been curious what might we learn from a species that is 100 million years old (we humans are only 100,000 to 1 million years old, depending on whose metrics you use). What might we learn from the bees that not only could sustain us, and create thriving cities—but contribute as much to all of Earth's species as the honey bee does?

Clues to this riddle come from Howard Bloom (2000)[26]—he discovered that the honey bee has developed a strategy for individual adaptation, hive innovation, and species resilience.

A beehive has about 50,000 bees in it—about the size of a small city. It uses goals and roles in its sustainability strategy that give us new insight for understanding the Human Hive.

GOAL—The beehive's goal is to produce 40 pounds of honey per year in order for the hive to survive. So, a beehive has a clear sustainability objective for the hive, measured in terms of energy production.

ROLES—In the beehive, five key Roles contribute to achieving the Goal. In our Human Hive I link these Roles to the Voices of the city (as I have done in parentheses below).

1. PRODUCERS—(Voice of the Citizen—How many readers speak with this voice?) Producers (foragers and workers) gather the nectar and pollen and produce the honey.

   About 90% of the hive are Producers or **Conformity Enforcers**. One of their jobs is to fly to flower patches and harvest as much nectar and pollen as they can. They use the "waggle dance" form of communication to let sister bees know where to find the resources. When 90% of the hive is doing the same dance—it's like a Rock

---

26 Thanks to Dr. Don Beck who in 2002 dubbed the 5 roles as Bloom's "Pentad."

& Roll rave—the energy produced attracts a lot of attention and reinforces successful finds.

2. ENTREPRENEURS—(Voice of the business/innovators—How many readers speak with this voice?)

Entrepreneurs source new resources and keep the Producers advised of all options.

About 5% of the hive are Entrepreneurs or Business **Diversity Generators**. Their job is to fly to different flower beds than the Producer Conformity Enforcers. As a result, their waggle dances contain different information—more like Irish jigs or step dances, than say, Rock & Roll. When the Producers are at peak performance, the Diversity Generators are not noticed because their communication is drowned out by the Producers having their "rave."

3. ADMINISTRATORS—(Voice of the Managers of City Hall and Agencies or Institutions, such as education, healthcare, justice, emergency responders, etc. How many readers speak with this voice?) Administrators allocate resources to reward effective performance. Only a small percent of the hive are Administrators or **Resource Allocators (RA)**. Their job is to reward the performance of Producers and Entrepreneur bees. When Producers' performance lags (after depleting the resources in one flower patch), Administrators withhold rewards until the point that the Producer/Conformity Enforcer bees are not only de-energized—they become downright depressed. You can imagine them walking around completely bummed out—the party is over (by the way, depression in bees can be determined by measuring their pheromones). Eventually when the Producers' energy is lowest, they finally take note of the Entrepreneurs/Diversity Generators doing their Irish jig (communication) and switch their resourcing flights to new locations.

4. INTEGRATORS—(Voice of the Civil Society/Integrators—How many readers speak with this voice?)

Integrators align all the other Roles for the achievement of the Hive Goal and survival.

Only a small percent of the hive **are Integrators or Inner Judges (IJ).** Some say this is even a hive intelligence. **The Integrators** work with Administrators to assess and reward performance, so that the hive can achieve its sustainability goals of producing 40 pounds of honey.

5. COMPETITORS—(Voice of the other Hives in the same eco-region—How many readers are visiting from another city today?)

Competitors ensure that the best survival strategies emerge and sustain the species.

This fifth role is a whole hive role—it is created through **Inter-Group Tournaments (IT)**. This role actually emerges from the competition between hives within the bee's eco-region; that is, the territory they share with other hives competing for the same resources.

These **five roles** create a resilience strategy that depends on performance and innovation to support the hive and the species (very much like the Panarchy model). But the bees have taken their sustainability strategy beyond the hive to scale at the regional level of resilience. Because of course, as they gather resources for themselves, they pollinate their eco-region, thereby creating energy renewal for next year. This means the bees have developed a double sustainability loop that supports hive survival *and* regenerates the energy resources in their eco-region, producing more than $90 billion worth of agriculture production per year for global human consumption (Benjamin & McCullum, 2009; Bjerga, 2007). The Inter-Group tournaments operate at the level of species survival—ensuring any hive that gets an edge in the innovation and evolution curve is the one most likely to survive and pass on its learning.

In terms of sustainability, I have wondered when homo sapiens sapiens will embrace performance goals and strategies that replenish the resources we use to sustain our human hive and our eco-regions, thereby adding value to the earth?

How can our capacity as Gaia's Reflective Organ help the human species contribute in a way that supports the whole of life on earth? In other words, **what is the equivalent, for the Human Hive of the bees' 40 pounds of honey?**

From the perspective of Spiritual Communities, here may be their special interest in the **Soul's calling** of our species: to act as the Integrators of the Human Hive in service as Gaia's Reflective Organ. Spiritual Communities have the opportunity (if not the purpose) to help cities find their Vision and its Goals (the equivalent of the bees' 40 pounds of honey) that will sustain them in good times and bad.

This opportunity exists not only at the local city scale, but has implications for the health of our whole planet. For, if humans as individuals are cells (and organizations are organelles) in Gaia's reflective Human Hive organs, then it is not too much of a stretch to consider that these reflective organs are like nodes on a planetary meridian system—our Planet of Cities. This may be how our cities or Human Hives can act as not just one organ, but an organ system for Gaia's reflective capacity.

If this is the case, then our reflective organs are at the stage of evolution where we need to learn how the principles the bees have learned in their practice of the **Master Code** contribute to the potential goals of individual cities, the Planet of Cities, and thus to the well-being of our planet, Gaia. **How might we on every level practice: *Take care of ourselves, each other, this place, and this planet?***

INQUIRY PRACTICE FOR SPIRITUAL COMMUNITIES: WHAT, HOW

WHAT

Spiritual communities play a very special role in the evolution of collective intelligence in human systems, with a calling (or commission) to be much larger actors than they have typically been imagining.

Spiritual Communities traditionally have attended to the spiritual awakening of individuals. Many also attend to the individual's and family needs. And they certainly often take energy and pleasure in the enjoyment of their own company. Many churches, temples, and synagogues even support global caring missions for others in need—where they minister to the suffering located in (other) neighborhoods, cities, and even countries. In order to explore how Spiritual Communities can expand their relationship—and service—to the city, the inquiry question for this practice is:

HOW CAN SPIRITUAL COMMUNITIES SERVE THE EVOLUTION OF THE HUMAN HIVE AS GAIA'S REFLECTIVE ORGAN?

HOW

Find a Goal or Vision

As we have learned above, each voice of the city has a particular role to play in achieving the goal of the city. One way to understand this goal is the discovery and realization of the city's vision, mission, and values. We explore this process in subsequent chapters (7, 8, 9, 10). For now, we assume the vision can be discovered and stated—as some of the world's more advanced cities have done in the following examples:

- To be the greenest city (Vancouver, Canada)
- To be the most walkable city (Copenhagen, Denmark)
- To be the most energy efficient city (Malmo, Sweden)
- To be Latin America's most bikable city (Leon, Mexico)

It should be noted that most current city visions are in service to the well-being of the Master Code at the local place scale, and are not yet in service to the planetary scale of Gaia's well-being. But even these place-based expressions are strong evolutionary indicators that we are moving in the right direction. For the purposes of this exercise even the intention to find a vision for the city is a sufficient starting point, and in fact, we focus the realization of the Master Code at the primary levels of Self, Others, and Place in the examples below. We believe the planetary scale will emerge when enough cities (or key cities) have implemented Master Code practice as a way of operating— probably 10% to 15% of the world's cities, if we take the lessons from complexity theory (De Landa, 2006; Eoyang & Olson, 2001; Gladwell, 2002; Holling, 2001).

4 Voices Release Integral City Intelligences

The first Integral City (Hamilton, 2008a) book explored in depth the 12 intelligences that give a city environmental context, integral wholeness, strategic responses, and evolutionary direction (see *Appendix* C for a summary of the 12 intelligences).

We are now in a position to propose that the 12 intelligences can be released by the 4 Voices of the city, practicing the Master Code (and guided by the city's vision).

In the summaries below, for each of the city voices, we propose 3 practices that embrace the Master Code and in so doing, result in the emergence of one of the 12 Integral City intelligences. We note that the examples we have used come from real communities who have practiced them, so they are not merely hypothetical. We also note, that although we have identified only one intelligence as an outcome for each practice, in fact multiple intelligences will be involved in the process and will reinforce one another (like activating synaptic connections through overlapping pathways in a neural network).

We propose that Civil Society has the special role of Integrator in the city. Because Spiritual Communities are located in this voice (in the Lower Left quadrant of the city) and they nurture the reflective capacity of people, we suggest that they have the greatest potential to step into the role of Integrators of the Human Hive. Many readers may consider this role is better played by the Government or Business voices of the city (who have assumed this role in the rise of Traditional and Modern cities), but the Spiritual Community has the greatest potential for success as Integrator in the Integral City because of its experience and skills in reflection, contemplation, and creating communities of caring people. Spiritual Communities have the reflective memes needed to catalyze and seed the city's attraction to the highest vision of itself.

Practice Examples

For each of the 4 city voices, we offer three practices that can release intelligences in the city. We start with the voices of the Citizen, then Business and Government, and finish with the voice of the Civil Society. Then we offer a specific methodology for Spiritual Practices to enact their role as Integrators for the city.

It should be noted that the person(s) whose voice belongs to Civil Society or Spiritual Community, no doubt will also belong to the Citizen and possibly even Business or Government voices as well. This possibility offers a multiplicity of opportunities to amplify the voice of the Spiritual Community and thus enable them to work more closely together with other city voices as Integrators of the multiple practices and intelligences in service to aligning care for all life.

At the same time, we observe that the other voices of the city may have opportunities to act as Integrators. (In fact as noted above, the voice of Government has typically played that role in the Traditional and Modern Cities.) However, because their "natural" contribution as we discussed above is to be Diversity Generators (Business) and Resource Allocators (Government), it is most likely their energies will not be focused and/or available to play the vital role of Integrators (especially employing reflective practice).

Keeping that in mind, let us examine some practices that increase intelligence in the city through practicing the Master Code through each of the 4 Voices. In the following tables we give specific examples of how each voice can practice the Master Code with an example of a city (in CAPS) where this has occurred. (To understand the methodology for each of these examples requires a full project report and is beyond the scope of this chapter or book; however, sources or reports are provided in the References section.) This overview is intended to paint a picture of the richness and opportunity available to spiritual communities to act as Integrators for their cities using the Master Code as an empowering guide.

Table 4 shows three examples of how **Citizens** can increase the intelligence of the city.

Table 4: Citizens Practice Master Code

Take Care of Yourself	Take Care of Each Other	Take Care of this Place
Individuals practise cleansing, connecting, and crowning personal energies for individual and collective clarity of expression. This produces Outer Intelligence for acting with authenticity.	Leaders improve their effectiveness with the "We" of groups, teams and organizations by integrating structures, cultures and caring for the system. This produces Integral Intelligence that allows you to align individuals and groups as you do your work in the city.	Activists work together with universities, business and city workers for common well-being of the city and the planet. This produces Ecosphere Intelligence that makes you aware of the context of the city's eco-region and how it is important to each and all of us.
ARGO/IZHEVSK	DURANT	TNS/WHISTLER

Table 5 shows three examples of how **Government/Institutions** can increase the intelligence of the city.

Table 5: City and Institutions Practice Master Code

Take Care of Yourself	Take Care of Each Other	Take Care of this Place
Individual designers and architects make their dreams for new city governance real by challenging the status quo with experiments in eco-villages and renewable energy production that engage the many individuals in new forms of engagement to achieve a goal. This produces Structural Intelligence that gives the Designer many new ideas and engages the Residents in co-designing city structures. STRATHCONA, CANADA EKURHULENI, S. AFRICA	Villagers in the developing world (and/or underprivileged city areas) discover how they can mesh themselves and message their story about how climate change affects them, so neighbors learn how to cooperate with each other and local governments, and also national, regional and global institutions. This produces Meshworking Intelligence where all the people, priorities, purposes and planet line up – connecting all the dots. EL SALVADOR	Investment fund managers using principles based on living systems open up whole new standards for economies, environments, social and cultural pillars of sustainability and resilience at all scales – from public, to private, city, nation, and globe. This produces Navigating Intelligence that uses metrics based on living systems, natural capital and strengthens city and citizen alike. AQAL INVESTMENT

Table 6 shows three examples of how Business /Organizations can increase the intelligence of the city.

Table 6: Business/Organizations Practice Master Code

Take Care of Yourself	Take Care of Each Other	Take Care of this Place
Leaders have the power to transact, translate, transform and transduce the entire supply chain of business interests and economies. This produces Evolutionary Intelligence where the city uses an economic metabolism so matter, energy and information flow through it to sustain prosperity and life.	Private Sector Employers use Appreciative Inquiry to unlock the energy of stakeholders, who: discover they have the wisdom to develop new transportation systems for the city: dream new technology solutions; design ways of changing mobility in the city; and deliver new decision making processes to connect private and public sectors with all city voices. This produces Inquiry Intelligence that allows for experiments, uncertainty and learning together.	Major banks redefine their service to the city in terms of catalyzing generative relationships and revise their collaborative functions accordingly. This produces Emergence Intelligence and releases the power of place, so that the intractable problems related to water, food, energy, climate and finance are approached with full human consciousness and greatest cultural values.
EINDHOVEN, NL	EDMONTON, CANADA	RABOBANK – AMSTERDAM, NL

Table 7 shows three examples of how Civil Society can increase the intelligence of the city.

Table 7: Civil Society Practices Master Code

Take Care of Yourself	Take Care of Each Other	Take Care of this Place
City faith leaders (from churches, temples and synagogues) invite citizens to see themselves as spiritually empowered contributors to the city.	Civil society members catalyze and support neighborhoods to build together art-based gathering places.	Citizen Observatories convene the collective WE even in bankrupt cities and cities under siege, so people can share how they discover capacities for city change.
This produces Inner Intelligence for the civil society members and citizens at the same time.	This produces Cultural Intelligence where people tell the stories that bond them together and build community.	This produces Living Intelligence where chaos and crisis can be used to grow resilience in difficult times.
VANCOUVER – CANADIAN MEMORIAL UNITED CHURCH	SEATTLE – POMEGRANATE CENTER, IMAGINE ABBOTSFORD	LEON, MEXICO

HOW: Spiritual Communities Act as Integrators for the Human Hive

Now having seen how each of the 4 Voices can expand Integral City Intelligence, let us look at the possibilities for Spiritual Communities to act as Integrators who create the conditions for city evolution. Here are some specific steps that Spiritual Communities can take to catalyze integration of their city in a series of gatherings (format to be native to their faith practice—e.g., circle, cell, group, family). These gatherings can occur sequentially over a period of days, weeks, or months and/or they can be convened at a conference or weekend.

1. Honor Circles of Care

   As you practice the Master Code you will discover that each level expands your Circles of Care. Each level is more complex than the one before. And as you learn to practice the basics of taking care of your Self, then you will develop the capacity to take care of Others. It is a practice that most Spiritual Communities already have ways for and it is the place to start the integration process. In your gathering, recognize how you are already taking care of Self and Others.

2. Honor Sacred Places

   The next step is to honor how you take care of the many places in your lives—whether that is your home (apartment, house), workplace, Spiritual Community (church, synagogue, mosque, temple), neighborhood, city, eco-region, or even the planet. As the scale of the Place increases, so do your Circles of Care. In your gathering, identify the Places you already care for. Create a visual record of these places by marking a City map or creating a mind map, collage, or mandala of your special and sacred Places.

3. Connect People to Places

   In Gathering 3 link the people from Gathering 1 to the Places in Gathering 2. If your gathering is large, invite people to self-organize into smaller groups (of 6 to 8 people) to work on different locations. Starting with the places you identified in Gathering 2, make a list of all the people who belong to those places. When you finish your lists, bring them all together on a wall or table. Notice the patterns where more people gather and others where there are fewer. Take an overview of the neighborhood and/or city, and notice the gaps. Ask, who else should be here to expand our picture of the whole city? After the gathering, reach out to the other 4 Voices of the city. Ask, who should be part of this conversation? Other churches, government/city hall, business, civil society members, citizens?

4. Care for What People Care For

   In Gathering 4, start with your lists from Gathering 3 and regroup to ask yourselves, what do people in these places care for? Consider the possibilities (from *Table 2: Levels of Complexity for Caring for Others, Chapter 3*). Take a straw-poll (also called wisdom of the crowd) and weight the size (or importance) of the cares on a scale of 1 to 10. Do this by place and/or neighborhood. Notice the differences from one place to the other. (An easy way to make this visible is to select different size dots and/or different colored dots to represent the different weightings.)

5. Identify Assets in People and Places

In Gathering 5, expand what you know about the values or assets that exist at the conjunction of people and places. Make a list for each dot of the Placecaring and Placemaking assets that are embedded in each dot. For each dot you can use the Integral City perspective of Placecaring for People-Centered Assets (like skills, professions, trades, knowledge, culture, etc.) and Placemaking for Habitat-Centered Assets (like housing, food distributors, buildings, government offices, communication systems, transportation, utilities, businesses, etc.). Before you move on, stand back from your asset map and look at the places in between your dots. Ask: What assets exist in the places-in-between?

6. Identify Needs for People and Habitats

In Gathering 6, explore what you know about the needs that exist at the conjunction of people and habitats. (You can use *Table 3: Place-based Objects of Caring* to identify broad classifications of needs and then expand into more detailed needs.) This time make a list for each dot of the needs that are missing at each dot location. As in Gathering 5, for each dot, use the Integral City perspective of Placecaring and Placemaking. For People-Centered Needs, identify lack of needed supports for consciousness and culture like missing skills, professions, trades, knowledge, culture, or experience. Related to Placemaking, identify Place-Centered Needs (like lack of materials, infrastructure and systems—missing from housing, food distributors, buildings, government offices, communication systems, transportation, utilities, or businesses).

7. Bring Together a Complete Picture and 4 Voices for Action

In Gathering 7, invite the 4 Voices of the city to attend a *Summit on the City for our Grandchildren*. Bring together everyone who has worked in the earlier 6 Gatherings and present your findings to the 4 Voices of the city, using the lenses of Placecaring and Placemaking Assets and Needs. Create the conditions for generative dialogue around creating a City that works for your grandchildren. Address the City Needs you have identified by building on the City Assets. Ask:

How can we work together to create a habitat that nurtures our grandchildren? How can we build on City strengths and assets and overcome City needs? What is our Vision for a City that works for today's generations and the generations to come?

8. Follow Up with Summit Vision

In Gathering 8, reconvene the Spiritual Community. Consider the ideas identified in the *Summit on a City for our Grandchildren*, and identify what are the steps that the 4 Voices need to take to realize the Vision? How can your Spiritual Community support those steps acting as an Integrator? How can the Integrator support each voice acting in the roles of Producers, Diversity Generators, and Resource Allocators? How can you act with others in the larger Spiritual Community to be the Integrators for the City as it moves forward to realize the Vision? How can the Spiritual Community care for the Spirit of the City in service to the future generations? (And for those communities where activists abound, how can you care for the Spirit of the City in service to the well-being of the eco-region and Gaia herself?)

CONCLUSION: WHY2

Spiritual Communities have special gifts and incentives to discover for the Human Hive: What are its Goals, Roles, and Souls? Spiritual Community members may be the most potently positioned in the whole City to bring their reflective intelligence to answer these questions because they care deeply about being in service to Spirit (as a source of Life). Individuals and individual Spiritual Communities can also ask this question in the company of other Spiritual Communities. They can be spiritually inspired even to discover if they care enough about such an opportunity in service to the City, that they bring their **collective** intelligence (e.g., as a ministerial association) to bear on how to add value to the City.

Within the living human hive, Spiritual Communities have the special purview of being habitats that grow caring capacity and also create the conditions to reflect on caring. They are purpose-gathered to bring people together for spiritual experience, awareness, caring, sharing, and development. As such, Spiritual Communities may be Evolution's purpose-designed playgrounds, rehearsal halls, and gardens for growing the capacity of Gaia's Reflective Organ.

Intelligence in the Master Code

In our research, we have discovered that the Master Code naturally leads us to call on the 4 Voices and to wake them up, grow them up, clean them up, and show them off, both individually and collectively as multiple intelligences of the city. Particularly relevant questions for the Spiritual Community are: How can we act as Integrators of the practices and intelligences of all the voices in the human hive? How can Spiritual Communities grow the Circles of Care in the Master Code?

Growing Caring Capacity

If Spiritual Communities take the challenge of acting as the Integrator voice of the city, they can generate many dividends for the quality of life and the capacity of resilience in the city.

It turns out that cities who develop their caring capacity for self, others, and place, are cities that develop their carrying capacity, which translates into resilience for good times and bad (e.g., manage their eco-footprint, develop policies for responses to climate change, care for the disadvantaged, open their doors to refugees).

Communities and Cities who care have the capacity to rapidly respond and evolve into new ways of being and becoming together. Moreover, we have arrived at a time in Gaia's evolution when the evolution of human systems needs to wake up, grow up, and take responsibility for the evolutionary role we have been created for—to be Gaia's Reflective Organ.

We have reached an evolutionary stage for Spiritual Communities to wake up their powerful voice to catalyze the evolution of the city itself. The voice of Spiritual Communities is the voice of the Integrator in the city. They have developed the practices and protocols to bring people together in unity around visions, values, and belief systems within their own faith systems and denominations and increasingly across faith divides. Now it is time for them to make a stretch into a whole new way of operating.

Spiritual Communities often have all 4 Voices of the city within their membership—so in essence, the whole city system gathers together on a regular basis. But now the purpose of that gathering can transcend and include all that Spiritual Communities have done historically and reach out to being of service to the future well-being of the whole city itself. It is time for Spiritual Communities to shift the scale from practicing as a community of individuals, or even as an organization (or collaboration), to practicing in service to a whole city.

REITERATION OF INQUIRY OBJECTIVES

The inquiry objectives of this chapter were:

1. Learn the evolutionary lineage of Integral City.
2. Understand Human Hive goals and roles.
3. Connect Human Hive roles to city voices.
4. Connect Master Code to 4 city voices and 12 city intelligences.
5. Identify practices for 4 city roles.
6. Suggest opportunities for Integrator Role of Spiritual Communities.

ACTION PLAN FOR PRACTITIONER, CATALYST, MESHWORKER

Review this chapter and make notes below of your impressions, insights, and questions. Locate yourself on the Integral City practice scaffolding. Notice what you have observed, thought, felt, and what you now want to do in any of the three possible practice configurations: as a Practitioner, as a Catalyst, as a Meshworker.

After you have made these notes, consider some of the Impact Questions (below). They also might help you reflect on how to generate impact through inquiry and action. Finally check out the Resources and Links suggested for this practice at the end of the chapter.

IMPACT QUESTIONS: DEEP, WIDE, CLEAR, HIGH

1. UL DEEP: How can I practice the Master Code (MC)—taking care of self, taking care of others, taking care of this place?
2. LL WIDE: How can you engage with all the 4 Voices of the city within your spiritual community and discover your beliefs about

city well-being, sustainability, and resilience as Gaia's Reflective Organ? How can you attract, convene, intend, pray, and play with and as the 4 Voices of the human hive?

3. UR CLEAR: How can I expand my individual practices to model the Master Code as an exemplar for others in the city—in small ways to begin with, and then grow them as I am able?

4. LR HIGH: How can you go beyond the spiritual community and reach out to all the other Voices of the city? (Start by learning how they live the Master Code.) How can you go on to convene dialogues with the 4 Voices and create the safe and spiritually energized space where you can co-discover your beliefs about city well-being, sustainability, and resilience as Gaia's Reflective Organ? How can you invite dialogue and exchange with spiritual communities in Gaia's other Reflective Organs in the eco-region?

CHAPTER RESOURCES AND/OR LINKS

Appendix B: Integral City Maps (1–5): **1, 2, 4, 5**

Appendix C1: Definitions of 12 Intelligences: **Ecological, Emergent, Integral, Living, Inner, Outer, Structural, Cultural, Navigating, Evolutionary**

Appendix C3: Integral City GPS Locator: **Resilient, Integral, Evolutionary**

Reflective Question for Whom /Where/ What I Could Use as:	Practitioner	Catalyst	Meshworker
What do I observe as I read?			
What do I think?			
What do I feel?			
What do I want to do next?			

SECTION III — *Assess the 12 Intelligences of the Integral City*

These two chapters explore the 12 Intelligences of the city—first in Chapter 5 by demonstrating how to assess them and secondly in Chapter 6 by sharing a case study that shows how the intelligences can be applied to assessing practical business ventures or city-scale prototypes of any kind. Exploring the 12 Intelligences of the city effectively translates the Master Code into inquiry and action practices that bring awareness to what it means to act, experience, relate, and create in the Human Hive.

5

FIND THE 12 INTELLIGENCES IN THE CITY

INQUIRY OBJECTIVES

The inquiry objectives of this chapter are:

1. Recognize the 12 Integral City Intelligences.
2. Take steps to discover the 12 Intelligences in your city.
3. Link 12 Intelligences to Master Code.
4. Understand how to assess 12 Intelligences.
5. Summarize assessment of 12 Intelligences.
6. Outline recommendations for Master Strategic Plan.

INTRODUCTION TO INQUIRY, ACTION, AND IMPACT FOR DISCOVERING THE 12 INTELLIGENCES

Integral City uses a set of **12 Intelligences** that identify the principles that emerge from the Master Code (see *Chapter 3: Amplify Caring Capacity with Master Code*). How many and how strongly these intelligences have emerged in the city determines its capacity for sustainability and resilience. These intelligences enable the city to balance its 4 quadrants of development for Quality of Life (as discussed below), engage the 4 Voices of the city, and interconnect city scales across individuals, families, organizations, and communities. These Intelligences and their principles can be divided into 5 clusters (See *Appendix* Cl for detailed descriptions):

1. **Contexting Intelligences:** Ecosphere, Emerging, Integral, Living
2. **Individual Intelligences:** Inner, Outer
3. **Collective Intelligences:** Building (Structural-Systems), Cultural (Storytelling)
4. **Strategic Intelligences:** Inquiry, Meshworking, Navigating
5. **Evolving Intelligences:** (the energetic impulse that drives all the other intelligences)

The presence and strength of these Intelligences reveals how a city is actually practicing the Master Code. The Placecaring that looks after Self and Others enables the sustainability of the economy, culture, and consciousness. The Placemaking that looks after Place and Planet sustains the systems, infrastructures, and environment. Altogether, the interplay of Placecaring and Placemaking is embedded in the relationships of the Master Code and they generate the human and living systems' "capital" that enables city resilience in good times and bad.

When a city invites an Integral City team to assess opportunities (for change, sustainability, resilience, and/or future development) we set out on a discovery mission to find the 12 Intelligences because they reveal the "capital" or capacities (strengths, opportunities, assets, and resources, or SOAR[27]) on which the city can build. The 12 Intelligences also suggest the life conditions that support or undermine development and indicate needs for strengthening, mitigation, or remediation.

The first step for the Integral City Assessor (s) (ICA) is to tour the city in question (which in research terms is the *system of interest*) to assess the presence of the 12 Intelligences. The purpose of this assessment

---

27   SOAR acronym shared by Choctaw Nation Chief Batton.

is to notice how strongly these natural and organic Intelligences have emerged. The ICA summarizes on a worksheet (see *Appendix* C2) three observations related to each Intelligence on a 4-point scale (Latent, Aware, Active, Advanced) discussed below. After the initial discovery tour of the city, and the preliminary assessment, the ICA can make preliminary recommendations for the next natural steps that the city might take to move forward along the cycle of inquiry, action, and impact described in this book.

FRAMING INQUIRY FOR THE 12 INTELLIGENCES: WHO, WHY1

WHO

- Facilitator
- Sponsors/Leaders from 4 Voices (Citizens, Civic Managers, Civil Society, Business)
- Recorder

Leaders from any of the 4 Voices of the city (energized citizens, government, civil society, or business) may sponsor an Integral City discovery tour. These voices may already be organized into active groups such as the Chamber of Commerce, Industrial Authority, Community Foundation, Taxpayer Representatives, or Arts Association. Usually, they have concluded through prior discussion that the city needs to improve, expand, revitalize, recover, or change in some meaningful way. Whatever the precipitating reason, the leaders suspect that the change they desire needs to engage the whole city and not just a minor part of it.

Sponsoring, organizing, and scheduling a professional discovery tour is an initial, low-cost commitment to the change process and starts the city on the road to expanding its capacity for future development in a way that is visible because it mirrors the participatory, integral, and evolutionary principles of the 12 Intelligences.

Regardless of which sponsor initiates the discovery tour, the ICA will ask for the involvement of representatives from the 4 Voices of the city seeking to form an overall group with balance across gender, generations, ethnicities, belief systems, and city locations:

- Active Citizens: (4–5)
- Government Bodies: Mayor, City Manager, County/State, Tribal Elders, Health, Education (K-12, university/college), Justice
- Civil Society: Faith Communities, Not-for-Profits, Arts, Environmental Activists
- Business Organizations: representative sectors of local economic drivers

In addition to the facilitator and 4 Voices, a recorder harvests the contributions from all participants.

WHY1

The discovery process is designed to reveal evidence from all participants regarding aspects of caring for Self, Others, and Place: what is working around here, what is not working, what our visions are for the future, and what we value individually and collectively. This evidence of the Master Code in practice can be translated into shared values, polarities, and the life conditions that make their particular city unique.

The discovery process also reveals the story that people tell about their city—and how that rests on the culture and history of the people who have made that place.

The ICA translates onto the worksheet the evidence gathered from the discovery process (including the stories) into the 12 Intelligences. The patterns on the worksheet reveal how strongly the 12 Intelligences have emerged as the city has matured as a living human system and suggests areas for recommending where the city can strategically develop its future.

INQUIRY PRACTICE FOR DISCOVERING THE 12 INTELLIGENCES: WHAT / HOW

WHAT

The inquiry question for the discovery process is: **For this city [name], how strong are and what is the evidence for the 12 Integral City Intelligences?** The sub-question is: **How do the Intelligences suggest recommendations for action and impact?**

HOW

Gather Evidence

The ICA undertakes these key evidence gathering steps:

- Researches the city through its online website and/or promotional materials
- Gains an overview of the city (a planet-view) from geo-spatial maps (e.g., Google Earth)
- Meets key city Leaders and Sponsors of the Discovery Tour
- Tours the city: sees the basic geo-spatial layout and key infrastructure features of the city
- Visits important city sites: city hall, high schools, hospitals, coffee shops in working districts, parks, indigenous peoples' neighborhoods, local art galleries
- Meets (dine with, if possible) important city representatives who coalesce authority, power, and influence (CAPI[28]) of the 4 Voices of the city (Citizens, Civic Managers, Civil Society, and Business)
- Explores in Dialogue Circle(s) with 4 Voices: What is Working; What is Not Working; Visions for the Future; and Burning Questions (Note: circles are ideally 16 to 20 people. If the city has multiple neighborhoods or communities, every key area of the city should have a Dialogue Circle. For more details see *Chapter* 10.)

Summarize Findings

The ICA summarizes Findings by using three integral frameworks that integrate the 4 quadrants for the development of Quality of Life, 4 Voices, and 4 Scales of Complexity in the City. These are described as follows:

1. The 4 lenses for developing **Quality of Life (QOL)** that impact everyone in the city:
   - **Individual Subjective QOL**: happiness, learning, and willingness to change

---

28   A term coined by Ichak Adizes, author of *The Secrets of the Corporate Lifecycle* (2006) and founder of Adizes Institute and Adizes Graduate School.

- **Individual Objective QOL**: how people act in healthy ways (accessing the basics of healthy living, including food, water, energy/sports/performing arts)
- **Collective Intersubjective QOL**: how people care for each other (including culture, beliefs, and stories)
- **Collective Interobjective QOL**: how people and systems work well together (through structures and infrastructures for work, housing, transportation systems, healthcare, schools)

2. The **4 Voices** who speak about the QOL in the city:
   - Citizens
   - Civic Managers (from City, Justice, Medical, ERT, Education)
   - Civil Society (NFP, NGO, Churches, Temples, Synagogues)
   - Business

3. The **4 Scales of Complexity** in the city (where each larger scale includes all the smaller ones):
   - Individual Person
   - Family
   - Organization
   - Community

Identify City Values

From the Findings and using the foregoing frameworks, the ICA identifies core values in the city. (Note: Values mapping is discussed in more detail in *Chapter 7: Discover Integral City Values*.) The **Individual Values** can indicate how strong is the **Quality of Life in the city** and therefore where it is stable or where it is in tension. Some people may want to hold on to key values and demonstrate resistance if they believe they cannot retain them as they move forward. Others are desperate to replace values that are not working for them and may demand action faster than others in the city are willing to tolerate (this can set up polarities as discussed below).

Collective Values can indicate how well people work together in teams, organizations, neighborhoods, and across systems. They provide a foundation for future expansion of both leadership capacities in people and infrastructure for the city. The ICA will look to see how and if people share a desire to align current (and often fragmented) plans and efforts around a future Vision and a city Purpose.

Identify Polarities in the City

When surveying the Values, Voices, and Intelligences of the city, the ICA can identify many polarities that exist across the dimensions of: Culture, Economy, Environment, City Hall and Civic Management, Workforce, Housing, Education, and Population (for an example, see *Appendix F8: Polarity Management Examples*).

These polarities are natural, as they have emerged from the dynamics of people interacting as people have co-created the city with their values, voices, skills, families, organizations, churches, and neighborhoods.

However, the polarities also create tensions that will have to be recognized and dynamically balanced as the city moves forward. Gaining the overview of the whole system (using Integral City approaches) reveals what is out of (or in) alignment and what shifts in direction might be needed to navigate and/or resolve these natural tensions. Whatever the case, from the Integral City's perspective, the use of polarities avoids or prevents labeling people or strategies as being right or wrong. Instead, polarity identification offers the perspective that they help define the extreme positions on a spectrum of realities. Moreover, polarity management suggests the likelihood that dynamic steering will be necessary not only for realizing any desired future but as a response that will always be demanded for resilience in the face of changing life conditions.

Track Visions for the City

In order to "have legs," any **Visions** for the city that emerge in the long run must include both sustainability for economic growth and wellness in individual, family, and organizational life. At this discovery stage the ICA makes careful note of the potpourri of Visions that typically emerge, without committing to any one of them.

The **Purpose for the city** may also emerge weakly or strongly from gathering evidence. The ICA will make a note of any hints and check for feedback with participants.

Summarize 12 Intelligences

From the tours and discussions with the city leaders, the ICA will record the first observations of the city using the **12 Intelligence Discovery Worksheet** (see *Appendix* C2).

Each of the Intelligences is unpacked by 3 "rules" that have been derived from the *Integral City* book 1: *What works around here; what doesn't work around here; what is the (implicit) vision for the city.* The ICA uses each of these rules as an indicator for the emergence of that Intelligence in practice, on a 4-point metric:

Latent: means the indicator has no or little evidence of practice.

Aware: means that some people demonstrate some general awareness of the indicator.

Active: means that many people practice the indicator actively.

Advanced: means not only do many people practice the indicator, but also track, monitor, and use it as a vital sign of well-being for the city.

In addition to each measurement, the ICA will record a comment and/or example to illustrate the indicator in practice.

Examples of such observations might include:

- Eco-Intelligence: Fear of water depletion of aquifer.
- Emerging Intelligence: City waste management system polluting ground water and causing toxic impact on ground water and local agri-businesses.
- Integral Intelligence: City using basic geo-spatial mapping but lacks comprehensive master plan to guide development and integrate strategic initiatives.
- Living Intelligence: Little awareness of Integral City Master Code—where people look after individuals, each other, and community for the well-being of all generations.
- Living Intelligence: Managing personal and leadership energy through wellness programs, personal practice, coaching, and healthcare system.
- Living, Inner, Outer, Intelligence: Succession planning needed for city hall, other city agencies, or the education system.
- Building/Structural Intelligence: City leaders are becoming active in interconnecting and linking city planning at different scales—especially individuals and organization workplaces.

- Inner, Outer, Structural, Cultural Intelligence: Need for strong leadership is being addressed in education, training organizations, and individual businesses.
- Cultural/Storytelling Intelligence: Strong promotion, announcements, and invitations for new initiatives; for example, arts-based programs, community sports events, technology innovation.
- Cultural/Storytelling Intelligence: Open encouragement of storytelling, listening to others, valuing history and traditions from different ethnicities, indigenous peoples, faith communities.
- Inquiry Intelligence: City has initiated multi-stakeholder dialogues to find out what is working for people.
- Meshworking Intelligence: City is limited by the silos between sectors (e.g., faith communities don't participate in an interfaith ministerial); retailers are refusing to cooperate on downtown revitalization; and homelessness is growing.
- Navigating Intelligence: K-12 education system has developed goals that every child will graduate from high school and tracking progress by child, school, and district.
- Evolutionary Intelligence: City responded to extreme weather forecast by putting emergency response system into practice: educating businesses and citizens how to make emergency response kits in advance of extreme incident, four days prior to incident warning citizens by radio and social media; opening emergency response shelters; and broadcasting for drivers to stay off the roads.

CONCLUSION: WHY2

Willingness and Readiness for Change

In just a few days to a week of taking a purpose-designed discovery tour of the city, the ICA will notice how people have indicated their **Willingness to Change**. This will often be evidenced by "can do" attitudes, or if the energy of the city is low, it may also show up as **Resistance to Change**.

Readiness to Change is often evidenced by the invitation for the review that precipitated an Integral City discovery tour in the first place. Many Burning Questions from the Dialogues may indicate that people want to move beyond the status quo into actively planning for organic future development. The ICA will note if people want to address key challenges but also realize that a status quo approach is not acceptable in order to do so. This will help indicate not only readiness for change—but who is ready for what kind of change. (It is very common for the ICA to learn that different groups may be ready for different scales of change in different timeframes.)

The ICA will note the **Kinds of Change** in the context of a systems cycle (using aspects of frameworks adapted from Adizes, Spiral Dynamics, and/ or Panarchy (Adizes, 1999; D. Beck & Cowan, 1996; Gunderson & Holling, 2002). Recognizing that many types of change may be ongoing in the city simultaneously, four major approaches to change will be characterized as:

- Maintain the status quo (little or moderate change, requiring gentle coaching).
- Allow the system to deteriorate (from old age and/or dysfunction) because it is past its prime (destructive change, requiring advanced hospicing).
- Explore the possibilities of new patterns, relationships, materials (creative change, requiring agile experimentation).
- Generate a new system to align with new life conditions (generative change, requiring complex, wholistic meshworking[29]).

Recommendations for Action Steps

With the survey of Values, Vision, Purpose, Polarities, and Intelligence Worksheet Summary, the ICA can suggest key recommendations for the city's next steps.

The ICA will note that these recommendations need to be aligned with the research and actions currently performed by other institutions in the city including but not limited to: Economic and/or Industrial Authorities, Education System, University, Health or Medical Center, City Hall, Chamber of Commerce, Arts Council, Indigenous Governments. In undertaking any

---

29   See Footnote 11

of the recommendations it is assumed that this information would be integrated, aligned, and "meshworked."

It should also be noted that although recommendations are suggested at this stage, how to accomplish the next steps is not made explicit, and will require further discussion, a long-term plan to create value and vision, and a strategy to realize the value through implementation. Nevertheless, there are some key steps that most cities will need to consider (even to determine the readiness, willingness, and kind of change they wish to engage). We suggest these steps as a start (and note that they reflect many of the chapters of this book).

1. Develop a City Future Core Team

   Create a Core Team to align the City Future process as it emerges. This should contain leaders from all the 4 Voices (with diversity of gender and generations) and have a Secretariat for continuity of action. Over time, this team would create a "meshwork" that would align the implementation of the City Future process (see *Chapter 13: Realize Meshworking Capacities in the Human Hive*). Many of the Dialogue Circle members would be effective candidates for such a team.

2. Create Ongoing Dialogues

   It is important to continue the dialogue among the key cultures within the City and City Hall started by this City Future discovery visit. It is important for key players to enable success of all as the City and communities develop together.

3. Visioning

   The City has started the Visioning process with this City Future discovery visit; however, it needs to involve the 4 Voices of the city in a further series of Dialogues to explore Economic, Education, Culture, Healthcare, Community, and Environmental contributions to create a Vision for the next 3 generations (100 years). In this series of Dialogues, it will be critical to identify a future destination point so the Values and Principles that are core to this Vision can propel the City beyond near-term "tinkering" to establish a long-term methodology for future scenario planning; for example, **City 2050** (time target) or **City 300,000** (population target).

4. Values Mapping, Vital Signs Monitoring

As part of the Visioning process, completing a Values Mapping survey of the city will identify wants, needs, and hopes that can coalesce authority, power, and influence for city change.

Another outcome of this process can be to identify the indicators for a Vital Signs Monitor for the City. This can track the Sustainability and Planning trajectories noted below and provide feedback to the city as it proceeds. (The ICA can provide examples and prototypes for review.)

5. Succession Planning

The City's growth may have outpaced succession planning at City Hall, City Agencies, University, Medical Center, and many businesses (and other organizations). It is imperative that succession plans be developed for these key organizations, as the leaders who take over in the City's institutions must contribute to aligning plans for moving forward.

6. Conduct Core Sustainability and Service Reviews

All of the core institutions of the City should undertake sustainability reviews. A unique opportunity exists to do this as an economic and/or supply chain that could align and would impact decisions for city planning, infrastructure growth, and industrial development. Integral City has key partners who specialize in this, using well-recognized processes like *The Natural Step* (Cook, 2005; Park, Purcell, & Purkis, 2009).

7. Develop an Integrated Master Sustainability Plan

With a Vision/Purpose, Succession Plan, and Core Sustainability Review, the City should develop an Integrated Master Sustainability Plan (Ling, Dale, & Hanna, 2007; Park et al., 2009) that uses the Principles and Values (noted above) to enable dynamic growth and success for the city that brings accountability and visibility for the goals, so all can participate in the outcomes and benefits.

8. Align Education Systems K-12 and early/mid/late Career Planning

Because of the many economic and job opportunities rapidly emerging in the city, aligning its education system to meet and serve these growth opportunities is imperative.

9. Engage Citizens and Landowners for Residential Redevelopment

Any felt need to upgrade the housing quality must be done with the engagement of both residents and landowners. The ICA can help to teach and coach how to facilitate processes that can accomplish participation, buy-in, and commitment to change that will build capacity for everyone involved.

Why Act?

When city leaders follow through on these recommendations, they will reap the dividends of assessing the city's 12 Intelligences and take the next natural steps to strengthening the integral capital of the whole city. This will set it on a path to creating well-being for both people and habitat. This will certainly demonstrate a deep commitment to living the Master Code.

REITERATION OF INQUIRY OBJECTIVES

The inquiry objectives of this chapter were:

1. Recognize the 12 Integral City Intelligences.
2. Take steps to discover the 12 Intelligences in your city.
3. Link 12 Intelligences to Master Code.
4. Understand how to assess 12 Intelligences.
5. Summarize assessment of 12 intelligences.
6. Outline recommendations for Master Strategic Plan.

ACTION PLAN FOR PRACTITIONER, CATALYST, MESHWORKER

Review this chapter and make notes below of your impressions, insights, and questions. Locate yourself on the Integral City practice scaffolding. Notice what you have observed, thought, felt, and what you now want to do in any of the three possible practice configurations: as a Practitioner, as a Catalyst, as a Meshworker.

After you have made these notes, consider some of the Impact Questions (below). They also might help you reflect on how to generate impact through inquiry and action. Finally check out the Resources and Links suggested for this practice at the end of the chapter.

IMPACT QUESTIONS: DEEP, WIDE, CLEAR, HIGH

UL DEEP: How do I rate my leadership in the indicators of Integral City's 12 Intelligences (latent, aware, active, advanced)?

LL WIDE: How can our organization reach out to other organizations in the city to explore the stories we tell about our city? How can we make those stories more positive, generative, and hopeful, and therefore attractive?

UR CLEAR: What measures do I use to give myself feedback about personal well-being? What actions do I take that support (or undermine) that well-being? What burning questions do I have about improving my well-being?

LR HIGH: What strategies for sustainability (from City Hall, Healthcare, Education, Justice, Infrastructure Providers) does our business community support or resist? What is one way our organization could contribute to city resilience in the face of disaster?

CHAPTER RESOURCES AND/OR LINKS

Appendix B: Integral City Maps (1–5): 1, 2, 3, 4

Appendix C2: Assessment Worksheet for 12 Intelligences: All 12

Appendix C3: Integral City GPS Locator: Integral, Smart, Resilient, Evolutionary

Reflective Question for Whom /Where/ What I Could Use as:	Practitioner	Catalyst	Meshworker
What do I observe as I read?			
What do I think?			
What do I feel?			
What do I want to do next?			

6

USE THE 12 INTELLIGENCES TO ASSESS BUSINESS OPPORTUNITIES

INQUIRY OBJECTIVES

The inquiry objectives of this chapter are:

1. Design a methodology to assess a business opportunity or plan based on the 12 Intelligences.

2. Identify the audience for the assessment.

3. Frame the integrating contributions to the methodology from:

   a. 4 Quadrants of the Quality of Life

   b. 4 City Voices

   c. 4 City Scales

   d. 5 Sets of Integral City Intelligences

4. Use integral metrics to determine:

   a. What is working?

   b. What is not working?

   c. How to improve the plan?

5. Summarize your assessment analysis with integral recommendations.

INTRODUCTION TO INQUIRY, ACTION, AND IMPACT IN USING THE 12 INTELLIGENCES

The purpose of using the 12 Intelligences to review a business opportunity or plan is to bring Integral City lenses to consider how the project might optimize alignment of their endeavor with a paradigm of the city that is integral, complex, operates like a living system, and is evolutionary.

The process described below assumes that the developers of the opportunity or plan have described it in written reports and/or graphics. The client for this assessment may be the original designer or another party with (or seeking) a vested interest in its success, such as a venture capitalist, potential partner, or even a city hall.

This assessment methodology explains how to obtain findings (evidence), frame conclusions, and offer recommendations to optimize the opportunity within an Integral City.

FRAMING INQUIRY IN USING THE 12 INTELLIGENCES: WHO, WHY1

WHO

- Integral City Assessor
- Target audience

It is important to consider who is the target audience for this assessment. It could be one, some, or all of these: actual or potential business opportunity developer, financier, partner or consortium, city agency.

Within any of those audiences, sub-audiences may also be interested parties, such as: owners, shareholders, designers, engineers, operations managers, talent/employment agencies, legal advisors, bankers, government departments.

Therefore, the first step for the Integral City Assessor (ICA) is to identify the intended audience(s) for the assessment so that the report can be addressed with appropriate language and levels of detail. If more than one audience will use the assessment, it should be noted that the ICA will need to produce more than one version of the report, or presentation summary (e.g., PowerPoint), so that the assessment can be translated into language that is meaningful to each audience.

A key consideration for the ICA success in appropriately communicating with any audience is to understand to what degree they are an "integrally informed audience." The description that follows assumes an "implicitly integrally informed audience," who requires some basic translation of integral constructs. Even if an audience is explicitly integrally informed, it is probably advisable for the ICA to review the basic constructs of an Integral City, so that they have an understanding of the application of integral principles to the assessment process.

WHY1

In reviewing the documents outlining the opportunity or plan (hereafter referred to as the *Project*) the assessor looks for the inspiration and intentions of its authors and/or designers.

We consider **Quality of Life (QOL)** through the frame of the 4 quadrants to discover weightings and balance of QOL.

When using the **4 Voices Frame,** we look for the Business Voice (for the purposes of this chapter, assumed to be the developer of the Project) and how it relates to the other 3 internal city Voices: Civic Managers, Civil Society, and Citizen. We also consider the 5th Voice as an external city Voice—the voice from other cities.

When considering the **Scales of Complexity in the City** we are most interested to see if the impact of the Project has been considered at all scales from individual to family to organization to the whole city. We will also note its possible impact at the scale of eco-region and planet.

When looking for evidence, we note the many **Polarities** that naturally exist across the dimensions of: Culture, Economy, Environment, Civic Management, Workforce, Infrastructure Networks, Education, and Population. We recognize that these Polarities create natural tensions that will have to be dynamically balanced as the Project interacts with its stakeholders.

When considering the 12 Intelligences for this kind of assessment, we translate them into a more strategic expression as the **5 sets of Intelligences** at a city-centric scale (as noted below). This helps paint a picture from the city meta-perspective of the Project's impact on Capacities and Readiness for change. In a Project which has not been designed from a fully, integrally aware perspective, the ICA uses the 5 sets of Intelligences to provide an overview of which Intelligences will need to be developed and resourced for Project success.

INQUIRY PRACTICE FOR USING THE 12 INTELLIGENCES: WHAT / HOW

WHAT

After establishing the target audience, the ICA must also determine the purpose of the assessment as this will determine the Inquiry Question. The purpose will usually be associated closely with the interests of the stakeholder(s). Some examples of Inquiry Questions follow.

- How does our design add value to the daily lives of citizens?
- Would this Project adapt to different cities (geographies, cultures, economies)?
- Should this Project become part of my (client's) investment portfolio?
- How could our organization partner with the Project developer?
- In what ways might marginalized citizens resist the Project?

HOW

Apply Integral City Lenses for Quality of Life, City Voices, City Scales, Intelligences

To view the Project, the ICA uses 4 integral frameworks that integrate aspects of Quality of Life, 4 Voices of the City, 4 Scales of Complexity, and 12 Intelligences of the City.

1. The 4 lenses for **Quality of Life, or QOL** (see Figure 10) that impact everyone in the city are:
   - **Individual Subjective QOL**: happiness, learning, and willingness to change.
   - **Individual Objective QOL**: how people act in healthy ways (accessing the basics of healthy living, including food, water, energy/ sports/performing arts).
   - **Collective Intersubjective QOL**: how people care for each other (including culture, beliefs, and stories).

- **Collective Interobjective QOL**: how people and systems work well together (through structures and infrastructures for work, housing, transportation systems, healthcare, schools).

It should be noted that each of these quadrants uses different metrics to measure success. The left-hand quadrants address the qualities of Placecaring and include individual and collective metrics like psychological well-being and cultural capacity. The right-hand quadrants address the qualities of Placemaking and include individual and collective metrics for bio-physical performance and systems efficiency.

Interdisciplinary research has demonstrated that each quadrant can be measured independently but in reality all the quadrants are interdependent and actually occur simultaneously—thus constantly interacting and interconnecting Quality of Life in these four major domains (psychological, cultural, bio-physical, systems/structures).

Quality of Life Map: Example

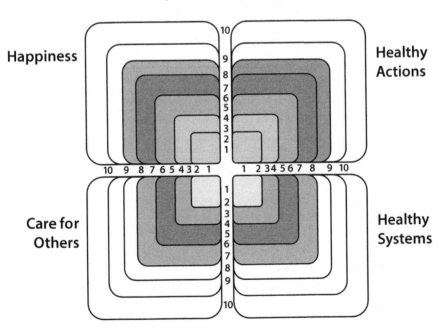

Figure 10: 4 Lenses for Quality of Life

2. The 4 Voices who speak about the QOL in the city are (see Figure 11):

- **Citizens**
- **Civic Managers** (from City, Justice, Healthcare, ERT, Education)
- **Civil Society** (NFP, NGO, Churches, Temples, Synagogues)
- **Business**

These 4 Voices are core stakeholders in the well-being of the city. Our research shows us that each voice can be a gateway to city well-being; but each voice must be willing and able to listen to, talk with, and learn from the other voices for optimizing quality of life in the city.

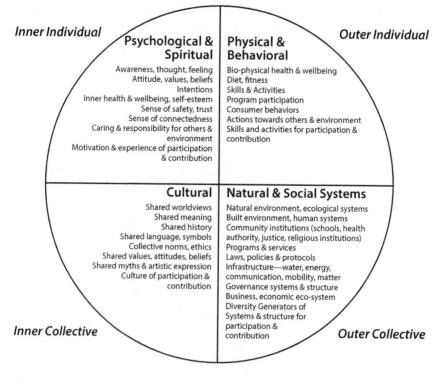

Figure 11: 4 Voices of the City

3. The **4 Scales of Complexity** in the city—where each larger scale includes all the smaller ones and scales larger than the city includes the city (see Figure 12, which is also Map 2 in *Appendix* B)

- Individual Person
- Family/Group/Tribe
- Organization
- City
- (Eco-Region, World, Kosmos)

The scales of complexity reflect the natural "fractal" patterns of human systems at increasingly greater scales. The city is the most complex system yet created by humans, and like other living systems, each city forms an ecology of the core scales (from individual, to family, to organization, to community/city) that coexist with each other. As a natural ecology, it mimics the biology of human systems (biomimicry) but it also mimics the consciousness of human systems (emotional-intellectual-spiritual-cultural mimicry).

Integral City Scales of Complexity

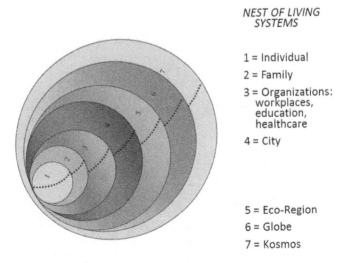

NEST OF LIVING
SYSTEMS

1 = Individual

2 = Family

3 = Organizations:
workplaces,
education,
healthcare

4 = City

5 = Eco-Region

6 = Globe

7 = Kosmos

Figure 12: Scales of Complexity in the City

4. The Integral City **5 sets of Intelligences** embrace the principles that enable QOL, engagement of the 4 Voices, and interconnection of City Scales. These Intelligences and their principles create a kind

of Integral City Compass that enables a whole view of the living city, in the context of its natural environment, energized by the people who make it up, and guided by the strategies they implement to optimize well-being and evolution. The 5 sets of Intelligences contain 12 individual intelligences that act at the city scale, like multiple intelligences at the individual scale. The Integral City Intelligences are:

- Contexting Intelligences: Ecosphere, Emerging, Integral, Living
- Individual Intelligences: Inner, Outer
- Collective Intelligences: Social (Building-Systems), Cultural (Storytelling)
- Strategic Intelligences: Inquiry, Meshworking, Navigating
- Evolving Intelligences: (the energetic impulse that drives all the other intelligences)

We have transposed these 5 sets of Intelligences into a GPS Locator for three city types that have emerged since pre-modern times. (Figure 13 provides an image of the GPS and *Appendix* C3 explains how it operates.)

Figure 13: 5 Sets of Intelligences on Integral City GPS Locator App

Integral City Findings

Discovery Tour and/or Document Review

In order to gather evidence, the ICA will scope out with the client the extent of the data gathering process. This may involve an onsite Discovery Tour as discussed in *Chapter 5: Find the 12 Intelligences in the City*.

It may also be limited to reviewing Project documents and/or media such as:

- Business Plans
- Business Plan Marketing Summaries
- Service or Product Plans
- Financing Plans and/or Draft Investment Prospectus
- Project Plans and/or Dashboards
- Stakeholder Profiles
- Websites

In reviewing the documents for the Project, the ICA takes the perspective of the designated audience (with consideration as to its level of understanding of the integral paradigm).

The ICA will produce a draft report addressing the designated audience, and report to them on the Project and its relevant aspects in terms of:

- **What Works**
- **What's Missing**
- **How to Improve**

CONCLUSION: WHY2

After analyzing and summarizing Findings, the ICA can produce a Quick Audit in terms of positive, neutral, or negative (+ 0—) ratings of the 5 Sets of Intelligences related to the Project; for example:

- **Contexting**: ecological (–), emergent (0), integral (0), living (+);
- **Individual:** inner (–), outer (+)
- **Collective:** cultural (–), social (–)

- **Strategic:** Inquiry 0, Meshworking (–), Navigating (–)
- **Evolutionary:** (0)

This audit is derived from the 12 Intelligences Worksheet discussed in *Chapter 5* and illustrated in *Appendix* C2.

The ICA then produces a set of Recommendations. These Recommendations will be similar in intention and sequence to those outlined for a reporting a city-scale assessment reported in *Chapter 5*, but will be scoped and targeted for the Project.

EXAMPLES OF RECOMMENDATIONS: PROJECT NEXT STEPS

With the survey of QOL Values, Voices, Scales of Complexity, Polarities, and 12 Intelligences, the ICA suggests recommendations to improve the value proposition of the Project to the target audience. The overall pattern to these Recommendations for Project success in many ways mirrors the sequence of inquiry and action mapped out in this book—not surprisingly since most of the patterns endemic to an Integral City are quite fractal.

In undertaking any of the Recommendations offered, it is assumed that this information would be integrated, aligned, and "meshworked"[30] with other diagnostics or stakeholder technical analyses.

It should also be noted that the Recommendations for this scope of assessment do not address how to accomplish the next steps. That level of implementation would typically require further scoping, analysis, and discussion. Here are some typical Recommendations:

1. Teach Project Team Integral Language and Meta Lenses

    The value of using basic Integral frames is that it provides a common language that can be shared by multiple disciplines, stakeholders, stewards, and Voices.

    Basic Integral languaging also allows for translation between and across values, worldviews, perspectives, and scales. The Project should also be able to be situated within a spectrum of related

---

30   See Footnote 11.

Projects, identified in the market, for the purposes of scaling up, and/or connecting to competitive services/products.

2. Create 4 Voices Discovery Research

   Collect data from and with all 4 Voices. This is core market information that informs product/service design, marketing, and even infrastructure.

3. Engage Citizens as User/Operators

   Develop product/service within the contexts of all 4 QOL realities and with the engagement of all 4 Voices. This knowledge can impact whole decision chains. It is important for the Project leaders to learn how to facilitate decision processes that can accomplish participation, buy-in, and commitment to change that will build capacity for everyone involved.

4. Articulate External Vision

   Most Projects need to build strategies for external communications related to their market and multiple stakeholders/Voices. This involves translating the internal vision, values, and mission of the Project into terms the external market can understand.

5. Complete Values Mapping, Vital Signs Monitoring

   As part of the Visioning process, completing a Values Mapping survey of target cities where the Project will be located will identify wants, needs, and hopes that can coalesce authority, power, and influence (CAPI) for city change in that city (see *Chapter 7: Discover Integral City Values*). By bringing together a preliminary CAPI group, the Project can involve future stakeholders in creating a climate of acceptance—or learn very quickly that there are blind spots that the Project developers might have missed.

   Another outcome of this process can be to identify the indicators for a Vital Signs Monitor used by the city critical for the Project to see/use as context for success. This can track and provide feedback to the Project and city stakeholders as the Project proceeds (such an exercise may also lead the city to build on this initial Vital Signs Monitor for general use to measure city QOL).

6. Research Generational Positioning

The Project may need to understand the demographics of its market, especially recent research on generational profiles, that shows how they make decisions differently and how they potentially flow/align together (but may also be blocking one another as a natural stage of inter-generational development). Most cities of the 21st century will contain four generations (and as life extension continues, perhaps five to six generations) dynamically interacting. As cities expand, the numbers of cultures within their boundaries, the cross-generational and cross-cultural mixes will greatly impact capacities and modes of both Placecaring and Placemaking.

For example, different cultures utilize housing and transportation systems very differently. Some desire private pods for nuclear families while others want three generations under one roof. As a result, they hold different expectations about access to public space in workplaces, healthcare facilities, and parks (Sandercock, 2000; Sandercock & Lyssiotis, 2003).

7. Conduct Core Sustainability and Service Safety Reviews

The Project needs to conduct research relating to sustainability and safety. Frameworks like *The Natural Step*[31] can provide this information and template, which will impact risk assessment, operations, and marketing of the Project.

8. Develop a Master Integrated City Sustainability Plan (ICSP)

In general, the market will perceive the Project's value and the Project will contribute to QOL in the city if developers can contextualize it within an ICSP. If one already exists, then the Project should be aligned with it. If an ICSP has not yet been created, overlooking a need for this geo-spatial analysis (and values integration) can impact long-term

---

31   The Natural Step uses a 5-Level Framework (5LF)as a comprehensive model for planning and decision making in complex systems based on whole systems thinking. It comprises: 1) System, 2) Success, 3) Strategic, 4) Actions, and 5) Tools. It can be used to analyze any complex system of any type or scale (e.g., human body, game, organization, sustainability concept) and helps to plan, decide, and act strategically towards success based on principles determined by the working of the system. Source: https://en.wikipedia.org/wiki/The_Natural_Step

Project success. The ICA may connect with city hall to review current conditions for an ICSP and/or make recommendations for its development (Ling et al., 2007).

9. Develop a CAPI Group for External Project Review

The ICA will look for and/or recommend that the Project define its internal Vision, Values, and Mission (thus characterizing the Project's core Purpose). In order to successfully translate the Vision, Values, and Mission externally to the city context, the ICA may recommend that the Project coalesce authority, power and influence (CAPI) to review the Project's potential for success.

10. Develop a PAEI Frame for Internal Project Review

The ICA will also be seeking an internal Project review to understand how its operations will mature through future organizational lifecycles. This can be framed as an Adizes-style organizational strategic plan with Production, Administration, Entrepreneurship, and Integration (PAEI) that integrates with Integral City evolutionary contexts (Adizes, 1999, 2006).

Such a CAPI/PAEI external/internal review will use Principles and Values that are likely to enable dynamic growth and success for the Project and the city. This combination can bring accountability and visibility for the Project goals, so all can participate in the outcomes and benefits. This needs to address the appropriate levels of complexity related to the Project and translated to multiple audiences so that messages can be effectively communicated to all stakeholders.

11. Find a Way to Align with 4 Voices of the City

Because of the core opportunities offered by the Project, the impacts will be widespread. The Project developers need to find a way to communicate the benefits of the Project and gain support for it from all 4 Voices of the city. Finding and assigning an integrally-informed communications expert to translate messages designed to communicate to each Voice (and even its spectrum of Values (as discussed in *Chapter 7: Discover Integral City Values*) will pay dividends to the Project developer early on in the Project lifecycle.

REITERATION OF INQUIRY OBJECTIVES

The inquiry objectives of this chapter were:

1. Design a methodology to assess a business opportunity or plan based on the 12 Intelligences.
2. Identify the audience for the assessment.
3. Frame the integrating contributions to the methodology from:
   a. 4 Quadrants of the Quality of Life
   b. 4 City Voices
   c. 4 City Scales
   d. 5 Sets of Integral City Intelligences
4. Use integral metrics to determine:
   a. What is working?
   b. What is not working?
   c. How to improve the plan?
5. Summarize your assessment analysis with integrally informed Recommendations.

ACTION PLAN FOR PRACTITIONER, CATALYST, MESHWORKER

Review this chapter and make notes below of your impressions, insights, and questions. Locate yourself on the Integral City practice scaffolding. Notice what you have observed, thought, felt, and what you now want to do in any of the three possible practice configurations: as a Practitioner, as a Catalyst, as a Meshworker.

After you have made these notes, consider some of the Impact Questions(below). They also might help you reflect on how to generate impact through inquiry and action. Finally check out the Resources and Links suggested for this practice at the end of the chapter.

IMPACT QUESTIONS: DEEP, WIDE, CLEAR, HIGH

UL DEEP: As Project Leader how do I rate my level of being integrally informed in relation to the 12 intelligences in this Project (rate each intelligence—/0/+)?

LL WIDE: How does our Project team relate internally? What partners might we need to collaborate with for Project success? What city Voices have we involved (or are missing) in our design process? How can we communicate about this Project to all 4 Voices for multiple wins in the city?

UR CLEAR: What metrics have I identified to measure Project success? How does project success contribute to city well-being? What actions will link measures of Project success to city success?

LR HIGH: How does our Project contribute to city well-being and sustainability? In what ways might our Project invite support or cause resistance to change in the city? How does our Project contribute to city resilience in the next decade? In the next 2 decades (to multiple generations)?

CHAPTER RESOURCES AND/OR LINKS

Appendix B: Integral City Maps (1–5): 1, 2

Appendix C1: Definitions of 12 Intelligences: All 12

Appendix C3: Integral City GPS Locator: Smart, Resilient, Integral, Evolutionary

Reflective Question for Whom /Where/ What I Could Use as:	Practitioner	Catalyst	Meshworker
What do I observe as I read?			
What do I think?			
What do I feel?			
What do I want to do next?			

SECTION IV — *Discover and Map City Values & Vital Signs*

These two chapters share some of Integral City's applications that have been longest practiced. They are based on Hamilton's original dissertation research into learning and leadership in self-organizing systems (Hamilton, 1999) and weave in the multi-source paradigms from the integral and Spiral Dynamics integral (SDi) authors and communities (D. Beck, 2000b, 2002b; D. Beck & Cowan, 1996; D. Beck & Linscott, 2006; Laszlo, 2006b; Wilber, 1995, 2000b, 2007).

Chapter 7 focuses on Values Mapping and reveals how this process profiles the city not just in psychological terms (as used by Richard Florida, (2008)) but also in developmental terms. This reveals city patterns that map bio-psycho-cultural-social qualities at 4 major stages of complexity (reflecting the Master Code) that are mappable on Global Information Systems (GIS). Such data becomes integral to effective implementation of any change in the city because it reveals how to communicate what to whom, in a values-based language they understand. In today's "mongrel" cities (Sandercock, 2000; Sandercock & Lyssiotis, 2003) that contain all the cultures of the world living cheek by jowl with one another, this is necessary intelligence to have for effectively implementing security, sustainability, and resilience.

Chapter 8 explores the possibilities of Integral Vital Signs Monitoring (IVSM). This inquiry and action practice suggests a possible platform on which the complex tracking of data could be organized. But the key value of this chapter is to demonstrate how to use the integral values assessment to seek out and choose relevant vital signs data (most of which already exist in organizational databases spread throughout the city). Examples are offered of how to assemble a dashboard and maintain it, and how to attract stakeholders and collect their data for a pilot project or prototype an IVSM dashboard.

DISCOVER INTEGRAL CITY VALUES

INQUIRY OBJECTIVES

The inquiry objectives of this chapter are:

1. Learn the Integral framework for mapping values in the city.

2. Demonstrate the value of mapping values in the city to identify the location of differences, cultural sources of misunderstandings, conflicts, and differing expectations.

3. Map the values of city populations to identify languages and age, to help locate the geographic clustering or distribution of subpopulations.

4. Learn how values help identify systemic interconnections or disconnections of city subpopulations.

5. Create a framework for a values-based capacity and asset map of the city, using the integral model that embraces Placecaring and Placemaking capacities.

INTRODUCTION TO INQUIRY, ACTION, AND IMPACT
UNDERSTANDING VALUES IN THE CITY

One of the major advantages of conducting values research in the city is that it is foundational to understanding Placecaring. Moreover, an inquiry into values adds to the more widely researched data on visible minorities and reveals the invisible differences that underlie human behavior in the city.

The Integral City values mapping process uses a framework that is developmental in nature. It assumes that each person has the potential for changing and growing ever more complex sets of values, given life conditions that demand and/or encourage the recalibration of values. The resulting sets of values are thus an outcome of the interactions between internal and external life conditions.

Graves (Graves, 2003, 2005) conducted research in the 1960s and 1970s (an 18-year study, whose conclusions came to be known as the "evolutionary complex levels of human existence") that showed that human behaviors arising out of one set of conditions created problems of existence that could not be solved at that level (echoing Einstein's proposition of the same nature).

As a result, new adaptive behaviors are called into existence for both Placecaring and Placemaking. From the developmental sequence of values, Graves recognized individual-centric patterns of behaviors he called "express self" values and group-centric patterns of behaviors he called "sacrifice self" values. Moreover, his research showed that these behaviors adapted and alternated with one another at an ever-increasing level of complexity, as life conditions changed. Graves used a set of identifiers to represent life conditions (designated by letters from the first half of the alphabet) and bio-psycho-cultural-social human development (designated by letters from the second half of the alphabet).

Subsequently, Beck (2002a), Beck and Cowan (1996), and Beck and Linscott (2006) devised a system of color codes to identify each level of complexity. Beige, red, orange, and yellow (i.e., warm colors) relate to "express self" versions of existence. Purple, blue, green, and turquoise (i.e., cool colors) relate to "sacrifice self" versions of existence (as shown in Table 8).

The color codes provide for neutrality and also an easy referencing system for the values sets and can be thought of as Placecaring and

Placemaking on a vertical scale—or elevation. The higher elevation one has, the more one can see wider circles of Placecaring, appreciate multiple perspectives, and connect to more Place Makers in the city (and the world).

Table 8: Levels of Values Complexity
Source: Hamilton, 2008, p. 86, Adapted from Beck, 2002.

EXPRESS SELF STAGE	ORGANIZING PRINCIPLE OF LIFE CONDITIONS	SACRIFICE SELF STAGE	ORGANIZING PRINCIPLE OF LIFE CONDITIONS
AN - Beige	Survival	BO - Purple	Belonging
CP - Red	Command & Control	DQ - Blue	Authoritarian Structure
ER - Orange	Economic Success	FS - Green	Humanitarian Equality
GT - Yellow	Systemic Flex & Flow	HU - Turquoise	Planetary Commons

In fact, another way to frame the developmental sequence is to define the value sets into three levels of increasing complexity:

1. SELFCENTRIC—focuses on "I"; also known as egocentric; care and concern for self. This generally spans from Level 1. Basics of Life / Beige to Level 2. Family/Purple to Level 3. Personal Expression/Red.

2. SOCIOCENTRIC—focuses on "We"; for example, ethnic group, religion, nation; also known as ethnocentric; care and concern for people "like me." This generally spans from Level 4. Order/Blue to Level 5. Results/Orange and early Level 6. Caring/Green.

3. WORLDCENTRIC—focuses on "all of us"; it is the ability to take into account multiple perspectives; care and concern for all people and the environment. This generally spans from Level 6. Caring /Green to Level 7. Wisdom/Yellow to Level 8. World Connectedness/Turquoise.

A single word description of the values sets is summarized in the first column in Table 9: Basics (of Life), Family/Belonging, (Personal) Expression, Order, Results, Caring, Wisdom/Flex-flow, and World (Connectedness).

Table 9: Summary of Positive Values Descriptions
Adapted from Spiral Dynamics (Beck & Cowan, 1996)

Value Sequence & Short Form	Orientation	Description	Spiral Dynamics Color Symbol
Basics	I	Basic needs of life and personal safety	1. beige
Family	We	Family traditions, belonging and kinship	2. purple
Express	I	Personal expression, optimal energy and pleasure expressed in healthy ways	3. red
Order	We	Order, respect for peace, and rules at home and play; working for stability, healthy routines and direction for a greater good	4. blue
Results	I	Results, plans and, strategic tools, technology and science that works	5. orange
Caring	We	Caring and sensitivity to others, embracing diversity (visible and some aspects of invisible), egalitarian fairness, partnering	6. green
Wisdom	I	Wise knowledge and integration of approaches, flexibility and spontaneity	7. yellow
World	We	World / global connectedness, balanced health, and wholeness	8. turquoise

Being able to map the values of any given city neighborhood (or household or street) informs strategic decision-making by civic managers and city developers related to resource allocation (for both Placecaring and Placemaking initiatives). In Figure 14, one can see different sets of 4 quadrant values mapped onto the city's neighborhoods.[32] We have learned from police chiefs, fire marshalls, and social service providers that this information makes all the difference in how they deliver services to specific areas, because they better understand the invisible differences underlying behaviors and cultures in the city, and can thus "connect the dots" in designing effective strategies to interact with different city populations.

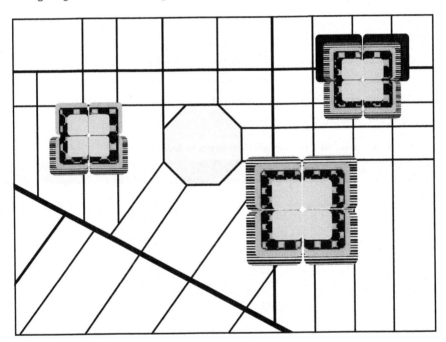

Figure 14: Different Values in Different Neighborhoods

Now that we have explained why values mapping contributes to managing effectively in the city, let's describe the process for framing the inquiry and gathering and analyzing the data.

---

32 The neighborhood data on this map is similar to the 4-quadrant analysis of city values shown in Appendix K: Abbotsford Values Flower Map

FRAMING INQUIRY: WHO, WHY1

WHO

- Research Sponsor (e.g., City Manager, Police Chief, Community Foundation)
- Project Team: Leader, Data Collection, Analysis, Report Production
- Data Gatherers: Interviewers—Phone, In-Person (by language), Online
- Random population sample for phone interviews
- Purposive population samples for in-person and online surveys
- In-Depth Interviewees: Thought Leaders from 4 Voices

Research Preparation

The Project Team Leader will work with the Research Sponsor to explain the research method and help identify populations and subpopulations for the research that will contribute to the sponsor's intentions for conducting the research.

Table 10: Summary of First Spoken Languages in Sample City

Language		
English	80,955	72%
Punjabi	14,550	13%
German	6,600	6%
Korean	630	1%
Chinese	535	1%
Dutch	1,865	2%
Spanish	795	1%
Other	6,166	6%
Total	112,096	100%

In preparing for values research in the city, it is useful to identify the language groupings by population in the city according to the most recent census data as in Table 10. From statistics like these, the languages can be selected in which to conduct the surveys discussed below. In addition, language can be used as a proxy for cultural contexts and differences that might otherwise be difficult to identify. (Another proxy for culture might include belief systems, such as are used in Singapore to create and administer values-based policy.)

Inquiry Participants

Selecting inquiry participants for values research in the city may employ several different data collection methods. Three different data collection methods follow: telephone surveys, face-to-face and online surveys, and interviews. The basic survey format for all data collection methods is included in *Appendix D*. Sample survey forms are available for license from Integral City.

1. **Random Population Sample: telephone survey** (sample 250)

   Telephone Surveys are generally well-suited to obtaining a statistically relevant, random population sample of the city, drawn from respondents whose gender and age distribution reflect the census data as closely as possible. This example shows a distribution by gender and age as shown in Table 11.

Table 11: Population Gender & Age Distribution

Gender	
Male	115
Female	135
Ages	
18–34	41
35–54	92
55–74	72
75+	40
DK	5
Total	250

Telephone surveys require particular attention to professional practice and are most effectively completed by professional organizations with properly trained staff. However, small surveys can also be completed by college or university students under the supervision of a teacher/professor who can use the data gathering project as part of a curriculum (e.g., for market research, social sciences, etc.) Survey forms for telephone data collection are adaptations of those used for in-person interviews (samples are available for license from Integral City).

2. **Direct in-person and online: SURVEY** (sample 217)

Surveys may be obtained by face-to-face methods (talking to people on the street, in the mall, at the market, etc.). The direct contact approach allows the researcher to sample particular populations (e.g., language groupings or age ranges) that are otherwise difficult to obtain.

Table 12: Survey Results by Gender, Age, and Language

Gender	
Male	113
Female	100
Declined	4
Language	
German	70
Korean	50
Punjabi	80
Mandarin	17
Ages	
13–18	69
19–28	70
29–34	8
35–55	58
55+	7
DK	5
Total	**217**

It is especially important in a city where significant language group-ings exist to obtain data in languages other than the primary "native" language, because different cultures relate to values in significantly different ways. When non-native language data is collected, the data gatherer will need to speak the designated language, record the data in the original language, and then translate the data into English (or the native language of the city), for aggregation with the whole city population set. (It should also be noted that careful attention must be paid to the subtle shades of meaning that can arise when translating one language to another, so that important expressions of values are not "lost in translation.")

An example of the results of a survey distribution targeted by gender, age, and language distribution (as compared to the random sample above) is shown in Table 12.

3. **Online Surveys** (sample 100)

Online surveys can also be distributed to selected populations by website platforms. Sample survey forms (for both direct and online surveys and in a variety of translations) are available for license from Integral City.

One of the advantages of online surveys is that they can combine open questions (which require qualitative data analysis) and closed questions (with multiple choice answers) for which the program can complete the data analysis automatically, thereby reducing time and costs for data collection.

4. **In-depth interviews**

In-depth interviews offer the researcher an expanded data set from each respondent that offers particular insight from individuals who are generally leaders in the community (and therefore tend to have more complex perspectives) into the qualitative responses that are either absent from or much abbreviated in the prior data gathering methods.

The Integral City researcher selects participants for interviews, using a purposive sampling method, whereby they invite a designated number of "Thought Leaders" from the Integral City 4 Voices of the city (see *Chapter 9*). These can be designated by both quadrant and/or sector, such as: UL/Education; UR/Healthcare; LL/Faith Community; LR/ Business Community. The total will therefore be divisible by 4 (e.g., total of 12, 16, 20, etc.). An example of in-depth interview respondent distribution might show gender and age distribution like this:

Gender: Male 5, Female 7
Age: 15–35 = 2; 35–55 = 7; 55–75 = 3

The purpose of the in-depth interview population sample is to gather both quantitative and qualitative data that is "deep, rich, and thick" and that both expands on the data from the random sample and short surveys, and can be triangulated with them. The interview format is structured as a guided interview with both closed and open-ended questions.

Sample survey forms are available for license from Integral City.

Project Team

For each of these methods, Project team members act as managers of their method, translators, and/or data collectors as follows.

Telephone Survey: Managed by a professional research company (or college/university professor) with a designated Project Manager and professional telephone surveyors.

In-Person and Online Survey: Managed by Project Manager, researcher; survey data gatherers (with a target number of surveys to deliver, e.g., 20); data translators for designated languages; professional translators for survey translation if required; data gatherers, transcribers, and data enterers for manually gathered data surveys.

Thought Leaders—in-depth interview: Managed by Project Manager, data gatherers.

WHY1

It is important to collect values data for the city, in order to understand both inner motivations and outer behaviors of city populations. Our understanding of human behavior assumes that the dominant behaviors we observe in the city arise in response to life conditions—as one would expect from any complex adaptive system (Capra, 1996; Gunderson & Holling, 2002; Stevenson & Hamilton, 2001)—each level of existence behaves with increasing levels of complexity in order to maximize the organizing principle (or value) of the current life condition. This behavior results in a tendency to protect the status quo at its current level of complexity (Hamilton, 2007; Hamilton & Dale, 2007). In Bloom's terms,[33] this could be interpreted as conformity enforcement that protects the organizing principle or value.

Thus, a tension in favor of the values and behaviors that are most coherent with the current life conditions will tend to be demonstrated by people in the city as conformity enforcement. The flip side of this behavior is that the dominant culture will also protect itself against diversity generation, until such time as life conditions require the solutions that diversity generation can offer to the problems, created by maximizing the values and organizing principles in play at any level of existence. Moreover, in the city, we can see the natural evolutionary cycles emerge at all levels of scale: individual, family, organization, society.

In general terms, we have found that the city and its citizens have a "center of gravity" (COG) to their values which tends to span three contiguous value sets as set out in Tables 8 & 9.

An analysis of values in the city can help to reveal the motivating patterns arising from the COG that underlie observable and often puzzling behaviors that relate to Placecaring (or indifference) and Placemaking (or destruction). With this in mind, it should be recognized that collecting the data is just the first step in correlating values to behavior. Analyzing the data in a way that reveals the underlying values patterns produces Conclusions that point to Recommendations for change that can be built on the city values in operation.

---

33   Bloom (2000) identified 4 roles in the beehive: Conformity Enforcers, Diversity Generators, Resource Allocators, and Inner Judges. These appear to be fractal and used by other systems such as Adizes' (1999) Producers, Entrepreneurs, Administrators, and Integrators, and at the city scale Hamilton (2008a) identifies them as Citizens, Civic Managers, Civil Society, and Business Developers.

INQUIRY PRACTICE: WHAT / HOW

WHAT

The key inquiry questions for discovering the values in the city are:

1. How do people experience city Quality of Life (QOL) in bio-psycho-cultural-structural realities?

2. What values support people in city life conditions? What is working around here?

3. What values impede people in city life conditions? What does not work around here?

4. What values do people aspire to change in the city? What do you imagine is possible?

5. How do you describe yourself?

HOW

Procedures/Study Conduct

Collecting values data from the city using the three methods set out above requires a detailed project plan for each method. Integral City has documented examples of each in reports published on the website http://www.integralcity.com/resources. For the purposes of this chapter, an overview of each method is provided for general understanding of how to use the telephone survey, face-to-face/online surveys, and in-depth interviews.

Telephone Survey

The telephone survey is conducted in a 1 to 2 week period. Calling is conducted from a random selection of all publicly listed telephone numbers within the city borders. Respondents are further screened to ensure they are at least 18 years of age and have resided within the city for the past 12 months or longer. The professional survey company will target the number of phone numbers to be dialed, to produce a statistically relevant pre-agreed number of qualified surveys. Calling is usually conducted over day and evening hours from a central facility where calls are subject to monitoring and supervision. All information collected in the survey, including names and mailing addresses, is handled in strict accordance with pre-agreed privacy policy, which aligns with the ethical guidelines for research used by Integral City.

The survey sample is generally set to produce a level of confidence at 95% certainty level that the results are accurate. For nearly all questions, the actual sample size is somewhat less than the total number of respondents due to some answering "don't know," "not applicable," or failing to provide a response. In these cases, the confidence interval or margin of error will be larger than for the entire sample.

Weightings, that may be applied to data to correct for over- or under-sampling certain members of the underlying population that ensure the data is proportionately representative, may also inflate the margin of error. For this type of survey, the margin of error on weighted data is generally targeted to be accurate to within plus or minus (n) percentage points of the stated value, 19 times out of 20.

Face-to-Face Survey

The Project team decides on translation for different languages based on the latest population scan of most prominent languages in the city (from census or other population data). The survey form translations are edited and finalized by professional translators. Surveyors with language skills (such as student interns) are selected. They collect and translate in the designated languages.

The surveyors are assigned to gather purposive data from designated population groups (e.g., by language, age, gender). They then gather the data, translate, and transcribe the qualitative comments into English (or the city's native language) and enter it into the online data collection and analysis platform.

In-Depth Interviews

The Project Manager may choose to act as the primary researcher (or assign another researcher with advanced interview skills) to conduct the in-depth responses from community leaders in the city. These interviews are generally conducted in the same time period as the telephone surveys noted above (and would exclude anyone who was part of any other data collection method).

The interviews are recorded on paper-based long-form survey forms (licensed for use by Integral City). Subsequently, the researcher enters the subset of the interviews into the online data collection and analysis platform, and transcribes the qualitative comments.

Research Journal

Throughout the research period, the Project Manager and researchers maintain a Research Journal, which identifies the sequence of tasks they undertake and also records key data and observations. This may be used in preparing the report to the client.

Data Analysis

The Project Manager (and/or designate) applies Action Research methodologies (Coghlan & Brannick, 2007; Glesne, 1999; Stringer, 1999, 2014) in interpreting and analyzing the data from the research (see *Appendix F3: Action Research*). The quantitative data from all three methods is downloaded into Excel (and/or SPSS) reports. The qualitative data is then transcribed into MS Word tables.

The first step is to review the coding and labeling of the quantitative data for each question. The researcher repeats this process for each of the research methods: the telephone survey, face-to-face or online surveys, and in-depth interviews. Then they translate key data sets into charts in Excel (or SPSS) that allow for pattern recognition within like data sets and comparison between different sources of the data.

It should be noted that not all data can be used for each section of analysis because some respondents decline to respond in some fields. In all cases, per APA style (Gasque & Jackson, 2011), the number analyzed is indicated on the chart or table.

After the process of checking the coding, categorizing and charting for the quantitative data, the researcher examines the qualitative data, looking for patterns that emerge from repetition, juxtaposition, association, and mirroring. From this process they identify themes and summarize them into tables. Then, they may (if such are available) compare the results to relevant comparative studies, such as the Abbotsford Values Map (Hamilton, 2003a, 2010a), Developmental

Assets: A Profile of Your Youth (anon, 2009) and the National Values Survey (Taylor, 2009).

The data analysis and summaries in each section of the surveys should be contextualized in relation to the method for obtaining the responses; for example, in this discussion, three different methods are used to obtain the quantitative results. (Examples of the analysis below are based on the survey forms that can be licensed from Integral City.)

Question 1: Quadrant analysis of bio-psycho-cultural-structural Quality of Life (QOL): The responses to the four questions are scored on a 10-point Likert scale. Responses from all participants are totaled and an average, min/max, and standard deviation are calculated.

Questions 2, 3, 4: Strengths/Difficulties/Improvements: For each question, the responses are single selections from eight multiple-choice options. The results are *not* averages but weightings expressed as percentages of the total number of responses selected for each question. Therefore, there are *no* average, min/max or standard deviation calculated.

Question 5: Self Description: For the Random Population Sample, respondents are asked to select the one best description of themselves from seven multiple-choice options. The results are *not* averages but weightings expressed as percentages of the total number of responses selected for each question. Therefore, there are *no* average, min/max or standard deviation calculated.

For the Face-to-Face Survey, respondents are asked to rank order seven descriptions from first to last choice as appropriate descriptions of themselves. The resulting graph shows the rankings in order of the most votes for first choice, second choice, etc. Therefore, there are *no* average, min/max, or standard deviation calculated.

For the Thought Leader In-Depth Interviews, Thought Leaders are asked to rank order seven descriptions from first to last choice as appropriate descriptions of themselves. The resulting graph shows the rankings in order of the most votes for first choice, second choice, etc. Therefore, there are *no* average, min/max or standard deviation calculated.

In all cases, the Centre of Gravity (COG) of the choices is determined by the top three rankings.

Trustworthiness and Reliability

Throughout this process, the researcher checks the trustworthiness and validity of the data, the methods that are used by the team to collect the information, the data-management systems, and the data analysis and interpretation. As Glesne (2006) put it, "The research process is collaborative and inclusive of all major stakeholders with researcher acting as a facilitator who keeps the research cycles moving" (p.17).

Validity is developed in the survey collection processes (and through the interviews with the Thought Leaders in their observations of the city) from 4-quadrant perspectives, which includes comparing the qualitative data with the quantitative data across the three methods. A final validity check can also involve a check with any predecessor research projects and/or recent literature.

Lincoln and Guba (as cited in (Stringer, 1999, 2014) identify credibility, transferability, dependability, and confirmability as procedural assessments to be performed throughout the study (p. 57). Throughout the research process, the researcher ensures the applications of trustworthiness and validity and records in their research journal each step they take to implement these principles.

Ethical Guidelines

In conducting this kind of research, the IC researcher uses a framework of guiding ethical principles that includes respect for person, concern for welfare, and considerations of justice (anon, 2010, pp. 8–9).

In practicing these ethical guidelines, the researcher ensures that: All research participants are provided detailed information to allow them to make an informed decision about participating; they are able to withdraw at any time without penalty or punitive action; the researcher considers all risks and benefits and eliminates potential risks to the participants; the research project and advisory team maintain confidentiality of participants; the researcher ensures all confidential information is securely stored; and the researcher obtains permission from participants to share information with others.

CONCLUSION: WHY2

This section sets out the substantive categories of Findings, Conclusions, and Recommendations that are typical of this research.

Findings summarize the key results of "**What did the data collection discover?**" The Findings of this type of research project can be classified in the following subheadings:

1. City Culture
2. Individual Values
3. Ratings of Well-being by Quadrants
4. Data Pattern Summaries by Method
    a. Telephone Survey, Random Population Sample
    b. Face-to-Face Survey: Purposive Population Samples
    c. Thought Leaders: In-Depth Interviews or Long Surveys
5. Comparing Methods Outcomes
6. Analysis by Subpopulation Groups
7. Analysis by Language Populations and Geo-Spatial Locations (e.g., postal codes)

Findings are summarized both in descriptions and Charts as shown on the next page.

Finding: What Would Work Better

The comparisons of what would work better (see Figure A) produce some striking similarities between the two large groups of 2010 Survey respondents, regarding more **(5.) Order** and **(6.) Caring** values. However, these two groups differ in **(2.) Family (belonging)** where the Telephone Survey group would like to see more of this value set, while the Interns Survey respondents give it a negligible rating. However, both groups concur with giving **(5.) Results (planning)** a very low rating. In contrast, both the Thought Leaders and the 2003 respondents proposed much higher ratings for **(5.) Results (planning)**.

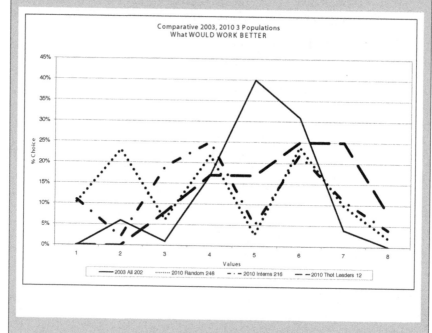

Figure A: Comparing What Would Work Better

Conclusions drawn from the Findings answer the question: "**So What is the Meaning of the Findings?**" An example of a typical conclusion is shown in the following inset.

Conclusion 7: What's not working — drugs, gangs, cultural silos — how are they related?

Both groups of survey respondents backed up their identification of what is not working—**personal Expression**) and **Order** (commitment)—with their qualitative comments. Appendices XX and YY summarize the themes from these comments and can be further clustered into **drugs, gangs**, and **cultural silos**.

These findings seem to be strongly corroborated by the School District #34 Developmental Assets Survey (anon, 2009), which identified all of the gang, drug, and violence behaviors with students who have fewer developmental assets. They identified high-risk behaviors that linked to low numbers of assets such as: alcohol use, binge drinking, marijuana use, smokeless tobacco, illegal drug use, driving while drinking, early sex, vandalism, inhalant use, smoking, shoplifting, using a weapon, eating disorders, skipping school, gambling, depression, getting in trouble with police, hitting another person, hurting another person, fighting in groups, carrying a protective weapon, threatening physical harm, attempting suicide, riding with an impaired driver. (p. 3)

A question that arises from the triangulation and intensity of these observations is: to what, if any degree, are they are connected to one another? There is enough evidence from violent crime reports to strongly link the connection of drugs and gangs. And certainly, some regional police strategies are aimed at gangs connected to particular cultures. However, it could be generative to explore how the values of particular cultures might influence individual and collective choices relating to respondents' perceptions of what does not work well in the city.

Recommendations based on the Conclusions respond to the question: **"Now What Can We Do as a Result of these Conclusions?"**

Typically, Conclusions and Recommendations will be framed through the values constructs outlined in the WHY1 section above.

Some examples of **Recommendations** are shown in the following inset.

It is recommended that:

The city develops well-being with a whole system, all quadrant, all levels, cross cultural, all faiths meshwork approach.

Policy makers across the city incorporate the results of this research into values-based strategies in their programs and services; for example, in policing, safety, social services.

Key city stakeholders collaborate to activate the prototype of an Integral Vital Signs Monitor (IVSM) to track effective changes to city well-being.

Key city stakeholders collaborate to create a Community of Practice to meshwork community organizations so that their services are aligned to solve key issues (e.g., homelessness, youth violence).

The city economic development council develops strategies for businesses to grow strategic planning capacities for success, results, and innovation at all stages. The Chamber of Commerce could be a key stakeholder in enabling this to happen.

The agriculture sector promotes the whole trajectory of jobs from the farm gate to the food plate to young people in an annual agriculture career fair.

The education system in the city from K-12 and college/university meet with the business sector to align workforce education and training programs so employers can hire qualified workers from the local population.

The healthcare system in the city develop a strategy to provide healthcare for specific challenges (e.g., HIV, water quality, etc.) aligned with subpopulation values.

In summary, the objective of this values-based research is to identify key recommendations that contribute to Placecaring and Placemaking as we recognize it in the well-being of the city and/or particular subpopulations. This data is analyzed into the 4 quadrants that measure Placecaring (Upper Left and Lower Left) and Placemaking (Upper Right and Lower Right).

In profiling the differences in Placecaring values—the "invisible" values—among key groups of subpopulations in the city (like immigrants and founding cultures) this research enables the creation of city values and asset maps that can be overlaid on geo-spatial maps (as illustrated above in Figure 14: Different Values in Different Neighborhoods). Overlaying values and asset maps on one another can reveal patterning that indicates to civic managers and civil society how to more effectively allocate limited resources for both Placecaring and Placemaking and to city developers how to design (Place Make) structures and infrastructure differently to suit different populations, based on their perceived values and needs. This can lead to greater perceived fairness (and justice) and satisfaction with city life.

Together with data from other sources (including anecdotal experience, national census data, and experience from related projects) the values mapping can reveal the tensions and dynamics of city culture in such a way that the cultural background of many projects can be better understood, and used to contribute to key decisions that improve the design and delivery of city projects and resources.

REITERATION OF INQUIRY OBJECTIVES

The inquiry objectives of this chapter were:

1. Learn the Integral framework for mapping values in the city.

2. Demonstrate the value of mapping values in the city to identify the location of differences, cultural sources of misunderstandings, conflicts, and differing expectations.

3. Map the values of city populations to identify languages and age to help locate the geographic clustering or distribution of subpopulations.

4. Learn how values help identify systemic interconnections or disconnections of city subpopulations.

5. Create a framework for a values-based capacity and asset map of the city, using the integral model that embraces Placecaring and Placemaking capacities.

ACTION PLAN FOR PRACTITIONER, CATALYST, MESHWORKER

Review this chapter and make notes below of your impressions, insights, and questions. Locate yourself on the Integral City practice scaffolding. Notice what you have observed, thought, felt, and what you now want to do in any of the three possible practice configurations: as a Practitioner, as a Catalyst, as a Meshworker.

After you have made these notes, consider some of the Impact Questions (below). They also might help you reflect on how to generate impact through inquiry and action. Finally check out the Resources and Links suggested for this practice at the end of the chapter.

IMPACT QUESTIONS: DEEP, WIDE, CLEAR, HIGH

UL DEEP: As researcher, how do I describe my values on the sample survey in *Appendix D: Sample Values Survey* Form? What filters do they set up to my collection and interpretation of data?

LL WIDE: What is the Center of Gravity (COG) of the values of our research team? How does that impact how we relate to participants, and collect and interpret data? What are the key language/culture groups in the city?

UR CLEAR: What behaviors in the city have motivated the research? What measures do the Quality of Life (QOL) quadrants reveal about tensions in the city between the 4 bio-psycho-cultural-social realities?

LR HIGH: Where are the neighborhoods and subpopulations of the city that reveal different values patterns? How do these neighborhoods and subpopulations interact with one another?

CHAPTER RESOURCES AND/OR LINKS

Appendix B: Integral City Maps (1–5): 1, 2, 3, 4

Appendix C1: Definitions of 12 Intelligences: Inner, Outer, Structural, Cultural, Inquiry, Navigating

Appendix C3: Integral City GPS Locator: Smart, Resilient, Integral

Reflective Question for Whom /Where/ What I Could Use as:	Practitioner	Catalyst	Meshworker
What do I observe as I read?			
What do I think?			
What do I feel?			
What do I want to do next?			

MAP & MONITOR VITAL SIGNS
IN THE INTEGRAL CITY

INQUIRY OBJECTIVES

The inquiry objectives for this chapter are:

1. Understand the purpose of an Integral Vital Signs Monitor (IVSM).

2. Understand the relationship of values mapping to IVSM.

3. Understand the connection between salutogenic data and Integral City well-being indicators.

4. Learn possible data sources from existing databases and/or geo-maps.

5. Create an integrated stakeholder group to collect IVSM data.

6. Create a Community of Research Practitioners (CORP) to administer an IVSM.

7. Select IVSM categories.

8. Create a draft IVSM.

9. Contribute to the strategic planning process of the city.

INTRODUCTION TO INQUIRY, ACTION, AND IMPACT IN MAPPING IVSM

The purpose of a vital signs monitor is to track city well-being using a set of vital signs, organized within the Integral City model, that provide feedback and feedforward data so that city managers, strategic planners, and decision-makers can set strategic direction and destination(s) for Placecaring and Placemaking and make course corrections to reaching the intended destination(s).

A precept of the Integral Model, used to design the Vital Signs Monitor, is its definition of "holon." A holon is both a whole system in its own right, while at the same time being part of a larger whole system. Such is the natural "order" of complex living systems—cells, organelles, organs, individuals, teams, organizations, communities, cities, nation/states—all of which have been well-studied by interdisciplinary research teams in *Panarchy: Understanding Transformations in Human and Natural Systems* (Gunderson & Holling, 2002; Miller, 1978) and *Living Systems* (Miller, 1978). Wilber (1995) coined such a set of nested holons, a "holarchy."

In addition, what Wilber's Integral Model added to the quantitative picture of the outer life of human systems was the qualitative picture of the inner life of human systems—namely, consciousness and culture.

It follows therefore that, in order for monitors and metrics of city well-being to be truly integral, they must integrate metrics from the 4 quadrants (as identified in the *Introduction* chapter).

Furthermore, as many complexity-oriented practitioners have noted, the city is a composite of many different scales that coexist and dynamically impact one another. So, it is a challenge to find a model that captures the complexity of the 4 quadrants, holons, and measures of well-being. (For the sake of this chapter, I am assuming that measures of well-being are identifiable and can be defined in terms of desired targets. The assumptions related to this have been documented; for example, see (Hamilton, 2008a).

The schematic presented as a starting point for this exploration has become what I call Map 2 (see *Appendix* B). In this holarchy, the nest of holons begins with the individual resident of the city, and locates him/her in all the other holons to which they are a member.

In this way, each holarchy starts with an individual, represented by his/her inner and outer realities (representing Upper Left and Upper Right quadrants); then is nested in a series of collective holons, to which the individual (simultaneously) belongs. Each collective is essentially a different scale of a human system that represents a different set of collective contexts for individual reality (but each represents a version of Lower Left and Lower Right quadrants). A simple way to see this is that Janet (our individual holon) belongs to the family Smith, baseball team A, workplace Task Force B, school class C, health district D, community E, and city F.

The Integral Vital Signs Monitor (IVSM) tracks the achievement of target indicators related to each of these holons that are selected by a community of stakeholders. Users of the IVSM collect data from existing databases and/or self-assess against standards and best practices. The standards and practices develop into a feedback-based governance system as outlined below in Figure 15 (Hamilton, 2008a, p. 234).

Governance, Monitoring and Organizational Learning Framework End-to-End Process

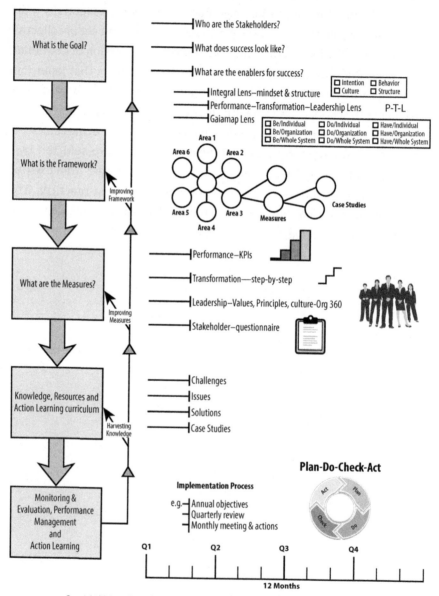

Figure 15: Governance Framework from IVSM Process

Chapter 7: Discover Integral City Values described the methodology for collecting the values-based indicators. The values indicators provide necessary lenses to create a prototype vital signs monitor that will be meaningful for a city to track progress against strategic objectives for Placecaring and Placemaking. The values-informed vital signs indicators include individual biological and psychological dimensions, and collective cultural and social dimensions (organized as qualitative and quantitative salutogenic indicators as shown in Figure 16).

Figure 16: Feedback Cycle for Salutogenic Indicators

In order to set up an Integral Vital Signs Monitor (IVSM) for a city, the place to start is with a review of available literature and research regarding indicators that the city, county/region, state/province, or nation might already have used. As noted in *Chapter 7: Discover Integral City Values*, a values map of the city provides critical information for framing an IVSM. Therefore, one logical place to start is with a review of studies examining asset mapping and/or values frameworks already applied to the target community or city (especially if any exist based on the Integral City Model). If such values mapping has not been completed, we recommend following the steps in Chapter 7 to collect this data to create an Integral City values map of the target city.

Planning the IVSM Project starts with reviewing the assumptions underlying the design (Hamilton, 2003b).

1. Our first assumption is that community develops as a result of individuals and groups organizing in the context of our Life Conditions. (Hamilton, 1999, 2008a).

2. Life Conditions contribute to core values of organization, community, city, culture, bio-region, province/state and country, at all levels of scale (D. Beck & Cowan, 1996; D. Beck & Linscott, 2006).

3. Core values emerge in a bio-psycho-social-cultural (integral) evolutionary spiral of ever-increasing complexity, as the success of one set of values co-emerges new life conditions that require a new set of values in order to solve the difficulties caused by the success of the previous set (Graves, as cited by (D. Beck & Cowan, 1996; Wilber, 2000b).

4. Life Condition indicators must go beyond (Placemaking) bio-physical, observable properties (e.g., factors tracked by census data and land use planning) in order to reveal they link to the (Placecaring) social development indicators of community (Wight, 2002).

5. The study of complexity informs the study of community, and vice versa (Stevenson & Hamilton, 2001).

6. Correlations between social and infrastructure conditions must be linked, to overcome disconnects between the different conditions (e.g., population explosion, pollution, and ecological degradation) and capacities and/or barriers for change (e.g., political decisions and belief systems (Wilber, 2000a, 2001, 2007).

7. Communities of today and the future require more complex values than communities of the past including those that enable the following outcomes (B. Robertson, 2016; R. Robertson, 2011; Smyre, 2012):

   a. Balancing action, thinking, productivity and relationship values

   b. Being open to new ideas

    c. Integrating multiple ideas with non-linear thinking

    d. Embracing connected individuality

    e. Emphasizing dynamic sustainability

    f. Expanding community development capacities for change & opportunity.

Using these assumptions, an IVSM can be prototyped as an Integral Scorecard or Dashboard that tracks the achievement of target indicators corresponding to levels of emerging capacity/complexity. Several prototypes of the Integral Dashboards that have been created from data in existing databases (e.g., Geo-Library, Healthy Community Indicators) were designed for users to self-assess against targeted standards and best practices.

The intention of the IVSM is to provide a knowledge base for storing and retrieving measures and interventions for each quadrant that can be used on-the-job, when needed. In the process of creating an IVSM users select the indicators and the standards they target and measure, across multiple metrics and timelines. (The standards and practices can be related to the four types of cities discussed in the *Introduction* chapter above: Traditional, Modern, Post-modern and Integral.) Because of the complexity and span of the information sources, we recommend that the IVSM be implemented as a web portal delivered thorough a web browser in an online environment that serves all the contributors and is available to all city stakeholders, including citizens.

Essentially, an IVSM displays a set of salutogenic (health generating) integral (bio-psycho-social-cultural) indicators and metrics. The IVSM serves as a community/city set of indices to measure overall health and well-being and whether those health indicators are moving towards greater or lesser health. What makes it successful is the premise that community partners select the indicators and distribute the workload of creating and tracking the data. Because partners contribute the indicators they "own," and a composite picture of the whole community emerges from the integral map they have a vested interest in its use. As a result, each community partner has a stake in the success of the IVSM and together, the community of partners gains insights of the interconnections that contribute to the well-being of the whole city.

FRAMING INQUIRY FOR IVSM: WHO, WHY1

WHO

- Project Manager
- Community of Partners: Stakeholders (4 Voices)
- Project Team (Data Collection, Analysis, Report Production, Communication)
- Data Maintenance and Communications Team

Producing an IVSM requires the leadership of a Project Manager. The project leadership may be initiated by any of the 4 Voices of the city (see *Chapter* 9), but will probably be most effective and most credible if it originates from civic management at city hall—largely because they will generally have the most developed technology base to coordinate such a function. The initiating organization will select a Project Manager (who may be an Integral City Assessor, ICA) who will assemble key stakeholders (representing the city's 4 Voices and core sectors) to identify sources of existing data and the categories for an IVSM through a brainstorming session.

Stakeholders can include department heads and/or technologists from city hall staff, health sector, school board, university, chamber of commerce, industrial authority, local foundations, financial sector, environmental activists, sustainability sector, civil society, and citizens (including youth and students). The purpose of the brainstorming session is to identify key indicators that can be used in an Integral Vital Signs Monitor (IVSM), including their metrics and potential owners (who have assembled the database and who will enter and maintain data).

After the stakeholder group selects the key indicators, it also nominates an IVSM Project Leader and creates Terms of Reference for an ongoing Project team or Community of Research Practitioners (CORP), outlining responsibility and authority to monitor, communicate, and revise the IVSM. (This may often default to city hall, but it could also exist at county/regional or state/province governance levels.)

WHY1

When the stakeholders first convene, the Project Manager can share data from the asset mapping and/or values mapping of the city. This will help identify possible categories and indicators for the Integral Vital Signs Monitor (IVSM) related to quadrants, levels, generations, locations, and sectors. This sharing process creates a condition among key stakeholders of intersubjectivity. It helps them explore what the data say, the questions raised by the data, and the interconnections within the possible data sources and sets. As information and perspectives are shared, new ideas, feedback and collaboration among the stakeholders naturally emerge.

After the first stakeholder meeting, the Project Manager drafts a version of the IVSM categories and circulates it to the stakeholders for their review and suggestions (see *Appendix G*). After receiving their input, the Project Manager revises the draft and proposes an initial version or prototype of the IVSM (in an Excel or Word document, as in *Appendix G*). The stakeholders provide further input and suggestions, which the Project Manager incorporates into the second draft IVSM.

At this point, generally speaking, the indicators from this draft IVSM may contain both a larger set to chart the well-being of the entire city and/or a subset with special focus on a target issue and/or population like youth or senior well-being in the city.

As noted below, the Project team will select an IVSM platform provider. The platform provider assists the data owners to upload the indicators, their descriptions, metrics, and proposed owners onto the online platform. (An example of a leading platform is Gaiasoft, which can be accessed at http://www.gaiasoft.com/index.php).

INQUIRY PRACTICE FOR IVSM: WHAT/HOW

WHAT

The key questions for the stakeholders to respond to are these:

I. What salutogenic indicators can you suggest that are already being collected for the following 9 scales of human systems:

   a. Individual Human Health (Internal/External)

   b. Families (Internal/External)

   c. Workplaces (Internal/External)

   d. Education System (Internal/External)

    e. Healthcare System (Internal/External)

    f. Civil Society (Internal/External)

    g. Recreation/Faith (Internal/External)

    h. City Hall/Infrastructure (Internal/External)

    i. Environment

2. Who is the potential source and/or owner of the data?

3. What is the appropriate metric for each data set?

4. How frequently should the data be updated?

5. What agreements exist for privacy of information and how might new agreements need to be drafted to share the data in an IVSM?

HOW

An Integral Vital Signs Monitor applies selected indicators within an Integral framework to monitor the progress of the city towards achieving strategic plans, goals, and optimal well-being.

The indicators should be chosen from the 9 key scales and the left and right-hand sides of the quadrant map at different scales (or fractals) of the city's human systems, plus its environment (as noted above under WHAT and illustrated in *Appendix G*). This will optimize community participation and commitment to maintaining and monitoring outcomes.

Each of the 9 scales will probably have indicators that are already being tracked by existing organizations. Using data that already exists in databases will minimize redundancy (because the data is already available) and maximize interconnections (because data collected by different organizations related to the same city will be reviewed as a whole for the first time).

From a quadrant perspective, it should be noted that the data is intentionally selected from Left/Internal quadrants (measuring Placecaring) and Right/External quadrants (measuring Placemaking). The Individual scale addresses the upper (individual) quadrants and all others (except Environment) address the lower (collective) quadrants. The Environmental indicators provide context for all of the others and will be based on the key sustainability indicators. *Appendix G: Integral Vital Signs Monitor—Composite*

Set of Indicators shows a composite sample of indicators, derived from the sustainability indicators used by multiple cities around the world.

When starting up an IVSM the number of indicators should be limited to 2 or 3 per scale (internal and external) so as not to overwhelm the learning process that will naturally ensue. Over time, both the selection of individual indicators and their interconnection with the overall IVSM will become refined as the stakeholders use the reporting system and learn how it contributes Key Success Factors (KSF) to measure the implementation of strategic plans.

INTEGRAL VITAL SIGNS MONITOR		

1. INDIVIDUAL
 	
Internal
HS Graduation Count   95%
 	
External
Reduction Incidents of
   Diabetes   50%
	2. FAMILY & FRIENDS
	
	Internal
	Reduction Incidents
	   Family Violence 10%
	
	External
	Housing 85%
		3. WORK PLACE
		
		Internal
		# Jobs Created for Youth 40%
		
		External
		Farm Gate Revenue $MM $m37

4. HEALTH SYSTEM
 	
Internal
Reductions Youth Mental
   Health Incidents   10%
 	
External
Reduction Youth
   Communicable Disease   30%
	**9. ENVIRONMENTAL
	   CONTROL**
	
	External
	Climate—GHG 90%
	Earth—Soil Quality 65%
	Water Quality 99%
	Air Quality 85%
	Biosphere Diversity 71%
		5. EDUCATION
		
		Internal
		Youth Literacy 72%
		
		External
		Number High School
		   Teachers 370

**6. CIVIL SOCIETY/
   COMMUNITY**
 	
Internal
Youth-to-Youth Volunteer
   Hours   1200
 	
External
NFP & NGO Count   20
	7. RECREATION & SPORT
	
	Internal
	Cross Cultural Events 1
	
	External
	Capital Investment
	   Rec Facilities 0%
		**8. CITY HALL, POLICE, FIRE,
		   INFRASTRUCTURE**
		
		Internal
		Safety Rating City Streets
		   at Night 75%
		
		External
		Ridership Public Transit 55%

Figure 17: Integral Vital Signs Monitor 9 Scales—Municipal Home Page

Technical Implementation

The Project team selects the required online platform and platform provider and implements the IVSM as an online web portal available in all stakeholders' workplace environments. The IVSM provides a knowledge base for storing and retrieving measures and interventions for each quadrant that can be used on-the-job, when needed.

The Municipal Home Page (Figure 17) shows an overview of municipal indicators for all the 9 scales noted above.

Progress of compliance and strategy execution as measured by targets for the selected indicators is available for all scales (and/or subscales). The Current Status of the indicators can be seen at a glance in a traffic light display (see Figure 18). The traffic light system allows for multiple targets and indicators, and enables a dashboard to show the current state of the city system at any time.

This traffic light reporting protocol reports on targets established by the reporting organization (based on the appropriate metrics). It is displayed as a universal traffic light system, where Green represents targets on track; Yellow as targets off track by a predefined moderate percentage; Red as targets off track by a predefined major percentage; and Orange as targets off track by a predefined amount, requiring immediate attention.

A personal view shows any manager everything they are accountable for—personal and business-unit transformation measures, outcomes, and actions.

A journaling feature ensures that there is an audit trail for key compliance and strategy execution decisions.

Charts show progress of key measures; for example, overall risk, or traditional financial, customer, or efficiency measures.

User Training and System Maintenance

The platform provider (in cooperation with the Project Manager and team) trains stakeholders to enter data related to the dataset that they own and are responsible for. The stakeholders enter the data into the web-based platform (often done as part of the on-the-job training).

The data for the IVSM that is maintained on a web platform consists of indicators that are each identified by Description, Metric, Frequency of Update, and Owner. This distributed ownership enables a division of responsibilities and investment of time/effort by the expert owners of each indicator. A prototype of this IVSM is shown in *Appendix* G and is typically provided by the platform provider.

INTEGRAL VITAL SIGNS MONITOR												
	Target	Jan	Feb	Mar	Apr	May	Jun	Jul	Aug	Sep	Oct	Nov	Dec
6. Civil Society/Community													
Internal													
Youth-to-Youth Volunteer Hours	894	900	850	850	700	950	975	995	950	905	905	900	850
External													
NFP & NGO Count	17.5	15	15	15	15	16	17	20	19	18	20	20	20
7. Recreation & Sport													
Internal													
Cross Cultural Events	1.8	1	0	2	1	2	3	4	3	1	2	1	2
External													
Capital Investment Rec Facilities	2%	0%	0%	0%	0%	0%	5%	2%	2%	3%	0%	10%	0%
8. City Hall, Police, Fire, Infrastructure													
Internal													
Safety Rating City Streets at Night	81%	75%	75%	75%	80%	85%	85%	85%	90%	90%	80%	75%	75%
External													
Ridership Public Transit	48%	50%	50%	50%	45%	45%	45%	45%	45%	45%	50%	55%	50%
9. Environmental Control													
External													
Climate - GHG	82%	90%	90%	85%	85%	82%	75%	77%	75%	80%	80%	80%	90%
Earth — Soil Quality	76%	79%	80%	76%	77%	79%	70%	75%	75%	70%	75%	79%	79%
Water Quality	90%	95%	99%	98%	95%	87%	95%	90%	85%	80%	80%	80%	95%
Air Quality	78%	89%	89%	85%	80%	79%	75%	70%	65%	70%	75%	75%	80%
Biosphere Diversity	72%	75%	70%	70%	70%	70%	71%	71%	71%	72%	75%	75%	75%
Eco-Region Sustainability	56%	60%	60%	60%	55%	55%	55%	50%	50%	55%	55%	55%	60%

Figure 18: Integral Vital Signs Monitor 9 Scales—Municipal Home Page

Create a Community of Practice to Administer the Integral Vital Signs Monitor

In order for the IVSM to serve its purpose, the owners of the specified indicators must commit to their maintenance. In addition, the IVSM needs a project coordinator to commit to its update and information distribution. Essentially, the data owners—all of whom are stakeholders in city well-being—must commence, commit, and continue the resourcing of ongoing participation.

One method of achieving this is to create a Community of Research Practitioners (CORP) who represent the stakeholders and owners of the IVSM. The CORP could meet monthly in virtual mode and quarterly in face-to-face mode to: review the status of the IVSM, report to the owners and public, select and apply the indicators, and recommend whether changes should be made to targets, interpretations, or indicators. The important perspective from which the CORP should operate is that the IVSM is essentially a learning system whose feedback and feedforward provides a whole system view of the city. Stakeholders and owners of the databases can start anywhere and gain experience as they operate the IVSM how best to learn from the system to support their strategic initiatives.

This CORP could be funded through a collaboration of stakeholder and owner agencies. As the data is collected and shared, the platform should be able to track and display a growing web of interconnections. Figure 19 shows an example of the IVSM Web of Interconnections view.

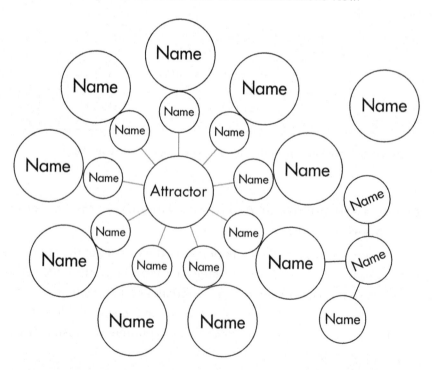

Figure 19: IVSM Web of Interconnections

An emerging function of this CORP would be to provide the data for feedback into strategic plans. Strategic plans for city development, community enhancement, educational, and healthcare improvement and geo-spatial planning all require key success factors (KSF) to track performance and successful implementation. The IVSM provides that data and the CORP is well positioned to become key players in designing the meshwork for the delivery of services to the community that are aligned in service to the well-being of the whole—as discussed in *Chapter 13: Realize Meshworking Capacities in the Human Hive*.

CONCLUSION: WHY2

An Integral Vital Signs Monitor (IVSM) reports on indicators that can enable the identification and maintenance of key contributors to the well-being of the city. The IVSM offers both an overall tracker of city well-being, with selective indicators that focus on the health of key populations and/or issues that derive from mapping the city values. A web-based Integral Vital Signs Monitor that tracks city well-being will contribute to the ongoing success of the city meeting its strategic goals.

Analysing the traffic light indicators from the IVSM provides integrated overviews of the city from the 4 quadrants of the Integral model that can contribute to Recommendations that are integrated through: actions (UR), learnings (UL), relationships (LL), and systems (LR) involved in the IVSM.

Another way to look at how the IVSM is designed integrally is to see how the indicators organized into the 9 scales of human systems, essentially embrace all 8 levels of complexity (outlined in *Chapter 7: Discover Integral City Values*). It is critical for the credibility of the stakeholders and the trustworthiness and effectiveness of the IVSM that indicators and recommendations address the 8 levels of complexity in order to optimize city well-being.

An Integral Vital Signs Monitor that is community-owned and community-administered supports the implementation and follow-through of strategic plans and achievement of city goals that optimize city well-being through attention to both Placecaring and Placemaking.

REITERATION OF INQUIRY OBJECTIVES

The inquiry objectives of this chapter were:

1. Understand the purpose of an Integral Vital Signs Monitor (IVSM).

2. Understand the relationship of values mapping to IVSM.

3. Understand the connection between salutogenic data and Integral City well-being indicators.

4. Learn possible data sources from existing databases and/or geo-maps.

5. Create an integrated stakeholder group to collect IVSM data.

6. Create a Create a Community of Research Practitioners (CORP) to administer an IVSM.

7. Select IVSM categories.

8. Create a draft IVSM.

9. Contribute to the strategic planning process of the city.

ACTION PLAN FOR PRACTITIONER, CATALYST, MESHWORKER

Review this chapter and make notes below of your impressions, insights, and questions. Locate yourself on the Integral City practice scaffolding. Notice what you have observed, thought, felt, and what you now want to do in any of the three possible practice configurations: as a Practitioner, as a Catalyst, as a Meshworker.

After you have made these notes, consider some of the Impact Questions (below). They also might help you reflect on how to generate impact through inquiry and action. Finally check out the Resources and Links suggested for this practice at the end of the chapter.

IMPACT QUESTIONS: DEEP, WIDE, CLEAR, HIGH

UL DEEP: How can I lead, collaborate, or contribute to the creation of a city IVSM? What does well-being mean to me? What metrics do I use?

LL WIDE: How can our organization lead, collaborate, or contribute to the creation of a city IVSM? What does well-being mean to our organization? What metrics do we use that could connect with indicators/metrics from other organizations?

UR CLEAR: What behaviors in the city are important to track? What metrics from the 4 quadrants of bio-psycho-cultural-social realities contribute to city well-being?

LR HIGH: Who are the organizational stakeholders who own and maintain indicators important for a city IVSM? What organization is optimally positioned and/or resourced to call together a city-wide Community of Practice to create, resource, and maintain an IVSM? What online platform could best serve a city IVSM?

CHAPTER RESOURCES AND/OR LINKS

Appendix B: Integral City Maps (1–5): 1, 2, 3

Appendix C1: Definitions of 12 Intelligences: Integral, Inquiry, Navigating

Appendix C3: Integral City GPS Locator: Smart, Resilient, Integral

Reflective Question for Whom /Where/ What I Could Use as:	Practitioner	Catalyst	Meshworker
What do I observe as I read?			
What do I think?			
What do I feel?			
What do I want to do next?			

PART 2
Placemaking

Part 2 of the book moves into the right-hand quadrants of the Integral City model and explores how to translate the Placecaring inquiry and action examined in earlier chapters into Placemaking inquiry and action. We effectively move from values creation into values realization.

SECTION V — *Engage the 4 Voices of the City*

These two chapters explore the 4+1 Voices of the City—Citizens, Civil Society, Civic Managers, and Business (and the +1 Voices of other cities).

Chapter 9 starts with the practical question of: How do you bring the 4+1 Voices to the table?

Chapter 10 lays out the elegant process of how to design a dialogue where the 4+1 Voices can respectfully listen to one another and take effective action.

9

ATTRACT THE 4 VOICES OF THE CITY

INQUIRY OBJECTIVES

The Inquiry Objectives of this chapter are:

1. Learn the living system source of the 4 Voices of the City.

2. Identify the 4 Voices of the City.

3. Invite the 4 Voices to meet each other.

4. Attract the 4 Voices in service to a Superordinate Goal.

5. Engage the 4 Voices for productive action and outcomes—overcoming conflict, finding new allies.

6. Recognize the distinctive qualities of each of the 4 Voices.

7. Learn how the 4 Voices work together for Placemaking (and Placecaring).

INTRODUCTION TO INQUIRY, ACTION, AND IMPACT THAT ATTRACTS THE 4 VOICES

As a complex adaptive human system, an Integral City is like a Human Hive (as discussed in *Chapter 4: Inspire Spiritual Communities to Serve Evolution of the Human Hive*, in terms of the roles played by different city functions.) In fact, the metaphor of the Human Hive lets us think about how to see the city as a whole living system, not only the roles that make it function but how those roles speak through the 4 Voices that naturally speak for, with, and as the living system.

I adapted the Human Hive metaphor from the story of complexity and the honey bee, told by Howard Bloom (Bloom, 2000)—he discovered that the honey bee developed a strategy for individual adaptation, hive innovation, and species resilience.

It is an amazing evolutionary fact that the honey bee (apis mellifera) is 100 million years old. That is 10 to 100 times the age of our species. The honey bee is also the most advanced species of the branch of the Tree of Life called the invertebrates. We are supposed to be the most advanced species of the branch called the vertebrates. So, with those credentials I have always been curious if the honey bee species has something to teach the human species?

A beehive has about 50,000 bees in it—about the size of a small city. Moreover, as a resilient living system, a beehive works to performance goals. It must produce a certain amount of honey per year in order to survive—about 40 pounds (20 kilos) per year.

Thus, a beehive has a clear sustainability objective for the hive, measured in terms of **energy production.** In fact, this objective becomes a **superordinate goal**[34] that the beehive is in service to.[35]

It is fascinating to learn how bees obtain the raw materials to produce honey. They do this by creating four roles within the hive (and one role between hives), and each of these roles serves the purpose and resilience of the hive.

---

34   A superordinate goal is a goal that transcends and includes other goals in a way that everyone supports because they see that their own interests are addressed by pursuing it. Superordinate goals are referenced frequently throughout subsequent chapters.

35   The concept of the superordinate goal and its importance originates with Dr. Don Beck and the Spiral Dynamics (1996) change methodology.

About 90% of the hive are **Conformity Enforcers (CE). In the city we can think of this role as the Voice of the Producers or Citizens.** Their job is to fly to flower patches and harvest as much nectar and pollen as they can. They use the "waggle dance" form of communication to let sister bees know where to find the resources. When 90% of the hive is doing the same dance—it's like a Rock & Roll rave—the energy produced attracts a lot of attention and reinforces successful finds.

About 5% of the hive are **Diversity Generators (DG). In the city we can think of this role as the Voice of the Business Entrepreneurs, Inventors, Artists, and Developers**. Their job is to fly to different flower beds than the Conformity Enforcers. As a result, their waggle dance contains different information—more like an Irish jig than rock & roll. When the Conformity Enforcers are at peak performance, the Diversity Generators are not noticed because their communication is drowned out by the Conformity Enforcer "rave."

However, a small percent of the hive are **Resource Allocators (RA). In the city we can think of this role as the Voice of the Civic Managers.** Their job is to reward the performance of Conformity Enforcer and Diversity Generator bees. When Conformity Enforcer performance lags (after depleting the resources in one flower patch), Resource Allocators withhold rewards until the point that Conformity Enforcer bees are not only de-energized— they become downright depressed. You can imagine them walking around completely bummed out—the party is over. (By the way, scientists can measure depression in bees by measuring their pheromones.) Eventually when the Conformity Enforcers' energy is lowest, they finally take note of the Diversity Generator Irish jig (communication) and switch their resourcing flights to the new locations discovered by the Diversity Generators.

An even smaller percent of the hive **are Inner Judges (IJ). Some say this is even a hive intelligence. In the city we can think of this role as the Voice of the Civil Society. The Inner Judges** work with Resource Allocators to assess and reward performance, so that the hive can achieve its sustainability goals.

Now, in the Human Hive, the percentage of Voices is probably different than in the beehive—but I have noticed that these 4 Voices play vital roles in city well-being and must all be functioning in alignment to one another—and to a common Purpose or Vision in order for the city to be well.

Incidentally, there is a fifth role in the hive that represents an external voice—it is created through **Inter-Group Tournaments (IT)**. **In city terms this would be the Voice of the other cities (competing) in the eco-region.** This role actually emerges from the competition between hives within the bee's eco-region—the territory they share with other hives competing for the same resources. In a similar way, cities in an eco-region compete for resources and strategic outcomes.

FOLLOW THE ENERGY

These five roles create a resilience strategy that essentially *follows the energy* in service to the superordinate goal of producing 40 pounds of honey annually. The strategy for well-being depends on performance and innovation to support the hive Purpose and the sustainability of the species. But interestingly, in pursuit of their superordinate goal, the bees have expanded their well-being strategy beyond the boundaries of the hive to the scale of a regional level of resilience. Because, of course, as they gather resources for themselves, honey bees pollinate the plants in their eco-region, thereby creating energy renewal for next year.

This means the bees have developed a double sustainability loop that supports hive survival and regenerates the energy resources in their eco-region. The inter-group tournaments operate at the level of species survival—ensuring any hive that gets an edge in the innovation and evolution curve is the one most likely to survive and pass on its learning.

In terms of well-being, I have wondered for some time—when homo sapiens sapiens will innovate sustainability strategies that will embrace superordinate goals (aka performance goals) and replenish the resources we use to sustain our human hive and thereby add value to the earth? I ask, what is the superordinate goal and energy equivalent of the 40 pounds of honey for the human hive?

4 VOICES CREATE RESILIENCE IN THE HUMAN HIVE

If we are looking for clues to answer this question, we will do well to look at how these 4+1 Voices work together for well-being in the Human Hive.

The 4 interior Voices each contribute to Placecaring and Placemaking. When we locate them in the Integral Quadrants (see Figure 20), we can more easily see how the 4 Voices co-create capacities of mutual benefit in the city. In the quadrants the Voices are situated as follows:

- The **Upper Left (UL) is the voice of the Citizen**—everyone is a citizen.
- In the **Lower Left (LL) are the voices of the Civil Society**—they represent the Not-for-Profits, NGOs, churches, temples, cultural organizations, and care-givers of the city.
- The **Upper Right (UR) is the voice of the City Manager**—these are the voices of City Hall, the institutions of Education and Healthcare, Justice, Emergency Response—any institution serving government or its agencies.
- In the **Lower Right (LR) are the voices of Business and Entrepreneurs**—these are the developers, innovators, and artists of the city.

4 VOICES OF THE HUMAN HIVE

Figure 20: 4 Quadrants and 4 Voices of the Human Hive

When we listen to the voices within the Integral City Quadrants we can recognize the many discourses and practices of human systems such as psychology, coaching, counseling, and organization development. All of these human practices exist at scales that are combinations of individual and collective human systems—leaders, teams, departments, organizations, and sectors. The city—or the "human hive" is the most complex human system yet created and contains all of these scales. But because the Integral framework is a "fractal"—a pattern that is repeated at multiple scales—we can see the quadrants and the voices can describe the city in terms of individual and collective voices who have capacities that are both interior and exterior. I think of the interior capacities (Upper Left, Lower Left) as **Placecaring Capacities**. I think of the exterior capacities (Upper Right, Lower Right) as **Placemaking Capacities,** as shown in Figure 21.

4 Voices in the Human Hive

Figure 21: 4 Voices: 2 for Placecaring and 2 for Placemaking

Next, we describe how we can open the discovery conversation that enables the 4+1 Voices in the city to recognize one another (and what qualities they bring to the conversation). In the following chapter, we build on these relationships and ask key questions of all the city Voices to discover how well-being shows up in the city.

As we create conditions for the 4 Voices of the city to convene and converse, we can notice the roles they play in the Human Hive—at work, recreation, and home. In many ways, these roles open gateways to the flow of energy in the city and we are better able to see how Citizen and Civil Society Voices contribute to Placecaring, and how Civic Manager and Business Voices contribute to Placemaking.

FRAMING INQUIRY FOR ATTRACTING THE 4 VOICES: WHO, WHY1

WHO

- Host / Sponsor
- Representatives of the 4 Voices
- Facilitator
- Action Co-Researchers

The participants in this inquiry include a sponsor or host and the representatives of the 4 Voices of the city. We have convened the 4+1 Voices of the city for exploring subsystem issues and opportunities and whole system goals, such as: for an individual city as a whole (e.g., seeking a unified vision); for exploring an issue in the city (e.g., how to elect more women to office); for groups of cities in the same eco-region (e.g., inquiring how to improve transportation systems); and for trans-national city representatives (e.g., discovering the different purposes of cities in the EU).

In order to attract the 4 Voices of the city, a representative of one or more of the Voices must step forward as a sponsor or host and extend an invitation to convene. Unlike Traditional, Smart, or Resilient Cities, where the invitation generally originates with the Voice of the Civic Manager, in an Integral City the invitation to convene may originate from any of the 4 internal Voices (or even from the one external voice for eco-regional or national interests).

Essentially, the 4 Voices of the city become gateways of attraction. As noted above, the impetus to step forward into this gateway role creates energy that is attractive to others belonging to the same Voice to follow. Moreover, it builds a field of attraction to the other Voices as informal (and formal) Placecaring and Placemaking leaders are attracted to follow the energy.

Profiles of the Action Co-Researchers

A fourth group of participants has helped us attract the 4 Voices of the city and learn their qualities. Co-researchers at three conferences (two designed for integrally informed interests and one for city sustainability interests) brought their own distinctive profiles.

- **The Integral Theory Conference 2013**, located in San Francisco, CA, attracted thinkers and theorists with a major interest and focus on integral points of view—a group that were heavily weighted in the Upper Left /Consciousness Quadrant of the Integral Model. At the same time, this group self-identified as being strongly biased in favor of Innovators and Business or Diversity Generators.

- **The Federation of Canadian Municipality Sustainability Conference 2014**, located in Prince Edward Island, Canada, attracted mayors, city managers, and civic leaders from across Canada with an interest in sustainability and action orientation. So, from an integral perspective this group was heavily weighted in the Upper Right/Action and Lower Right/Systems Quadrants of the Integral Model. This group by definition, were Civic Managers or Resource Allocators.

- Finally, the **Integral Europe Conference 2014**, located in Budapest, Hungary, attracted a diversity of cultures and actors from across Europe (with smaller representation from other non-European nations) who were heavily weighted in the Lower Left/ Cultural Quadrant of the Integral Model. This group had a strong predisposition to be Inner Judges from Civil Society (with a strong showing from Business as well.)

INQUIRY PRACTICE FOR ATTRACTING 4 VOICES: WHAT / HOW

WHAT

The core question of an inquiry that attracts the 4 Voices is: **How can the 4 Voices of the City discover the conditions that enable caring for and making a place that provides well-being for all?**

It should be noted that an infinite number of variations of this question may also serve to anchor the inquiry.

HOW

This section describes the basic workshop for convening the 4+1 Voices. Attracting the 4 Voices starts with an invitation to join a conversation. Then the conversation is designed and delivered in four parts.

Invitation, Introductions, Agenda

The invitation from the host/sponsor outlines an agenda, and opens the doors for introductions by all participants before they assemble (by learning participant names, relationships, and associations) and when they assemble through a check-in. The Facilitator invites in the Knowing Field (see *Chapter 1: Activate Inquiry for Knowing Cities* and *Chapter 2: Cultivate We-Space Inquiry for Human Hive Mind*), as the energy field where we will discover how city Voices can be gateways that are open, arrested, or blocked. Participants are asked to consider: **How are you a gateway to the city?**

Gate 1: The Voices—prepare, notice, deepen

The facilitator frames the workshop by:

- Telling the story of the human hive and the 4+1 Voices.
- Sharing the importance of the city to the planet (more than 50% of humans live in cities and in the developed world 90% live in cities).
- Asking participants to reintroduce themselves and identify how their Voice is a gateway to the city.

The participants as 4 Voices start to work together by:

- Self-organizing into mixed groups of 4 (one of each Voice).
- Telling a story of a time when the participant has felt the aliveness of the city, the pulse that makes it thrive. They talk about a particular community, a particular story.
- Discuss how the 4 Voices brought aliveness to the community.

Next, participants reorganize into like Voices (4 groups: Citizen, Civic Manager, Civil Society, Business) and collectively notice the qualities of each voice, including values, worldviews, capacities, roles, etc.

- They record what they find on a flip chart.
- They select a "receiver" to remain behind and add to their record during the following Gateway Tour.

Next participants, as explorers, take a Gateway Tour of the other Voices.

- They go to each other's Voice, and notice and add to its values, worldviews, capacities, roles, etc.
- They return to their "Home" Voice Gateway.
- They notice discoveries related to their "Home" Voice in relation to other 4 Voices.
- The Recorder adds any notes from discoveries on the tour.

Gate 2: The Values in the Voices — Spiral values and conflicts

The facilitator offers a quick teaching of the values in the Voices through the lens of Spiral Dynamics integral—explaining the 4 quadrants and the key levels (see Integral City Maps in *Appendix* B).

Participants are then led to understand and experience the values in their communities.

- In groups of 2 (each from the perspective of different Voice), participants tell a story of two values in conflict in their community.
- In Groups of 4 they debrief together—what roles did values have to play in their stories? How did healthy and unhealthy ways for the values show up? (Open, Arrested, Closed)

Participants then discern how values appear in healthy and unhealthy ways.

- Staying in their group of 4, they choose one of the stories and retell it, so that each person speaks *as* a Representative of one of the values in that story. Who was saying, doing, relating, creating what?

Participants notice how speaking as a Representative of a value changes their perception and understanding of that value and how that understanding can shape how they now see their work, their roles, and how to work more effectively in the city.

- In the Group of 4, they draw out the 4 quadrants, and label them; and then draw a spiral of the values showing up in each quadrant. They locate the players (Voices) in their stories on their quadrant/ spiral map; Where are the Citizens, Civil Society, Civic Managers, Business Voices?

Gate 3: Seeking the Superordinate Goal–Re-Storying Conflict. Learn How Our Voices & Values Work Together as Gateways... the bee story encore.

The facilitator retells the story of the bees, with emphasis on the Superordinate Goal (the 40 pounds of honey).

Continuing in their mixed Groups of four, participants explore how Voices and Values can enable flow through Gateways of Change. They discuss:

- What is the City's Superordinate Goal?
- When one or more Voice(s) blocks other Voices what happens?
- When one or more Voice stops contributing (becomes arrested) what happens?
- When the Spiral of Values does not serve a Superordinate Goal what happens?
- What Life Conditions create flow?

Gate 4: Dynamic Steering (Serving our Cities as Gateways of Intelligence)–The concentric circles, discussion, and a personal reflection.

The facilitator introduces the Master Code as the key to working together to discover the Superordinate Goal—as the key to opening the city gateways.

The facilitator organizes the room as a fishbowl (small circle in the center for speakers, surrounded by a larger circle for listeners) and asks the questions to those who enter the Inner Circle in sequence:

- How am I a Gateway to the Highest Good of the City?
- Who do I commit to work with to open City Gateway(s)? (other Voices, Values, Conflicts)
- What do you know and understand differently about city Voices as Gateways?
- Thank each person for being Gateways for the exploration of the 4 Voices.
- Release them from their Voice/Role. Return to the field of the Highest Good where working together opens the flow of energy in the city.
- Participants are invited to carry forward the Master Code as their Key to Opening Gateways of the City towards a superordinate goal.
- The facilitator completes the process with a check-out question (e.g., What valuable experience(s) or insights am I taking back to my city?)

CONCLUSION: WHY2

When we started our practice of convening the 4+I Voices, we realized that we should collect key data about the qualities of the Voices.

Three Action Research Groups from the three conferences noted above (where Integral City workshops were convened as Learning Lhabitats) explored the 4 Voices of the city in the United States, Canada, and Europe. These Learning Lhabitat research groups helped expand our understanding of the role of each Voice in the city.

As a result of convening the 4 Voices in these research groups we have been able to describe the qualities of the Voices of Citizens, Civil Society, Civic Managers, and Business as summarized below. The value of understanding the qualities of these Voices is that they provide clues to what attracts them to the conversations, agreements, and strategies in which we want to engage them. In other words, the qualities of the Voices tell us how to design the communications we need to connect directly with them to create the conditions for Placecaring and also how to design bridges that bring them together in collaboration for Placemaking activities (explored in more detail in the following chapters on Meshworking).

Qualities of the Citizen Voice

The three research groups gave us an in interesting sampling of the I/We/It/Its perspectives on the Citizen in the Integral City. Table 13 sets out the comparison of the 3 Groups as they identified qualities of the Citizen.

Table 13: Qualities of Citizen Voice

QUALITY	ITC2013 US/World	FCM2014 Canada	IEC2014 Europe
Citizen Voice			
Cityzens come in all flavours/colours/expressions of worldviews	x		
Leaders drive change and people power change		x	
Role of Citizens—engage in POSITIVE ways (Be free of the solution)		x	
Innovative		x	
I—WE—All of Us—the Planet			x
Higher purpose			x
Idea seed			x
Cityzens want a sense of being home and belonging	x		
Passion—bring emotional impetus/protecting what's valuable to community		x	
Love energy			x
Connect			x
Communicate			x
Cityzens just want to have fun!	x		
They can be action-oriented, doing what they have to do	x		
Willing Citizens—need to know path forward and rationale		x	
Power of the many			x
Adaptation/flexibility			x
Revolution		x	
They protest change and can stand up for their own preferred Quality of Life	x		
They can also feel powerless, apathetic and isolated	x		
People with "Inside Knowledge" of the systems try to use the system to their personal ends (eg., Former Staff, Councillors)		x	
Settled established groups/people in Community are often the most resistant to change		x	
Conflict makes you think/forces you to REASSESS		x	

Each Learning Lhabitat was asked to define the qualities of the Citizen Voice. From comparing results across the three data collection occasions, we learned that Citizens are appreciated for the many "Spiral Colors"[36] that they represent. Citizens are growing into the "new normal" as a positive force of change.

Citizens represent **innovation** in many ways connected to a higher purpose, that even goes beyond the usual polarities of I/We into "**All-of-Us**

---

36   See Spiral Dynamics (Beck & Cowan, 1996) and Chapter 7: Discover Integral City Values

and the Planet." They can be "**idea seeds**" for a higher purpose with a strong need for "**being home**" and a **sense of belonging**.

With this in mind, not surprisingly, Citizens want to **connect to others** and bring a **passion for community**—even a love energy to how they communicate. One group thought that "Citizens just want to have fun." But this also makes them action-oriented and even willing to follow a path that will work.

Other participants pointed out that Citizens, taken as a whole, have the "**power of the many**" which can be joined into teamwork that is adaptable and flexible.

However, Civic Manager researchers flagged the propensity of Citizens to lead "**revolutions**" and protest change that does not support their sometimes self-centered and narrow views. They warned of NIMBYism (not in my backyard) and flagged a special order of Citizen shadow, called **PANE** (people against nearly everything).

Even some positive thinkers identified the **ineffectiveness of Citizens who feel powerless and isolated**. They may show signs of apathy because "people with Inside Knowledge" who know the system (such as former Civic Managers or Councilors) can be the triggers and/or the source of resistance to change.

However, as one group pointed out, **conflict can make Citizens think and reassess situations**. Change is inevitable and Citizens who are able to practice the positive qualities embedded in higher purpose and positive connections can use conflict as a creative force to move forward.

Qualities of the Voice of Civil Society

The qualities of the Civil Society Voice are set out in Table 14.

In defining the qualities of the Civil Society Voice, the research groups characterized this Voice as a "**visionary spirit of pioneers**."

Civil Society is able to **set the focus** for conversations and act as integrators of diverse value systems in the city. They can create a "climate change" where all Voices share a mindset that is open to future focused thinking.

They are credited with being **good listeners** who can **align all voices on a shared track**. They have the capacity to be in **right relationship** with each other and the city. Moreover, they have the astuteness to discover who are the key stakeholders of the other three Voices in the city. In doing so they can **create a sense of "home"** in the city so that everyone gains a **"feel"** of the city.

Table 14: Qualities of Civil Society Voice

QUALITY	ITC2013 US/World	FCM2014 Canada	IEC2014 Europe
Civil Society Voice			
Visionary		x	x
Focus Setters		x	
Creating a "climate change" where all voices share a mindset that is open to future-focused thinking	x		
Integrators	x	x	
Good listeners		x	
Aligning all voices on a shared track	x		
Creating a sense of "home" in the city	x		
Love			x
Reflective, meditative capacities			x
Philanthropists		x	
Conscious (Integral)			x
Pragmatists			x
Social Network		x	
Community builders		x	x
Collaborators		x	
Champions		x	
Facilitators		x	
Organizers of intergroup exchanges within the city; e.g. art, science, business	x	x	
Discovering needs, purposes, and values of city voices, groups and cultures	x		
Greater Good		x	
Resiliency		x	x
Spark Plugs		x	
Shit Disturbers (leaders of the pack)		x	
Change agents		x	
Strategic thinking			x
Problem solvers		x	
Money spenders/Savers		x	
Cynicism		x	
Vocal		x	

This voice conveys **love**, as well as **reflective and meditative** capacities. They are known as both pragmatists (tough love?) and **conscious philanthropists**.

As builders of **strong social networks, collaborators,** and **facilitators,** they join forces to **build community** and organize intergroup exchanges, thereby **breaking down silos**. This voice searches for and discovers the needs, purposes, and values of city voices, groups, and cultures and they take the time and effort to check in with the intentions of citizens.

Civil Society aims for the **Greater Good**, demonstrating the stamina of "long distance runners," overcoming apathy and isolation, enabling **resilience** to emerge in themselves and the city.

Some called Civil Society "**spark plugs**" and others saw the same qualities as "**shit disturbers**"—but in either case they are active **leaders of the pack**— change agents with creative, innovative, pattern-busting capacities for change.

Even as free thinkers, Civil Society is seen also as **strategic thinkers, problem solvers,** and more than willing to spend money (and less often save it).

On the shadow side, Civil Society was seen as **cynical, vocal, self-interested,** and adamant about getting their way.

Qualities of the Voice of Civic Managers

The qualities of the Voice of the Civic Managers are summarized in Table 15.

Each Learning Lhabitat was asked to define the qualities of the Civic Manager Voice. This voice was driven by the value of **structure** in service to the **bigger picture** and **finding out what is best for the community**. Civic Managers were called "**bridge builders between the unconnected.**"

The Voice of Civic Managers often **triggered the next steps** to a larger or spiritual consciousness.

This voice acted as **connectors** to the community and the resources required to build structures as well as **allies with the Inner Judges** of Civil Society. Acting as a hub or **centerpiece** between Council, Citizens, and Developers, Civic Managers can **guide the Citizen Voice for collaboration** on community interests.

In its **bureaucratic systems,** Civic Managers can advocate toward **long-term visions** (including **sustainability**) while using access to information to **frame an objective view of issues** that assists in **staying on course**.

Civic Managers can **build consensus** in an intelligent way, fearlessly **delving into root causes** of concerns, dispelling misconceptions, and providing a **synopsis** of the issues to expedite workable solutions.

At their best, Civic Managers operate on a principle of **majority** [rules], but as professionals, they make sure they **listen without pushing their own agenda**.

Table 15: Qualities of Civic Managers

QUALITY	ITC2013 US/World	FCM2014 Canada	IEC2014 Europe
Civic Manager's Voice			
Build bridges between the unconnected			x
—>For the bigger picture			x
Connection			x
Find what best for community		x	
Spiritual consciousness			x
Advocate toward long term visions			x
Trigger potential consciousness steps			x
Centre piece of Council, Citzens, Developers		x	
Guide Citizen Voice		x	
Allied with Integrators/InnerJudges	x		
Integration between Resources and Community			x
Staying on course		x	x
Build consensus		x	
Hearing Feedback		x	
Bureaucratic system		x	
Have an objective view orientation		x	
Knowledge, information	x	x	
Build on expertise and assets		x	
Balance the new with valuable heritage	x		
Insight on sustainability	x		
Innovate change/improvement		x	
Support unpopular position if best		x	
Systemic thinking—identifying and "fixing" key points with high impact		x	x
Planning—short, mid, long term		x	x
Processes			x
Consider responsibilities in decisions and expenditures		x	x
Keep the structures that work in place with justice	x	x	
Organization			x
Allow for flexibility		x	
Ensure "wheels on bus keep turning"		x	
Motivate staff		x	
Voice of the skeptic	x	x	
Measurers of results	x		
Rewarders of success	x		
Punishers of failure	x		

As Resource Allocators it is the job of Civic Managers to innovate and **introduce change and improvement**, even **supporting unpopular positions** if that makes most sense. In doing so they must use **systemic thinking**, identifying the highest impact leverage points. At the same time, they are called on to **balance new approaches with the values of heritage**.

It is the job of Civic Managers to act as **responsible decision-makers** (and expenditure managers) to **plan** for short, mid-, and long-term change, using processes (and motivating staff) that allow them to **frame, deliver, and maintain structures that work** (implemented with considerations for justice and flexibility).

Civic Managers were seen as ensuring that the "**wheels on the bus keep turning**," utilizing expertise and assets for **measurable results**.

While Civic Managers were viewed as positive Resource Allocators, they were also recognized as speaking from the Voice of the **Skeptic**. They are always **balancing the needs** of the community with a **diversity of opinions**. Thus, they hold powerful positions that enable them to **reward success**, as well as **punish failure**.

Qualities of the Voice of Business

The qualities of the Voice of Business are summarized in Table 16.

Each Learning Lhabitat was asked to define the qualities of the **Business Voice**. This voice was unanimously described as **innovators**, who "**dare to see what is and learn from the past to create the future.**" Business is seen as able to take the overview with an **optimistic**, spiritual consciousness. Advanced business leaders practice **servant leadership**, but at the same time can be **unattached** with a preference—even an expectation—for working with **freedom**.

As **creative entrepreneurs**, Business Voices are both **Purpose and Goal oriented,** organizing their plans to achieve both. As **profit generators** and **risk takers**, they also can **demonstrate social conscience**, with growing awareness of the importance of sustainability, practicing the "**3 Rs**" (reuse, recycle, redevelop) and generating wealth with a **triple bottom line** (People, Profit, Planet). Business both **drives the city agenda** with a focus on **producing results**, that **don't reinvent the wheel**, often **challenging the status quo**, and **changing policy** but somehow **finding the middle ground**.

Business can **redefine the very meaning of success** (e.g., developing ways to build community that **improves work/play and walkability**).

While Business **moves quickly** and is always aware of the **importance of time**, it also **demands clear process**. Business **asks clarifying questions** like: Where does the funding come from? Who can sponsor this? How do we change the car culture? What are the best practices already?

Table 16: Qualities of Voice of Business

QUALITY	ITC2013 US/World	FCM2014 Canada	IEC2014 Europe
Business/Developers/Inventors/Artists			
"dare to see what is and learn from past to create the future"			x
Optimistic			x
Overview			x
Spiritual consciousness			x
Shifters of systems and leadership	x		
Servant enterprise + leadership			x
Freedom—unattached			x
Innovators	x	x	x
Creators	x		x
Entrepreneurs	x		
Goal oriented	x		x
Goal aligners	x		
Structuring/planning			x
Risk takers	x		x
Social developers	x	x	
Profit generators	x	x	
Wealth generators for the sustainability of Triple P: People, Profit, Planet	x		
Able to reuse, redevelop, recycle	x		
Challengers of the Status Quo	x	x	
Demand clear process.		x	
Analyzing		x	
Results producers	x		
Drive the agenda—or what can I see the easiest?		x	
Finding middle ground		x	
Not reinventing the wheel		x	
See connections between things pushes city policy		x	
Re-definition of Success			x
Huge change underway to build community—developers are understanding this more—like work play, etc.; walkability		x	
Problem solving		x	
Timing is important—move quickly to get things done		x	

Summary: The Value of Multiple Perspectives

These Learning Lhabitats action research groups helped us see how all 4 Voices see themselves, each other, their city, and the world. In these Learning Lhabitats, each Voice discovered their power-making force in the Integral City, and how to confront the shadows that can reduce quality of life for any and all Voices. They also frequently surprised themselves in discovering the challenges facing the other Voices and the merits of having different perspectives for bringing a greater collective intelligence to the strategic Placemaking table.

In summarizing how Integral City Voices attract well-being to the City, we can say they act as gateways that enable the following outcomes.

- They attract other Voices of the city as they express both Placecaring and Placemaking qualities.
- By working together, they support the Strategic Intelligences of Inquiry and Meshworking (as discussed in *Chapter 6: Use the 12 Intelligences to Assess Business Opportunities*).
- They navigate with Integral Vision and Values the qualities of Well-being for the City.
- They evolve the collective intelligences of the Human Hive by working, playing, living together (Placecaring and Placemaking) thus acting as Gaia's Reflective Organ.

When Integral City Voices open such gateways to the city, they offer many advantages for thriving in the Human Hive. In fact, they form themselves into a community of practice that is informed by the Integral City Compass of the 12 Intelligences (as discussed in *Chapter 5: Find the 12 Intelligences in the City* and *Chapter 6: Use the 12 Intelligences to Assess Business Opportunities*). These Voices become powerful communicators and modelers of the practices and tools that guide and build the capacities of a city to work more willingly and effectively together. Working together, they create the conditions to discover that the secret to attaining superordinate goals and finding the human equivalent of 40 pounds of honey is to practice **the Master Code: To take care of yourself, so we can take care of each other, so we can take care of this Place and this Planet.** (See Chapter 3 and 4 in the Section *Embrace the Master Code*.)

REITERATION OF INQUIRY OBJECTIVES

The Inquiry Objectives of this chapter were:

1. Learn the living system source of the 4 Voices of the City.
2. Identify the 4 Voices of the City.
3. Invite the 4 Voices to meet each other.
4. Attract the 4 Voices in service to a Superordinate Goal.

5. Engage the 4 Voices for productive action and outcomes—overcoming conflict, finding new allies.
6. Recognize the distinctive qualities of each of the 4 Voices.
7. Learn how the 4 Voices work together for Placemaking (and Placecaring).

ACTION PLAN FOR PRACTITIONER, CATALYST, MESHWORKER

Review this chapter and make notes below of your impressions, insights, and questions. Locate yourself on the Integral City practice scaffolding. Notice what you have observed, thought, felt, and what you now want to do in any of the three possible practice configurations: as a Practitioner, as a Catalyst, as a Meshworker.

After you have made these notes, consider some of the Impact Questions (below). They also might help you reflect on how to generate impact through inquiry and action. Finally check out the Resources and Links suggested for this practice at the end of the chapter.

IMPACT QUESTIONS: DEEP, WIDE, CLEAR, HIGH

UL DEEP: How can I lead, initiate, or convene the 4+1 Voices of the city? What might I consider as a superordinate goal of the city? How could the superordinate goal motivate the 4 Voices to work together?

LL WIDE: How can our organization lead, initiate, or convene the 4+1 Voices of the city? What Gateway of the city does our organization serve? What might our organization consider to be a superordinate goal of the city? How could the superordinate goal motivate other stakeholders in the 4 Voices to work together?

UR CLEAR: What values-based actions in the city are important to its energy flow and well-being? How do the core values from the 4 quadrants of bio-psycho-cultural-social realities reveal themselves as behaviors practiced by the 4 Voices?

LR HIGH: Who are the organizational stakeholders who affirm, influence, and maintain city values and levels of complex development? What organization is optimally positioned and/or resourced to convene the 4 Voices so they can meet, learn about, and develop conditions to work together? What city systems strengthen individual and all Gateways of the city? How can we work together to keep Gateways open and overcome or prevent Gateways that are arrested or closed?

CHAPTER RESOURCES AND/OR LINKS

Appendix B: Integral City Maps (1–5): 1, 2, 3, 4, 5

Appendix C1: Definitions of 12 Intelligences: Integral, Inner, Outer, Cultural, Structural

Appendix C3: Integral City GPS Locator: Smart, Resilient, Integral

Reflective Question for Whom /Where/ What I Could Use as:	Practitioner	Catalyst	Meshworker
What do I observe as I read?			
What do I think?			
What do I feel?			
What do I want to do next?			

DIALOGUE WITH THE 4 VOICES OF THE CITY

INQUIRY OBJECTIVES

The Inquiry Objectives of this chapter are:

1. Create the conditions for a series of dialogues with key city stakeholders.
2. Learn how to have a successful dialogue.
3. Understand the importance of dialogue.
4. Learn the sequence and purpose of 4 variations of dialogue with the 4 Voices.
5. Learn the structure of the dialogue of city Voices and stakeholders.
6. Outline the framework for reporting on the dialogue.
7. Learn why to communicate the outcomes of the dialogue.
8. Follow up and follow through dialogue outcomes.

INTRODUCTION TO INQUIRY, ACTION, AND IMPACT FOR DIALOGUE WITH THE 4 VOICES

The Integral City discovery processes described in earlier chapters (Intelligences, Values, attracting the 4 Voices) usually set the stage for an Integral City dialogue process. At the same time, a basic dialogue can be part of the discovery process that an Integral City Activator may use to discover the willingness and readiness for the city stakeholders to engage in a city-scale change process.

The Integral City dialogue process is a way of having many conversations on the city's future. The objective of the dialogues is to discover which stakeholders in the city have energy for change. The dialogue process creates both a container and a catalyst for that change. A safe and open forum for ongoing dialogue creates conditions to reach individuals from all sectors across the community.

DIALOGUE SEQUENCE AND PURPOSE

An Integral City dialogue process convenes the 4 Voices of the city in a series of dialogue rounds. The first **Discovery Dialogue** brings together representatives of the 4 Voices in the city as part of the discovery process that can include an assessment of the 12 Intelligences (*Chapter 5: Find the 12 Intelligences in the City*), a values assessment (*Chapter 7: Discover Integral City Values*), and/or an opportunity assessment (*Chapter 6: Use the 12 Intelligences to Assess Business Opportunities*).

After the initial Discovery Dialogue that embraces the city as a whole, the next rounds are focused on one or a combination of themes that impact the city's well-being—such as economy, environment, city systems/infrastructure, culture, community, health, and education.

Typically, a round consists of **3 dialogues** in this sequence with the following stakeholders:

1. **Thought Leaders** (about 24 people selected by invitation) representing the 4 Voices explore the themes of interest.
2. **Public** (by an open invitation to citizens in a venue that can hold 100+ people) explores similar ground and responds to the Thought Leaders dialogue.

3. **Policy Makers** (by designated roles as resource allocators in relation to the theme) receive the reports of the Thought Leaders and Public and learn what they have discovered so that Policy Makers can enable the desired changes to happen.

How to Have a Successful Dialogue

Each dialogue begins with creating a safe and respectful environment by sharing these rules of dialogue:

- Listen compassionately
- Honor and respect each person's contribution
- Speak from your own experience
- Avoid criticism and persuasion
- Be aware of how often and how long you speak
- Seek to understand and learn
- Make sure everyone has a chance to talk

The Integral City dialogue facilitator speaks to the importance of each ground rule and includes the rules on a hard copy agenda. Where the city has appointed a staff person for the change process, the rules can be printed on the back of their business cards (or handed out on business card-size cards). It is a generative action to make these rules widely available and encourage participants to use them in their own organizations. By this means many leaders, organizations, and communities in the city can gain from the power of mutual trust and respect that the dialogue rules create.

FRAMING INQUIRY FOR DIALOGUE WITH THE 4 VOICES: WHO, WHY1

WHO

- Initiators/Hosts, Leaders of Dialogue Team
- Lead Facilitator(s)
- 4 Voices of the City
- Harvest Scribe or Reporter
- Small Group Facilitators

- Preparation and Delivery Team: Registrar(s), Supplies Person, Room Organizer, Refreshments Host

Dialogues need to be anchored by one or more facilitators. In general, their job is to create an agenda for the dialogue, set the conditions for a safe and mutually respectful environment before, during, and after the dialogue and organize the other small group facilitators, harvest reporters, and other team members. Each of the dialogues described below use similar roles and requires similar organizing efforts.

WHY?

A dialogue is usually initiated by representatives from one or more Thought Leaders (representing one or more of the 4 Voices of the city) who want to explore possibilities for and/or commit to make a difference to changing the city's capacity to develop and evolve into a (more) prosperous future. This can be motivated by many precipitating conditions such as: sustainability (economic shifts, environmental threats), culture (worldview and racial conflicts), or resilience (energy or water resource vulnerabilities).

It is not unusual that a particular event triggers this inquiry. The event may be negative—like a natural disaster, a lost industry, or a terrorist act. But it could also be positive—like a new industry, a new discovery, or a change of city demographics.

In fact, we could even go so far as to say, if a city is stable and most things are working well, city stakeholders are less likely to initiate an inquiry about change and are more likely to maintain the status quo.

INQUIRY PRACTICE FOR DIALOGUE WITH THE 4 VOICES: WHAT / HOW

WHAT

A key inquiry question must be developed for each dialogue as an invitation to attract stakeholders and as an anchor for the conversation. The structure of the question is typically like this: **How can the 4 Voices of the city work together to create the conditions to improve the well-being of the city? We invite you to dialogue on the theme of (x) in exploring this question.**

HOW

This section describes a basic format for the **Discovery Dialogue** followed by a basic format for a **round of 3 dialogues**. Each of the 4 formats is described below.

Discovery Dialogue Format

The initial Discovery dialogue can be located in a public space, like the local library. The initiator(s) selects and invites 16 to 24 city Voices to gather for a Dialogue. The psycho-graphic of the invitees should be multi-generational, balanced across gender, and representing a balance of the 4 Voices of the city—Citizens, Civic Managers, Civil Society, and Business. The purpose of the Dialogue is described in their letter of invitation and participants are asked to think about how to respond to four question sets:

1. What story can you share about a time when you felt a positive connection to the city? How did that influence your relationship to the city?

2. What is unique to your city? What makes it special in terms of economic, environmental, cultural, and social systems?

3. What future do you imagine for the city? What are your biggest concerns, hopes, and dreams?

4. What are the burning questions you have about a prosperous future for your city?

When the participants arrive at the dialogue location, the initiator, facilitator, and team greet them, offer light refreshments,[37] and ask them to find a seat in a circle of chairs.

The facilitator starts the dialogue by reviewing the agenda (based on the 4 questions above); introducing the role of the harvest scribe (to record the key points of the conversation); and explaining the report that will be

---

37   Note that providing refreshments at the dialogues is not optional. Breaking bread or enjoying a drink releases the bonding hormone oxytocin, which increases trust and a sense of belonging.

produced from the dialogue. The facilitator responds to any questions and then guides the conversation through the four questions.

The responses to **Question 1 (Story) tend to reveal much about Personal Values that underpin the Quality of Life (QOL) in the City.** (These relate to Map 1, *Appendix* B). When the number of stories for each of the 4 QOL quadrants are almost equal, it may indicate a healthy balance of Quality of Life dimensions in the city. When the stories are weighted in fewer quadrants, it may indicate an imbalance or strong polarities at play in the city.

A post-dialogue analysis will identify recurring themes in the stories such as: **Pride, Family, Church, Stability, Hard Work, and the Importance of college education to the community.**

Examples of Typical Stories

> - Our city is like a "positive black hole" that we call "home" – so many good things are here.
> - When I moved to the city I was "received here" by business, church and clan.
> - I was embraced by community in a way that I could expand myself and the next generation.

The responses to **Question 2 (Uniqueness) may reveal unique aspects that create the life conditions for the interconnection of people at different scales in the city**: individuals, family, business, and community (these relate to *Map 2, Appendix* B).

A post-dialogue analysis will identify important themes such as: **Unique Geographic Location; Family, Pride; Character and Religious Opportunity; Leadership; Culture of Caring; Quality of Life.**

Examples of What Is Unique to This City?

> - Citizens step up to the plate.
> - We have a culture of caring.
> - We have access to capital and financial support.

The responses to **Questions 3 (Hopes, Dreams and Concerns) and 4 (Burning Questions) often reveal much about the perceptions of how to interconnect people scales in the city for the future:** individuals, family, business, and community within the city (See Maps 2 and 4 in *Appendix* B).

Recurring themes may include: **Desire for Healthy Behaviors; Maintaining Value of Character; Planning for Careers, Housing, and Infrastructure; Controlling Sustainable Growth of City; Designing Recreational Facilities for Multiple Generations (Youth, Seniors); Stewardship of Natural Resources; Beautifying the City.**

Examples of What Are Your Hopes, Dreams, Concerns?

- The city needs to become a container where we can control growth.
- I want it to be safe to run – every morning I take my life in my hands running on the road – even at 5 a.m.
- We need a regional approach to water – especially related to nearby lake.

Examples of What Are Your Burning Questions?

- Would we consider a 1 cent wellness tax?
- I wonder why we don't merge with an adjoining city?
- What will be our population in 2050?

Format for 3-Round Dialogue Process

The 3-Round Dialogue Process starts with the initiators (and their local advisory board or team) selecting two themes as a focus for dialogue exchange (e.g., the economy and community). As described above, the design and delivery team then organizes the process for three dialogues (spaced about 2 months apart): with Thought Leaders, then with the Public, followed by a Policy Makers dialogue. Integral City experience shows that the complexity and demands of these are best managed by a minimum of two facilitators for each dialogue (and may have as many as four co-facilitators). Outlines for the basic formats follow.

Thought Leader Dialogue Format

Similar to the Discovery Dialogue, the facilitators review the agenda, explain the importance of dialogue, and create the conditions for safety and mutual trust and respect.

On Day 1 (evening): The dialogue begins with reflections among participants over an **evening meal where they each share stories** of their personal connection with the community. The meal is important, because it creates natural conditions for traditional sharing (breaking of bread) in a relaxing atmosphere. The stories are equally critical because they open both the storytellers and the listeners to learning about the invisible energies and cultures that coexist in the city. It is not unusual that people who have known each other for decades learn intimate details that they had never realized impacted the storytellers in the circle. The shared experience builds a natural field of mutual trust and respect—not the least because typical stories are often poignant, insightful, humorous, and even surprising. By planning to have the meal and storytelling on the opening evening, the energy of the people and the stories create a field of attraction that inevitably expands overnight and builds anticipation and curiosity for the agenda of the next day.

On Day 2: On the following morning, **a panel** of four or five participants offers an overview of key issues related to the selected themes that impact city growth and prosperity. Examples could be: impact of rapid development on city water infrastructure; the impact of recent immigrants on local job market; or the lack of facilities for senior recreation.

This kind of expert information is intended to energize participants, and also solidify the need for visioning and planning as the city faces challenges to its growth and development.

After the expert panel, **small groups** are created by the facilitators who organize participants into conversation circles (using a modified World Café process), where they engage a series of questions and also rotate among the groups to cross-pollinate their explorations. The small-group facilitators keep the conversations focused, encourage participants to draw, doodle, and illustrate their conversations on the paper tablecloths (and record key points on flip charts).

The following questions guide the conversations:

- What do we imagine for the city's future?
- What are your biggest hopes and concerns for the future of the city?
- How are we preparing the city for resilience?
- What examples in the city can you identify as signs of progress?

After this exploration, **participant groups summarize their discussions with a creative report and reconvene in plenary** to share their insights about the key themes (e.g., a healthy economy and community) as they will impact the city 50 years from now. They then consider what actions must take place in the present day in order for an imagined future to be achieved. (This is a form of back casting.)

Typically, an imagined future for the city is broken into overlapping but unified ideas such as:

- A healthy environment
- A diverse, thriving economy
- A community built around people

Facilitators also address participants' fears about the city's future. A post-dialogue analysis may identify fears categorized as follows:

- Strategic Planning Concerns
- Economic Concerns
- Social Concerns

Facilitators also **tap into the experience and expertise of the participants, asking them to identify other communities** that could serve as models of success during the planning phases of developing a city strategy in subsequent phases.

Signs of progress can act as strong counter-perspectives to fears that can block hope and freeze generative action. So, facilitators encourage participants to identify aspects of well-being already evident in the city that indicate existing signs of progress. This inquiry often identifies how living, learning, working, and relating as a community contributes to a sense of wholeness and belonging.

This line of exploration then opens the discussion into: **How are we creating our future today?**

After lunch, on the second day, facilitators guide participants to form **three mixed groups (of the 4 Voices)** to discuss several possible realities for the city: the darkest possible scenario, the status quo, and the ideal future. Each group prepares a creative presentation. (We have tapped into the fun of creating: Blog posts; Tweets; Hashtag for city2050: playlists; and guided tours).

The final stages of dialogue identify signs of hope and progress already visible throughout the city. (A post-dialogue analysis can categorize these indicators of signs of progress into categories relating to the 4 quadrants of the Quality of Life: personal intentions, personal behaviors, cultural/social experience, and economic/systemic structures).

In the final hours of the afternoon (or on the morning of Day 3), facilitators guide participants to consider: **What are the next steps to take together?**

This exploration is frequently inspiring because it reveals to participants that they are not in it by themselves but they have a whole community who are interested in changes for the better.

Finally, facilitators guide the dialogue to a close by asking everyone to **reflect on burning questions, offers, commitments, thoughts, and insights discovered throughout the process.**

Frequently, a number of participants gain optimism for the visioning process that this dialogue has started and are refueled to tackle the challenges identified.

Participants often agree that in order to move forward, **additional partners must be identified**. These partners may include business, organizational, and public policy partners as well as citizenry. These insights create the conditions for the next two dialogues in this round—with the Public and then, the Policy Makers.

The visioning process can ignite sparks of motivation within participants. As the dialogue concludes, facilitators invite them to **champion the cause and volunteer their time and resources in taking the first step towards an imagined future.**

The intention of **educating key partners and citizens about the vision for the future city** is necessary to move forward—which invites the need to **develop a communication strategy**. As outcomes of these aspirations, it is not unusual for participants to volunteer time, treasure, and talent for the development of logos, t-shirts, publicity events, websites, and QR codes.

Another critical outcome is to find a project that can act as an **"early win"** for committing to the visioning process and the strategic planning that will follow it. Early wins will be unique to each city but they might include plans for a trans-city walking trail; designing an art walk; convening a workshop on citizen engagement; or planning a community information website.

Following the dialogue, facilitators, initiators, and the harvest scribe will organize the production and publication of the Harvest Report. This is released on the project website. Inviting the contribution of a local community newspaper to publish the report and deliver in hard copy to all households (as well as on their news website) creates a powerful feedback loop into the community that attracts the energy for the next dialogues in this round (and future rounds on different themes).

Public Dialogue Format

The format for the Public Dialogue is condensed to a half-day session. It is usually offered on a Saturday morning at a location that is accessible by public transit for the convenience of as many people as possible.

Advertising, invitations, and promotions are released by all media possible, through students in the public school system and usually include the involvement and/or endorsement of the Thought Leaders from the previous dialogue. Key Thought Leaders are also invited to bring forward their expertise and share the experience and value of the dialogue process with the Public.

The Public Dialogue Agenda provides a basic framework for an open dialogue that guides discussion, enables differences to be expressed, connects to the Thought Leaders' Harvest Report (often given as a handout), and pays forward conclusions to the third dialogue with the Policy Makers.

The basic agenda is set out as follows.

Public Dialogue Basic Agenda & Questions
Initiators/Hosts Explain the Intention of the Day:

1. Meet people you don't know; circle up with new acquaintances; make new friends.

2. Create interpersonal connections across the diversities of the city: age, gender, students, workers, employers, ethnicity, race.

3. Create connections between people's perspectives of the economy and community.[38]

4. Discover common ground to build on and respect differences that make a difference.

5. Imagine how in 30 years we can improve the quality of the city's community and economy in a way that neither set of improvements is at the expense of the other.

Please turn off cell phones unless you are an emergency response person.

Facilitators Guide the Discussion:

Welcome, Introductions, and Why are we here?

What is the city's current and future situation (select related to themes)?

- Economy?
- Infrastructure?
- Community Vibrancy?
- Diversity?

Thought Leaders Share 3 Scenarios

- Dark Days Ahead
- Status Quo
- Our City Leading the Way

---

38 Or other theme sets such as Education & Culture or Health & Environment.

What is dialogue?
Small Group Dialogues
- Confirm or Choose Small Group Facilitator
- Choose Recorder for Q2, Q3
- Q4 Post-Its & Pen
- Q1, Q2, Q3, Q4—See Below

Fishbowl
Rearrange room into fishbowl
(concentric circles with 6–8 chairs in the middle)

Fishbowl Q5, 6, 7

Wrap: Checkout, Commitments, Offers, Discoveries, Next Steps

Questions Used by Facilitators for Small Groups and Fishbowl
These are the guiding questions for the small group discussions and Plenary Fishbowl.

Public Dialogue Small Group Questions:
1. Tell us a story about a time when you had an emotional connection with the city. How has that or does that influence your relationship to the community?
2. What level of growth do you think is sustainable for the city in the next 30 years?
3. How will balancing the economy and the community matter to the city's children or grandchildren?
4. What are the burning questions (for this group) about the city's future economy and community? (write on large post-its or cards)

Public Dialogue Plenary Fishbowl Questions:
5. Imagine yourself 30 years from now, talking to the next generation—what will you tell them about how you approached these burning questions?

6. What would you tell policy makers we should do now?

7. In the next month, what is one step you will take to move from contemplation to action regarding these questions?

Policy Maker Format

The format for the Policy Dialogue is condensed to a half-day session. It is usually offered on a Friday morning because many policy makers may be working outside the city at county, state/provincial, or federal locations, and Fridays are typically the day that they will return to their home city.

Policy Makers are identified by their influence on the theme being explored and their capacity to make decisions about it. They are often thought of as belonging to the voice of Civic Managers, but these days Policy Makers can as often come from Civil Society and Business as well. A letter of invitation is sent well ahead of time, so that Policy Makers can get the Dialogue on their agenda. The letter is typically followed up by a phone call to confirm attendance.

The Policy Maker Dialogue Agenda provides a basic framework for an open dialogue that guides discussion and offers a non-adversarial environment for exploration. This is often a very different environment than what Policy Makers typically experience in the adversarial-by-design governance structures where they work on a daily basis. The Policy Maker dialogue logically connects to the predecessor Thought Leaders' and Public Harvest Reports (often distributed to them with their invitation as an Executive Summary) and brings forward the key questions for Policy Makers that have emerged from those dialogues.

The basic agenda is set out as follows.

Policy Makers Dialogue
Basic Agenda & Questions

Initiators Welcome

- Policy Makers, Introductions, GM and GB, Facilitators/Scribe—framing & housekeeping.

Facilitator(s) Opens the Circle

- Introduces all Participants and Organizations.
- Reviews Dialogue Ground Rules & Process.
- Explains difference between Dialogue and Debate with key points.
- Facilitator compares Dialogue to Debate.

Dialogue	Debate
Work toward common understanding	Two sides oppose to prove the other wrong
Listen to understand	Listen for flaws
Reveal assumptions for re-evaluation	Defend assumptions as truth
Open minded – suspend judgment	Hold tight to certainties
Demonstrate concern for others even when holding different perspectives	More important to hold position than respect feelings or perspectives

- Summarizes the main points of the Executive Summary from Thought Leaders and Public.

Facilitator(s) Guides Conversation with These Questions

- "What do you notice about [2 themes like the Economy & Community] through the eyes of the Thought Leaders and the Public (in the reports and people in room)?" Opportunity for individual reflection and reaction to these points.
- "From where you sit, what will make a difference to the Economy & Community in the city in the future?" Opportunity for individual and collective reflection.
- "What is the key theme you heard today? How can Economy & Community interests in the city best communicate with you and/or support you to support a vision for the city's best future?"

Facilitator(s) Closes Circle and Seeks Insights

- Check out reactions to the work done today. Consider the implications of our discoveries. Consider our next steps, and note opportunities for alliances and further discussion.
- Thanks and wrap-up.

Harvest Reports

One of the precepts of Integral City is that "if you want to improve the health of a system, connect it to more of itself."[39]

Each of the four types of dialogue described above sets out to connect the participants (and thus parts of the city) to others. As a result, each dialogue deserves to be harvested for its fruit, the new connections that arose, and to transform the intangibility of the conversations into a tangible record or artefact. Each dialogue participant, in fact, deserves to be recognized for their contribution to this harvest in a report.

For each dialogue, a local scribe (who can listen attentively, take notes, assemble all the raw data from flipcharts and reports, analyze themes, and synergize a summary report) offers an inestimable service by effectively amplifying the impact and outcomes of the dialogues through creating a report. Producing a harvest report is no small accomplishment; it creates one of the first tangible outcomes of the dialogues and the report becomes an object or artefact to which people can point to remind them of their contribution, questions and collaboration. Moreover, the sequence of the harvest reports becomes a track record of what the city's "well-being team" is accomplishing.

Each report will have some unique qualities to it because of the culture of the participants. A general framework for the final documents will reflect the originating agendas and generally embraces the following sections.

- Participant Names and Organizations
- Introduction to Dialogue
- Participant Stories
- Exploring present conditions
- Expressing hopes for future
- Acknowledging fears, concerns, threats
- Identifying Signs of Progress
- Visioning Future Possibilities
- Identifying Early Wins as Pilot Projects to Show Success
- Suggesting Next Steps

---

39   I ascribe this precept of Margaret Wheatley from whom I learned it in the 1990s.

- Committing to Personal Responsibility and Action
- Appendices with 4 Quadrant Analyses

Communicating and Sharing the Harvest

The effort of convening the dialogue(s) and publishing a report (series) should also be amplified by sharing the experience as widely as possible. The reports should, if possible, be published and distributed through community newspapers because they are then delivered to every household. The first time this occurs they may be ignored—but the second, third, or seventh time this occurs, people will start to notice, anticipate the next one, and be prompted to step forward and become involved.

A multiplicity of media to publish the report or story, can also be brought into the communications strategy including a city or community website, Facebook, Twitter, podcasts, radio, TV, etc. Most Civil Society organizations will welcome presentations and talks from facilitators, team organizers, and other participants to the process. With a variety of people available, it is advisable and helpful for the Dialogue Team Leaders to create speaking notes (and PowerPoint presentations) that everyone can use.

The bottom line for multiplying the harvest is to keep the story alive and circulating and acting as a natural attractor to the evolution of the next step—moving from dialogue and inquiry to action.

CONCLUSION: WHY2

The dialogue process is a powerful way of thinking together as a community and a city. Dialogue ignites a flame within participants. As dialogue sessions conclude, participants typically offer to champion the cause and volunteer their time and resources in taking the next steps towards an imagined future for the city. However, as they have connected with others, they realize they cannot do it alone. But now they see they can work together to identify what they need to start working on now, in order to reach a long-term goal.

The dialogue discovery and visioning processes are all conversations about the city's future with the 4 Voices who can make it happen. The objective of the dialogues is to create a container and a catalyst for the realization of a future vision. The safe and open forum provided by dialogue allows individuals from all sectors across the community to interconnect. It is an action research type of process that changes the participants just because they have participated and through the new connections naturally improves the health of the community and city.

The basis of dialogue's powerful effect on people is the very stories they tell. As one of our facilitators, Beth Sanders, captures in a poem harvested from a Thought Leader's dialogue in Durant, Oklahoma: Story is sacred food!

SACRED FOOD
Harvested by Beth Sanders

Story is
sacred food
a sacred pride
in community
in personal generosity
I'm a live one
serving, giving
the spirit of home
in my heart
to the promise of Durant
to the promise of being here
where I choose to be
to grow
with our family of well-being
standing out
(out of our own way)
we are live ones
embracing the village story
on our shoulders
our sacred food

REITERATION OF INQUIRY OBJECTIVES

The Inquiry Objectives of this chapter are:

1. Create the conditions for a series of dialogues with key city stakeholders.
2. Learn how to have a successful dialogue.
3. Understand the importance of dialogue.
4. Learn the sequence and purpose of 4 variations of dialogue with the 4 Voices.
5. Learn the structure of the dialogue of city Voices and stakeholders.
6. Outline the framework for reporting on the dialogue.
7. Learn why to communicate the outcomes of the dialogue.
8. Follow-up and follow-through dialogue outcomes.

ACTION PLAN FOR PRACTITIONER, CATALYST, MESHWORKER

Review this chapter and make notes below of your impressions, insights, and questions. Locate yourself on the Integral City practice scaffolding. Notice what you have observed, thought, felt, and what you now want to do in any of the three possible practice configurations: as a Practitioner, as a Catalyst, as a Meshworker.

After you have made these notes, consider some of the Impact Questions (below). They also might help you reflect on how to generate impact through inquiry and action. Finally check out the Resources and Links suggested for this practice at the end of the chapter.

IMPACT QUESTIONS: DEEP, WIDE, CLEAR, HIGH

UL DEEP: How can I lead, initiate, or convene a Discovery Dialogue or a Dialogue Series for the City? What might I consider as a triggering event for such a dialogue? How could the dialogue introduce me to other perspectives?

LL WIDE: How can our organization lead, initiate, or convene a Discovery Dialogue or a Dialogue Series for the city? What strengths, opportunities, assets, or resources do we see emerging in the city that call us to take a wider view of the city's future possibilities? How might our organization catalyze a conversation for change? How could we attract other organizations to join us in the conversation?

UR CLEAR: What supply-chain issues and impacts in or around the city are important to its energy flow and well-being? How do the threats and fears that threaten the work force require a conversation that can support positive change?

LR HIGH: Who are the organizational stakeholders who act as primary communicators to other organizations in our city economic ecology? What organization has influence and recognition to invite others to the table so policy makers will listen? What city systems need to be connected to improve the health of the whole system?

CHAPTER RESOURCES AND/OR LINKS

Appendix B: Integral City Maps (1–5): 1, 2, 3, 4, 5

Appendix C1: Definitions of 12 Intelligences: Integral, Inner, Outer, Cultural, Structural, Inquiry, Evolutionary

Appendix C3: Integral City GPS Locator: Integral

Reflective Question for Whom /Where/ What I Could Use as:	Practitioner	Catalyst	Meshworker
What do I observe as I read?			
What do I think?			
What do I feel?			
What do I want to do next?			

SECTION VI — *Prototype Design for Learning Lhabitats, Pop-ups, and Sustainable Community Development*

These two chapters build strongly on all the foregoing chapters in the book. They are advanced applications of working with multiple stakeholders (4+1 Voices of the city) to prototype possible solutions without having to commit huge investments.

Chapter 11 describes two ways to engage the 4 Voices to learn together in Learning Lhabitats and Pop-Ups.

Chapter 12 describes how to prototype Sustainable Community Development through a longer-term (6 month) course—where a cohort of students can work with a real community to bring collective wisdom to a real issue.

EMPOWER PEOPLE WITH LEARNING LHABITATS AND POP-UPS

This chapter is based on the articles describing the harvesting process designed by Integral City for Integral Theory Conference 2013 (Hamilton & Sanders, 2013) and Integral Theory Conference 2015 (Hamilton et al., 2015). Contributors to the conferences and these processes included: Marilyn Hamilton, Alia Aurami, Diana Claire Douglas, Alicia Stammer, Anne-Marie Voorhoeve, Joan Arnott, Cherie Beck, Beth Sanders, Linda Shore, Ellen van Dongen, Mathias Weitbrecht, Nick Hunley-Moore.

INQUIRY OBJECTIVES

The objectives of this chapter are to:

1. Learn the history and value of prototyping.
2. Understand the role of design and deep design in prototyping.
3. Differentiate between the prototyping purposes and processes of Learning Lhabitats and Pop-Ups.
4. Describe the purpose and role of a Learning Lhabitat.
5. Develop a Learning Lhabitat for Practitioners to influence Citizen Voice.

6. Design a Learning Lhabitat for the Citizen Voice of the city.

7. Learn the role of Pop-Ups as a mode of prototyping.

8. Describe the Pop-Up preparation and delivery process.

9. Synthesize the lessons from Learning Lhabitats and Pop-Ups for action through Memory, Meaning, and Momentum.

INTRODUCTION TO INQUIRY, ACTION, AND IMPACT WITH LHABITATS AND POP-UPS

Design Principles

This is the first chapter that explores the phenomenon of prototyping as a vital aspect of Integral City design.

Designing on, with, and as the Integral City derives from our understanding of the developmental capacities that evolve in the people who act as designers. In the Smart City[40] those designers are typically technically trained professionals and experts like architects, engineers, city planners, and information technology (IT) experts. Their designs are focused *on* the city as an external object or artefact over which they have expert control. In the Resilient City[41] their designers embrace stakeholder input so they design *with* a design team lead by a Chief Resilience Officer (CRO) who seeks input from a broader group of contributors. In the Integral City those professionals and stakeholders transform themselves into designers who can experience, act, relate, and co-create *as* the living system that is the city itself.

In order to make this transition through the essential purposes and outcomes of design, the designers redesign themselves to enable the emergence of ever-increasing design capacities. Architect and Professor, Mark DeKay, captures the qualities and stages of the designer's journey in his book, *Integral Sustainable Design* (DeKay, 2011). He describes key aspects of the Integral Designer in *Appendix H: Qualities of an Integral Designer.*

---

40   Smart City is a term popularized by IBM and other large Information Technology (IT) firms for framing their IT solutions for cities.

41   Resilient City is a term popularized by the Rockefeller Foundation as they identified 100 cities where they supported resilience through funding a Chief Resilience Officer for selected cities.

Role of Prototyping

Ironically, one of the earliest models of integrated leadership development arose from the field and study of architecture through the work of Chris Argyris and Donald Schön (Argyris & Schön, 1974). Desiring to create the conditions where their design students could demonstrate their ideas in practical and realistic prototypes, they developed the concept of a *charrette*. Borrowing from the French "cart" that delivers pastry and produce to customers, they asked their students to produce working models of designs (displayed as a charrette model on the cart) produced by design teams, who competed with one another for qualities, outcomes, and aesthetics. The success of this early practice of prototyping in the classroom transferred not only to a design process that has become widespread today—but also to the leadership literature, and schools of leadership, because the impact that the prototyping had on the designer's own capacities was enormous; that is, their individual and collective leadership development was accelerated because of the prototyping charrette experience that combined individual contribution with collective learning (and intelligence).

In the prototyping phase of Inquiry and Action, Integral City builds on the previous definintions of Placecaring and Placemaking by recognizing the inevitable need for alignment of the designer, the design, the stakeholders, and the city systems (see *Introduction*). The natural co-arising of these elements translates into the very fabric of the city itself and therefore demands a method with enough flexibility to experiment with options; enough rigor to utilize an appropriate selection of materials, methods, and standards; and enough competition within the system to discover the greatest sustainability, resilience, economy, efficiency, and effectiveness. The method that seems best able to meet these requirements is prototyping.

Prototyping is the act of designing and building an early working model of the intended design. It provides a proving ground for the designer, design, production team, and contexting systems in which the design must exist. Prototyping allows not only for early wins, but also for "fast failures." The latter are as important as the former, because they can save enormous investments in time, effort, and resources and accelerate the learning of possibilities by showing designers what won't work. (Inventors like Edison, Bell, and Musk have histories of multiple failures that showed them hundreds of ways *not* to accomplish their intended outcomes.)

Prototyping, Deep Design, and Triple Loop Learning

Deep Design lies at the heart of how Integral City practices prototyping. Ken Wilber (Wilber, 2006, p. 33) says Integral Methodological Pluralism (IMP) involves:

... at least 8 fundamental and apparently irreducible methodologies, injunctions, or paradigms for gaining reproducible knowledge (or verifiably repeatable experiences).... the quadrants [with their inside and outside, and individual and collective dimensions]... are often represented as I, you/we, it and its... [as well as] the Good, the True, the Beautiful; or art, morals and science... . (p. 33).

Inspired by IMP, it appears that each quadrant's methodologies call forth different epistemologies that Integral City has learned to apply in a process of Deep Design. "Deep Design" is a term coined by Hamilton and Aurami to describe the methodology for integrating design with delivery so that inquiry, action, and impact emerge (as used by the Integral City team for the Integral Theory Conference 2015, (Hamilton et al., 2015)).

This methodology relies on how we interpret Integral Epistemological Pluralism, which we defined for our purposes as:

Integral Epistemological Pluralism, is the concurrent employment and availability, for the purpose at hand, of all faculties and capacities of consciousness (especially those related to "knowing") available to a given individual or group at a given time, employed in priorities optimal to accomplishment of the purpose.

Deep Design is made possible when an individual or group has access to the consciousness-capacities of intuition and inspiration, and to the consciousness-capacities of the conscious uploading and downloading of design information (both plans and principles of design) to and from, a particular morphic field which receives, integrates, evolves, and then in-forms/in-spires the deliverers in the moments they are delivering, as they have the capacity to *be* in-formed/in-spired by all that was held in or evolved within, that field. This is related to but perhaps another level beyond Third Order Learning or Torbert's Third Level of Feedback (William R. Torbert, 2015).

Deep Design enables the shaping of the delivery in an emergent way, both from within the deliverers but also those who might be at a distance and also in relationship to that morphic field. As it unfolds naturally, Deep Design frees deliverers from having to work from notes or to memorize aspects of the delivery and may reveal unanticipated surprises in the process.

Deep Design is an all-quadrant (AQAL) process: Deep Design includes (a) research of the past geological and social history and current conditions/situations/circumstances of the land on which delivery takes place; then (b) sensing into that history and the current subtle energetics of the land; and then (c) allowing that to both explicitly cognitively and subtle-energetically inform the design and delivery of the workshop or presentation. In particular, the current situation of the land (Mother Earth) is brought into the momentary decisions during delivery.

In many ways, this aspect of Deep Design is a process that unpacks the **Master Code** of caring for self, others, and place/ planet (including through 4 levels of evolution—ego, ethno, world, kosmic) through the lenses and expansion of AQAL, by including the land and people as context for both design and delivery. We use both dynamic steering (B. Robertson, 2016) and Orders of Love (Douglas & Hamilton, 2013a; Hamilton et al., 2015; Hamilton et al., 2016) to guide the way. The Integral City team uses this Deep Design implicitly and explicitly at all points in the design and delivery of the Learning Lhabitats and Pop-Ups.

In a fractal way, the same can be true for the larger context of whatever organizations/factions/groups are active in the conference and/or city context. We work with those, starting well ahead of delivery time, in our Deep Design process, and that continues throughout the delivery and debrief time.

One way to grasp Deep Design is to consider the metaphor that Deep Design is like making coffee. The designed plan and design principles are like the coffee machine, the grounds, the water, the electricity, the filter. The field is like the percolating; it changes what went in. The delivery is like pouring out and drinking the coffee, and is customized at that point or evolved even further, by creamer, sugar, whatever!!!

As a result, what is delivered is a changed version of what was designed—changed both during the percolating *and* during the delivery time itself, as adapted to the situation during delivery. Deep Design enables delivery to be done with more influence by the factors of the moment. Deep Design is emergent in delivery, and thus more flowing than in ordinary design. What is said and done during delivery is informed by all that went before in the design process.

Deep Design involves the deliverer *embodying* the design, rather than executing or carrying it out. This seems to be a subconscious process, guided by inspiration and intuition. (This is how we design *as* the city.)

From the beginning of our designing process, We-agreements have formed part of our Deep Design, because they create energetic fields/grooves/information that inform the field in which the design is delivered, to the extent the deliverers "listen." (Essentially our Integral City team meetings involve everyone at some point during the design phase, so we all contribute to the design.) As a team hosting the Spirit of a Planet of Cities, we hold the following agreements in working together:

1. When we meet, we first discern the purpose of the meeting, the outcomes, and impacts we seek from meeting.
2. Designers might or might not become deliverers, but deliverers are designers.
3. The deliverers explicitly hold the learning that is taking place (the designers do so implicitly).
4. We hold the Learning Lhabitat and Pop-Up, and Master Code in the Knowing Field as metaphors for our design guides.
5. We activate the Master Code as we work together.

As we describe below, we also embrace the complexities of designing for impact that include:

1. **Graduated or differing Levels and Fractals of Impact**; for example, traditional, modern, post-modern, integral impacts at the scales of individual, group, organization, conference, culture(s).
2. **Quadrants and stages of Impact**; for example, AQAL impacts at ego/ethno/world/Kosmic stages of maturity.

3. **How to measure impact**; for example, gross, subtle, causal outcomes in the 4 quadrants.

With this understanding of the role of Deep Design, it is time to explore our two prototyping processes: Learning Lhabitats and Pop-Ups.

ROLE OF LEARNING IN LHABITATS AND POP-UPS

The Integral City Core Team has discovered two models for prototyping that empower people in the process. We call them Learning Lhabitats and Pop-Ups. These two models have given us the keys to empowering the 4 Voices of the city regardless of who turns up in the room. The Learning Lhabitat draws on our appreciation of dialogue and the structure of the 4 Voices to design *with* "the whole city system in the room." The Pop-Up draws on the improvisational rehearsal space of systemic constellation work (SCW) to reach deep into the invisible field of energies that influence outcomes and designs *as* the city. (SCW was explored in *Chapter 1: Activate Inquiry for Knowing Cities* and *Chapter 2: Cultivate We-Space Inquiry for Human Hive Mind.*)

The rest of this chapter unpacks the models of the Learning Lhabitat and Pop-Up, framing, describing, and summarizing the conclusions of the inquiries, that each prototyping method enables.

FRAMING INQUIRY FOR LEARNING LHABITAT: WHO, WHY1

WHO

- Host
- Integral City Facilitator(s) Learning Guide
- Break Out Group Facilitators
- Meeting Maestro Coordinator
- Integral City Practitioners, Catalysts, Meshworkers
- 4 Voices
- Scribe/Reporter

Learning Lhabitats are designed for people who describe themselves in any (or many) of these ways:

1. Represent one or more of the 4 Voices in a specific city

2. Able to differentiate, integrate; differentiate, integrate ... (recognizing the iterative process of human development)

3. Care about their work, relationships and the city they live in—maybe even have a spiritual calling for doing good in the city

4. Are the 5% who want to make a "damn difference" in their city

5. Already value collaboration on a variety of scales

6. Love life (wide area of concern)

7. Already value wisdom and not just knowledge

8. Have the capacity to appreciate that efficiency can be gained by zooming out, in addition to zooming in

9. Have the capacity to appreciate the value of intelligence, wider perspectives, systemic views

10. Already value ongoing learning

11. Have participated in Integral City 2.0 Online Conference or other Integral City learning activities

12. Have an interest in responding to city-based issues, including but not limited to the 6 big challenges that face all cities: culture, climate, water, energy, food, finance

13. Want to work at the scale of the city:

    a. to improve Quality of Life for more than one kind of stakeholder

    b. to create an Integrator Organization that strengthens the voice of the Citizen

    c. to use existing skills/experience gained from Civil Society, Civic Management, or Business

14. Serving dynamic and/or public city celebrations such as:

    a. Olympics

    b. Sporting Events (e.g., National, Regional, International Events)

    c. Festivals, Conferences, etc.

15. Have a desire and/or a mechanism for ongoing learning *as a* group, such as:

- Integral City 2.0 Online Conference
- Art of Hosting
- Hellinger Systemic Constellations
- Huebl Practice Groups
- Vistar/Conscious Evolution
- Houston Social Artistry
- Centers for Human Emergence

WHY1

Learning Lhabitats help people learn how to mitigate, adapt, or resolve any challenge in the city (e.g., the 6 Big Threats challenging cities related to culture, climate, energy, water, food, and finance) through:

- Applying the principles of living systems
- Developing the special intelligence which hastens evolution
- Applying the 4 Voices of the City: citizens, civil society organizations, civic government/institutions and business
- Using theMaster Code of increasing cares (self, others, place, planet)
- Applying the 12 Intelligences of an Integral City

Learning Lhabitats not only serve the 4 Voices of the city, but their participatory action research design develops the skills of people who choose to become Integral City Activators—Practitioners, Catalysts, and Meshworkers (see *Introduction*).

The following example of a Learning Lhabitat process demonstrates how activators can attract, strengthen, and engage the Citizen Voice in the city and teach them how to strengthen the Citizen Voice and engage with the 3 other Voices operating to influence and create cities.

INQUIRY PRACTICE FOR LEARNING LHABITAT: WHAT/HOW

WHAT

The key inquiry question for this Learning Lhabitat is: **How do Practitioners attract, strengthen, & engage the Citizen Voice?**

HOW

We use a design and practice methodology based in whole living systems that is built on the Master Code for the Human Hive, a code which acts as the DNA of transformation (discussed in more detail in *Chapter 3: Amplify Caring Capacity with Master Code*):

- Take Care of Yourself
- Take Care of Each Other
- Take Care of This Place/Planet

In this Learning Lhabitat, Practitioners learn how to attract, strengthen, and engage the Voice of the Citizen to be a key player in the quartet of City Voices:

1. Citizens
2. Civil Society (including Not-for-Profits, NGOs, CSRs)
3. City Government/Institutions
4. Business/Organizations

Learning Lhabitat Objectives:

The objectives of this Learning Lhabitat are to create a learning system to:

1. Prepare Practitioners for Integrator jobs in their city, jobs which don't yet exist.

2. Create a new civil society Integrator Organizationthat works to support Citizen Engagement.

3. Empower Citizens for Citizen Engagementas a great need of their city (and all cities in the world).

4. Create a regular forum to bring together the 4 Voices of their Local City.

5. Support, develop, and deliver on a regular/iterative basis, the Voice of Citizens to express what they want (so their voice(s) is/are as strong as the other 3 City voices), at the same time that others can get what they want.

6. Create capacities for Commoning[42] so that as Citizens we can become awake, become conscious to engage and interact with the other 3 Voices.

7. Create the laboratory and habitat (Lhabitat) where all Voices discover their (superordinate) common goal that reveals the vision and purpose for the City.

CURRICULUM DESIGN AND OUTLINE

This Learning Lhabitat is really a series of Learning Lhabitats and has a 12-week curriculum design and outline:

These are the core elements of the curriculum:

- 12 weeks of modules, delivered every 2–3 weeks.
- The sessions are 2-hour phone calls (using a platform like Maestro Conference). Participants have specific mp3 or pdf preparation work assignments from Integral City Resources.
- Each session will have a Host, Learning Guide, Break Out Group Facilitators, and Meeting Maestro (conference call) Coordinator.
- Each session will have this general format:

Time	Leader	Activity
20 min	Host	Introductions/Report from Pre-Work Caring Commitment
20 min	Guest Guide	Guest Speaker
10 min	Maestro Coordinator	Set Up Break Out Groups
30 min	B/O Facilitators	Break Out Groups
20 min	Host & Guest Guide	Plenary Reports from Breakouts
15min	Participants	Personal Commitments to Caring
5 min	Host	Announcement & Next Session Preparation Work

42 Sharing common resources.

PRACTITIONER TRAINING: DRAFT CURRICULUM

The Draft Curriculum for 12 weeks is designed in 4 segments: The Basics, The City as Human Hive, Living the Master Code, and Core Practices for a Local Learning Lhabitat. (The content for these modules is discussed in earlier chapters of this book.) The key topics of each session are set out below.

Sessions 1–3: Integral City Learning Lhabitat: The Basics

1. What is an Integral City Learning Lhabitat?
2. What is the Integral City Master Code?
3. What are the 4 Voices of the City?

Sessions 4–6: The City as Human Hive

4. Human Hive as Biomimicry
5. 4 Roles as Innovation Generators
6. Passion, Priorities, Purpose, Prosperity, Praxis

Sessions 7–9: Practitioners Learning & Living the Master Code

7. Take Care of Yourself
8. Take Care of Others
9. Take Care of this Place/Planet

Session 10–12: Core Practices for Designing a Local Learning Lhabitat for Citizens

10. Attracting Citizens with Values & Purpose
11. Strengthening Citizens in Linking Priorities and Engaging with the 3 Other Voices
12. Engaging Citizens as the Vital Power for Prosperity in the Human Hive

CITIZEN TRAINING

Following the last session, Participants will deliver the training that they have designed for Citizens. The basic curriculum to train Citizens to strengthen and engage their voices with other city voices is formatted in 3 sessions.

Each of the 3 sessions will be delivered in 2-hour classes, in a local classroom-style Learning Lhabitat. (Much of the material for these sessions is included in the chapters on the Master Code, and Dialoguing with the 4 Voices.)

1. Take Care of Yourself: Learn Your Purpose
2. Take Care of Others: Link Priorities and Engage with the 3 Other Voices
3. Take Care of this Place/Planet: Create Prosperity Feedback Loop

Citizen Evaluation

Following the Citizen Training, Citizen Participants will be asked to evaluate the course training through these survey questions.

In taking this course, how strongly have you been rewarded in the 4 ways described below? (rate each question on a scale from 1–5 where 1 is low reward and 5 is high reward)

1. You are living at a new level of You as a caring individual.
2. You have increased your capacity to make a positive difference in the world as all of us "WE's" work together.
3. You are part of a vibrant community of mutually supportive relationships by connecting to People Who Care.
4. The Power of We operating as the Master Code in your city (caring for yourself, others, place, and planet) contributes to the well-being of all the cities on our Planet of Cities.

Practitioner Evaluation

As a final bookend to the whole Learning Lhabitat process, we recommend Integral City Practitioner/Students create an evaluation. The Integral City Practitioner Evaluation is grounded in our understanding that cities who develop their caring capacity for self, others, and place/planet, are cities who develop their carrying capacity and thus their resilience for good times and bad.

Communities and Cities Who Care have the capacity to rapidly respondand evolve into new ways of being and becoming together.

The natural power of the Master Code enables daily life and local and global well-being to:

- Care for yourself
- Care for each other
- Care for this place (on all scales up to the planetary level)

Evaluation Designed at the Beginning, Revisited at the End

At the beginning of Practitioner Training, Practitioners will be invited to co-create (with course leaders) the evaluation system for their successful completion of Practitioner Training. Here are three questions for Practitioners to consider in developing the evaluation framework:

1. In the next 6 months what/how will you live the Master Code in your own life and practice?

2. How will you evaluate the positive impact of training Citizens to strengthen their voice? (See the Framework for Citizen Evaluation above.)

3. What will it take to move from the current stage of Taking Care of Yourself and Taking Care of this Place to the next stage of Caring for your City's Resilience (and/or the well-being of the Planet)?

CONCLUSION—LEARNING LHABITAT: WHY2

Learning Lhabitats are prototyping structures that build on the Master Code, the 4 Voices of the city, and its 12 Intelligences, in ways that support the city to connect people for purposeful outcomes. They can be designed as single events or offered in a series, as we have outlined here. Learning Lhabitat prototypes use aspects of appreciative inquiry, participatory action research, and adult learning development theory to discover structures that serve living systems. As Integral City prototyping processes, Learning Lhabitats have evolved into research projects, collective learnings, and inquiries and experiments that have revealed insights into the next natural steps for participants to take in their city. They have opened gateways that enable collaboration among unlikely allies.

Furthermore, as we have shared here, each Learning Lhabitat not only serves its local city Voices but creates opportunities for learning laboratories for developing and honing the skills of Integral City Practitioners, Catalysts, and Meshworkers to research and develop a lineage of skillful means to wake up Passion, Priorities, Purpose, Praxis, and Prosperity for the Human Hive in Service to our Planet of Cities.

Our practice of Learning Lhabitats has shown us the potential for:

- Designing and amplifying the city's unique capacities to cogenerate innovation locally so that local contributions can impact a regional and global scale by integrating locally, regionally, and globally. We have learned that creating Learning Lhabitats optimizes innovation in the city/eco-region.
- Co-creating and nurturing conditions for personal change and transformation with supportive environments for personal choices that engage local and global challenges. We have learned that an adult learning cohort (like the one described here to support the Citizen Voice), choosing to consciously change, evolve, and affirm life, produces a corollary outcome of supporting and learning from each other as a community of practice.
- Co-creating the conditions for inquiry as a collective intelligence. The field of collective intelligence is alive in cities and is at the early stages of gestation. To support collective intelligence, it is necessary to enact inquiry in the morphic field. As a contribution towards this end, we have learned that the collective expression of both action inquiry and enaction inquiry designed into a Learning Lhabitat enable the Master Code and spiritual dimensions to serve a local need and by doing so, serve a Planet of Cities (and perhaps their morphic field).
- Drawing the "map" of the planet's local networks of Integral City Voices enables the Planet of Cities to begin seeing itself. Learning Lhabitats offer prototyping structures that can be co-created, as necessary, to support local leadership in cities. We have learned that the global impact of this has potential to become a mass amplification

of collective intelligence and wisdom in the cities of the planet and result in a shift by humanity to a higher level of consciousness.

Our Learning Lhabitats are learning laboratories/habitats where we can inquire and experiment how "practivism"—practical, evolutionary action—can create conditions for the 4 Voices of the city to co-develop, co-create, and co-emerge as self, with others and with place. We are creating laboratories and habitats to research and develop how we can live to our highest potential in the context of the human hive on our Planet of Cities. Learning Lhabitats can support individuals, organizations, and cities to emerge their purpose and goals in service to a sustainable, resilient Planet of Cities. At a cosmic scale, our experiments in prototyping new structures help us figure out what is wanted, how to implement it, and how to recognize and measure success. Our ongoing inquiry invites the minds, bodies, and spirits of all to reach out to unknown possibilities for, with, and as the human hive.

Given the foregoing description of the Learning Lhabitat, now let us frame, describe, and summarize the Pop-Up prototyping process.

FRAMING INQUIRY FOR POP-UP: WHO, WHY1

WHO

- Lead Constellator for Systemic Constellation (LC)
- Co-Facilitator(s) Team
- 4 Voices/Workshop Participants
- Graphic Recorder/Photographer
- Harvest Scribe

Facilitators' Roles

Integral City uses the guidance of a Lead Constellator (LC) who is applying (and evolving) the Systemic Constellation Work (SCW). Holding the palpable dimensions of SCW and through her embodiment of its philosophy and premises, she calls participants to reflect on and trust in the Knowing Field (morphic field). Prior to leading a given Pop-Up, she typically communes with the Knowing Field and is given the possible questions/issues to be constellated at the Pop-Up. By intention, they derive from the context in which the Pop-Up is occurring (which may include conference and/or speakers' topics). With input from the Integral City team, initial inquiry questions are chosen and refined.

The Integral City facilitation team as co-facilitator(s) holds the dimensions in the Knowing Field of the city where the Pop-Up is occurring. They also apply any information received from the field in the IC Community of Practice and in other work with cities.

The process steps for the SCW are described in Chapters 1 and 2. An explanation of how to use the SCW in a Pop-Up follows.

WHY1

The specific design of Integral City Pop-Ups incorporates the concept of Pop-Ups as a recently ubiquitous crowd experience found in many city locations, the practice of Systemic Constellation Work, and setting intentions for positive change impacts in the city.

What are Pop-Ups?

In modern cities Pop-Ups are a new phenomenon; they can be anywhere—they Pop-Up in train stations, parks, street corners, and conferences.[43]

One version of Integral City's Pop-Ups was designed as conference "playgrounds" to attract spontaneous, unexpected, unplanned diverse people to discover in the moment what they can do together in service to the themes of the conference. All of a sudden, the city's voices Pop-Up together in an instant, forming bonds among the 4 Voices of the city—citizens, community and cultural organizations, the business community, and civic institutions. As prototypes, our Pop-Up Playgrounds are intended to remind us of our capacities for joy, creativity, acting as a "we," and rediscovering our brilliance. They brighten our day and remind us of the interconnections among all sentient and non-sentient beings, that we are so often blind to.

What is an SCW?

Systemic Constellation Work (SCW) is a core process methodology that Integral City uses to do research, development, and prototyping, to expand our ways of knowing the archetype of Integral City as a reflective organ

---

43   See https://en.wikipedia.org/wiki/Pop-up_retail

for Gaia. SCW supports presencing, prototyping, and processing for the Integral City Community of Practice. (Our Lead Constellator, Diana Claire Douglas, Founder of Knowing Field Designs, uses SCW to inquire, prototype, and codesign with the IC Team on a regular basis.)

INQUIRY PRACTICE FOR POP-UP: WHAT / HOW

WHAT

Pop-Ups arise from a question that emerges from the discerning process just described. An example (from the Integral Theory Conference 2015) of a Pop-Up question is: **What happens when we speak as Mother Earth?**[44]

The intended impacts of the Pop-Up provide: a **place** (e.g., location like train station or the conference Pop-Up Playground), a **process** (SCW), and a **purpose** (e.g., showcase local artists, or capture a spontaneous conference harvest) to tap into the Knowing Field to reveal what participants don't know they know about a given question. Pop-Ups help make the invisible energies visible and therefore available for taking action.

More specifically, the Pop-Ups offer a way to:

- Amplify the impact of the context/conference (especially stories circulating in the zeitgeist) on the 4 Voices who become the Pop-Up participants (and by energy diffusion, everyone in the city).
- Harvest the stories from the context/conference and thus increase their long term impact on the world.
- Be a non-linear process for people to work together in the moment, which fosters a deep, almost subliminal (because non-linear) sense of community. Non-linear in the context of Pop-Ups means Integrally Epistemologically Pluralistic, (see definition above), thus involving 2nd and 3rd order learning.

Our Pop-Ups create a habitat for participants to harvest their deep knowing by:

---

44   Several versions of questions for the SCW typically arise. Three possible questions which could have been constellated are: What happens when we listen to Mother Earth? What happens when Mother Earth speaks? And, in the context of climate change, what happens when we speak as Mother Earth?

- Experiencing Systemic Constellation Work as a collective way of playing and knowing (aka prototyping).
- Learning from "Knowing Field Designs" Lead Constellator and Integral City Activators.
- Experimenting with how we learn, think and play together.
- Energizing our We-place and Activating questions, relationships, curiosities.
- Deepening connections with a community of integrally informed impact makers.
- Digesting all that is flowing through individuals and through the collective.
- Discerning the impact that the context/conference realities are having on self/others/place/planet.
- Harvesting personal and collective insights to take away for action and impact on self, work, family, community, and city.

HOW

After the preparation described above, the LC worked with a Pop-Up participant to define a question and then agree to sponsor the question. In this example, an Integral City Team Member sponsored the question for approximately 23 participants.[45] The question used in this example was: **What happens when we speak as Mother Earth?**

The LC (with input from the sponsor) defines the Elements that were to be represented in this example as: force of creativity, force of destruction, adaptability, Gaia, animals, birds, plants, insects, water beings, sun-moon-stars, fire, water, air, earth, 4 humans plus 1 conscious human, mystery.

Three Rounds progressed with significant energy and insight being offered by the elements of Creativity and Destruction. SCW rounds are typically recognized as: Initial Placement of representatives; First Move (usually triggered by a question or representative motivated to change position); Final Placement of representatives (resulting from the outcomes of the preceding Move(s)).

---

45   It should be noted that the actual delivery details of this Pop-Up were documented in the ITC2015 Harvest Report, Appendix C (Hamilton et al., 2015)

After the Pop-Up, the LC noted these observations:

I *have been asked about the number of elements included especially all the elements representing Life (animals, birds, insects, fire, water, air, earth, etc.). In preparation for the constellation, I was "shown" an image of all these elements sitting in a circle—the circle of life—with the forces of Creativity and Destruction in the center and to just watch what would happen. The magnetic attraction between Creativity and Destruction – their love and joy in each other, stays with me. As does Destruction's message, "I am here to serve."*

Rather than interpretation, as a Facilitator I am looking for movement, even small movements. Karen O'Brien (the conference speaker who was exploring climate change within an Integral context) had commented that in the (high-level) discourse on climate change we had not discussed the impact of human consciousness on the Earth and that this was a necessary step to include humanity's collective assumptions, beliefs and mindsets on climate change so that we can adapt to the changes. I was guided (by the Knowing Field) to place all the representatives for humans outside the circle of Life (as humanity has done) and to observe what happened and whether they were connected with adaptability. In the final image they were all inside the circle of life.

CONCLUSION: POP-UP—WHY2

The spontaneous nature of Pop-Ups means that outcomes are rarely predictable. Unlike the Learning Lhabitat, the process proceeds so rapidly self-documentation (like flip-chart notes and group reports) is not a usual or practical harvest method. However other technologies can be used to harvest the process and outcomes. Videoing the process is one method commonly available on one or more smartphones. If this mode is used, it should be consented to by participants early in the process.

A second "low tech" but "high expertise" mode of capturing the energy of Pop-Ups is graphic recording. The graphic recorder draws the Pop-Up as it moves through its three stages. Finally, the LC can document the Pop-Up with positional drawing and observation notes (for details, see Appendix E).

All of these forms of documenting lead to a series of syntheses that give meaning to the experience of the Pop-Up. This synthesis can in turn be translated into a summary of the key outcomes as framed in AQAL impact terms (as we have used at the end of each chapter of this book). A table can summarize an overview of the impacts that transformed mindsets, relationships, behaviors, and systems in the course of the Pop-Up. The table can also summarize related any Pop-Up harvest records and any post-Pop-Up debriefs that have occurred.

This final analysis (often occurring post-Pop-Up and off-site) can bring people together in contexts or habitats that reveal the non-linear, emergent creativity that emerged from the powerful messages in the Pop-Up. It weaves together through instant but intimate explorations, the whole Pop-Up experience set out as Deep, Wide, Clear, and High Impacts.

CONCLUSION: HARVESTING PROTOTYPING OUTCOMES FROM LEARNING LHABITATS AND POP-UPS

An integrally informed (AQAL) harvest analysis reveals how rich are the design processes of Learning Lhabitats and Pop-Ups.

As a way to summarize the AQAL richness we have used three modes to savor the beauty, goodness, and truth of the impacts from both prototyping processes. These modes have the qualities of time and learning built in:

- **Memory:** frames time Past, like a photograph of the moments. It embraces first-order learnings of observation and practical action.
- **Meaning:** frames time Present, with the ways we understand and share through our stories of what happened. It embraces second-order learnings (of constructive goals and strategies to achieve them) and third-order learnings (of imagination and visionary intentions).
- **Momentum :** frames time Future, with the impulse to move forward and make a difference. It creates a kind of "spin" on first-, second-, and third-order learnings.[46]

Memory is captured in the Learning Lhabitat and Pop-Up Harvest records including written, audio-recorded, art, and artefacts. It is both individual and collective, tangible and in cyberspace. Also, it is what is learned and remembered—essentially *first-order learnings*. By publishing

---

46   This framework of Memory, Meaning, Momentum has been contributed by George Por and Alia Aurami.

and distributing any particular prototyping Harvest report we make the Memory Harvest widely available to many people, so it contributes to the wider community/world to use for the aspects/impacts of harvest involving meaning and momentum. An important impact of memories is that they leave for further prototyping or actual implementation, artefacts, histories, and records for use in the future, enabling greater impact by future efforts because they can build on the past. (As an example, to create an online gallery of all the ITC2015 Memory Impacts we assembled in a Google Folder as many artefacts as we could compile.

Meaning can be usefully regarded as having several phases: response, reflection, and re-formation/reconfiguration/recalibration.

- **Response** includes feeling-reactions: elated, intrigued, disgusted, frustrated, jumping for joy, surprised, etc. Responses are momentary impacts, but the memory of them, and the effects of them, can be long-lasting, and can even change the Being of the person (see Reconfiguration, below).

- **Reflection** includes such things as poetic and other consequent (but immediate) creations, and both inner and conversational chewing/digesting, relating the content to one's life, to the world, etc. Reflection includes what we might call *second-order learnings*; not content learned, but what one learned about approaching the matter, conceptual re-organizations, etc. (Note: Reflection is a kind of impact because it can change a person's future doings and/or their Being.)

- **Reconfiguration** extends beyond conscious reflections, how one (or a "we") is actually impacted and changed on the "being" level by the event (and by the harvesting process, the reflections themselves.) This is 3rd-order learning (and perhaps even higher orders of learning). This can be an especially potent impact if there is a learning loop such that future iterations of the event itself are reconfigured because of the reflections (and momentum.) Reconfiguration also includes the impact when contributors/contributions to the prototyping event are morphed/developed further based on feedback from the event (such as might happen with a reader of the Harvest report or this chapter).

Momentum is the impact characterized by ripples forward and outward from the space-time event and the objects generated therein. It includes (for example) interpersonal, transpersonal, and intra-personal connections, new and deepened, sparks of synergy begun, new endeavors and/or collaborations emerging either for individuals or groups, new learning curves inspired or undertaken, people feeling supported, encouraged, and heartened to continue or increase their work in the world.

- Ideally, momentum-impact is as strong, as immediate, and long-term, and as wide as possible! Momentum includes, if looking at the event energetically, a strengthening of the morphic field (s) related to the purposes and intentions, shared and individual, around and for the event.
- Momentum in our Harvest lens can be captured most dramatically by the written and spoken commitments people often make at the end of the prototyping processes (either Learning Lhabitat or Pop-Up).

Combining Memory, Meaning, and Momentum with AQAL Impacts (as we encourage at the end of each chapter) allows organizers to gain an overview of the prototyping event and/or the context or conference across time and scale.

Memory highlights the mementos of photos, conversations, posters, pre-, and during the prototyping process, promotional materials, and delivery notations.

Meaning highlights the Response, Reflections, and Reconfigurations from participants' responding to the Learning Lhabitat and Pop-Up calls for participation, reflecting the system as a whole, and the reframing of wider-context messages into personal and shared meanings that can be translated into actions and strategies.

Momentum highlights commitments to join a direction of energy (like mitigating climate change), the multitude of inter-/intra-/trans-/personal connections made during the prototyping process and especially any commitments to personally act/impact.

REITERATION OF INQUIRY OBJECTIVES

The objectives of this chapter were to:

1. Learn the history and value of prototyping.

2. Understand the role of design and deep design in prototyping.

3. Differentiate between the prototyping purposes and processes of Learning Lhabitats and Pop-Ups.

4. Describe the purpose and role of a Learning Lhabitat.

5. Develop a Learning Lhabitat for Practitioners to influence Citizen Voice.

6. Design a Learning Lhabitat for the Citizen Voice of the city.

7. Learn the role of Pop-Ups as a mode of prototyping.

8. Describe the Pop-Up preparation and delivery process.

9. Synthesize the lessons from Learning Lhabitats and Pop-Ups for action through Memory, Meaning, and Momentum.

ACTION PLAN FOR PRACTITIONER, CATALYST, MESHWORKER

Review this chapter and make notes below of your impressions, insights, and questions. Locate yourself on the Integral City practice scaffolding. Notice what you have observed, thought, felt and what you now want to do in any of the three possible practice configurations: as a Practitioner, as a Catalyst, as a Meshworker.

After you have made these notes, consider some of the Impact Questions (below). They also might help you reflect on how to generate impact through inquiry and action. Finally check out the Resources and Links suggested for this practice at the end of the chapter.

IMPACT QUESTIONS: DEEP, WIDE, CLEAR, HIGH

UL DEEP: How can I influence, lead, initiate, or convene a Prototyping process for my community or city? What design questions am I curious about prototyping? How might I explore the value of Learning Lhabitats or Pop-Ups?

LL WIDE: How can our organization use prototyping to discover how we contribute to city success? How might prototyping give us a deeper and/or wider view of the city's future possibilities? How could prototyping invite other organizations into the process for change? How could we attract other organizations to participate in a Learning Lhabitat? When and where might we surprise others with the fun of a Pop-Up?

UR CLEAR: How could prototyping with Learning Lhabitats engage the city's supply chains that contribute to its metabolic flow and well-being? How could a Pop-Up break down barriers within my organization to new solutions for one of our intractable problems?

LR HIGH: How might a Pop-Up attract unusual or unlikely allies to the table to explore city infrastructure issues? What organizations already use prototyping in design phases? How could we use their experience to design more effectively for the city systems?

CHAPTER RESOURCES AND/OR LINKS

Appendix B: *Integral City Maps (1–5)*: 1, 2, 3, 4, 5

Appendix C1: *Definitions of 12 Intelligences*: *Integral, Inner, Cultural, Structural, Inquiry, Evolutionary*

Appendix C3: *Integral City GPS Locator*: *Integral City*

Reflective Question for Whom /Where/ What I Could Use as:	Practitioner	Catalyst	Meshworker
What do I observe as I read?			
What do I think?			
What do I feel?			
What do I want to do next?			

PROTOTYPE SUSTAINABLE COMMUNITY DEVELOPMENT

This chapter is based on a course designed and delivered for Royal Roads University (2010–2012) as a 6-month graduate certificate in Sustainable Community Development.

INQUIRY OBJECTIVES

The objectives of this chapter are to:

1. Frame prototyping as a practical, informal, and/or formal academic process and outcome.
2. Apply Integral City frameworks to the design of a sustainable community development course.
3. Outline a course design and key curriculum.
4. Describe how students work together as a prototyping team.
5. Understand how the 4 Voices of the City can sponsor, review, and contribute to the prototype.
6. Evaluate the prototype for practical implementation.

INTRODUCTION TO INQUIRY, ACTION, AND IMPACT FOR SUSTAINABLE COMMUNITY DEVELOPMENT

An academic (or non-academic) program in Sustainable Community Development (SCD) can build the foundations for developing both sustainability practices in practitioners and community capacity in a city location. This chapter draws on many of the preceding chapters and shares a design to prototype an SCD project for a real Community of Interest.

The design for this prototype places emphasis on the development of the people skills in sustainable communities because this approach can design in multiple experiences of team building, learning in community, and actually working for a real Community of Interest. This kind of prototyping uses aspects of action learning to offer dynamic, evolutionary, intelligent practices, tools, and frameworks that develop practitioners who can gain the capacities to build a prototype and then apply the lessons learned to build resilient communities. As a result, graduates can go on to expand their own practices and expertise and/or work alongside experts in the hard sciences and economic specializations to bring insight into why and how human systems in communities develop capacities for sustainability and well-being.

Over and above the classroom, onsite and distance learning, this prototype design can include the use of a distinctive online Gaiaspace Meshwork to enable the connections among the cohort, the community, experts and practitioners (discussed in *Chapter 13*). Over time, this combination of prototyping methodology and technology can develop an archive of Practitioner Profiles, Tools, Best Practices for Community Engagement and Sustainability, and Case Studies for Sustainable Community Development.

The SCD prototyping program is focused around three leverage points:

1. Understanding Community in the context of its environment, eco-region, and evolution to date.
   - It explores systems in terms of the community's economy, environment, social and cultural life.
   - It considers the developmental and evolutionary nature of life and human intelligence acting in community.

2. Designing Capacity Building Systems aligned with paradigms in people, organizations, communities, and cities.

- It utilizes the Integral City framework's 4 quadrants of community (inner and outer for the individual, and interior and exterior for the collective) and 4 major levels of development to discern how human systems grow.
- It challenges and designs bridges across the silos, stovepipes, and solitudes[47] that fragment current community sectors.

3. Developing Strategies for Evaluating, Decision-Making, and Civic Engagement.

- It identifies and provides foundations for actions that build social capital.
- It provides strategies for inquiry, meshing networks, and navigating community change.
- It offers designs and tools for community engagement.

This program in the field of Sustainable Community Development goes beyond the post-modern framings (that have been more widely delivered since 1987, and the Brundtland Report which identified the three-legged sustainability stool of economic, environmental, and social capitals) to use an Integral City paradigm. This paradigm is grounded in: complexity and systems thinking, an embrace of evolutionary approaches in all the keystone domains, and the recognition that subjective and intersubjective development play an equal and necessary role with the objective and interobjective terrains.

FRAMING INQUIRY FOR SUSTAINABLE COMMUNITY DEVELOPMENT: WHO, WHY1

WHO

- Program Designer
- Curriculum Developer

---

47 This trio of fragmentations—silos, stovepipes, solitudes—was originally coined by Dr. Ann Dale (Dale, 2001; Dale & Onyx, 2005)

- Faculty
- Students
- Community of Interest
- Community of Interest Resource Person(s)
- Community of Interest Stakeholders (Evaluation Panel)

The SCD program design assumes the collaborative efforts of designers, faculty, students, and a Community of Interest. It was originally designed as a certificate course, earning credits at a post-graduate university. However, it can also be delivered in a non-academic environment (like an Impact Hub) where motivation is high and producing a prototype is a self-motivating opportunity in itself. The SCD program creates the gateway for the learners to apply their learning directly into a Community of Interest whose Resource Person starts the program by sharing a challenge they face. Examples of challenges are offered below under **WHAT**.

Whatever the challenge, it becomes the focus of each of the SCD courses and culminates in the production of a prototype capstone project. The Community of Interest generally introduces its challenge in the first residency (or introductory distance course) and continues to be a focus of applied learning in two distance learning courses—the first focused on Community Engagement, the second on Exploring Structural Foundations of community, and the final Prototype Capstone Project.

WHY1

The SCD program is necessarily interdisciplinary and may draw from faculty and/or experts and research in the domains of: Leadership, Environmental Management, Peace and Conflict Studies, Communications, and MBA, all of which operated as faculties at Royal Roads University (RRU) at the time of the initial SCD design. This program is also competency-based and reflects the strengths of collaborative and experiential learning and action research (also RRU strengths, as well as a growing number of other action learning-based universities).

INQUIRY PRACTICE FOR SUSTAINABLE COMMUNITY DEVELOPMENT: WHAT / HOW

WHAT

The inquiry question for the SCD program will be stated in the Challenge Summary that the Community of Interest describes to the faculty. The Challenge will be expressed in a question like:

How can city hall improve the participation rates of a solar panel installation program for residential homes? or How can the regional transportation system attract citizen engagement from multiple municipalities to improve and expand the pedestrian and bicycle path network?

HOW

On a practical level the SCD program engages students to develop a proposal for sustainable development with a real Community of Interest who reviews and accepts the proposal as the basis for the prototyping process and as the framework for receiving recommendations for action (see below for how the Community of Interest is selected). The proposal then becomes the container in which all the courses are delivered and the basis for the delivery of the final prototype recommendations.

The SCD program is designed to integrate different elements of prototyping (contexting, capacity building, and strategic development), experiences of the integral framework, appreciative inquiry, multiple scales of engagement, and practical applications. Each course of the program focuses on a different combination of these elements as summarized in Table 17 (below) under the headings Course Name, Program Elements, Integral Quadrants, Appreciative Inquiry (AI) Phase, Human System Scale, and Practical Applications.

The Pre-Residency introduces the SCD to learners by opening the window into their own capacities for sustainability, community, and development. They assess their subjective (Upper Left) and objective (Upper Right) self-knowledge; opening an Appreciative Inquiry through the Discovery phase; embracing human systems at the scale of self and other classmates; and practically applying their learnings to developing nodes of practice (implicated in the challenge question), values assessments, and a team charter (see *Appendix I* for a sample form).

In the Residency, the focus is on understanding what development means. It expands the Integral quadrants to the intersubjective (Lower Left) and interobjective (Lower Right) terrains; the Appreciative Inquiry phase moves beyond Discovery to Dream; and the human systems widen to embrace the Community of Interest which they meet and explore. Outcomes from this course include practical applications that result in mapping networks, developing the structure of the online Gaiaspace Meshwork, and engaging in large group processes that open up the cohort learning field beyond individual intelligences to collective intelligence.

In the third course, which is generally delivered on a distance-learning platform (like Moodle), the focus is on building sustainable community and what that means. The Integral quadrants expand into the subjective (Upper Left) and intersubjective (Lower Left) terrains and the Appreciative Inquiry process continues more of the Discovery and Dream phases but also progresses to the Design phase. The human system scale is focused on the Community of Interest and the practical applications include community engagement practices (like Open Space, World Café, Dialogue, and Circle Work). As the students work together, they form a Community of Research Practice using the toolbox included in the Gaiaspace Meshwork platform.

The fourth course (also delivered as a distance course) focuses on sustainable development. It switches to the Integral right-hand quadrants with a focus on objective (Upper Right) and interobjective (Lower Right) perspectives. Within Appreciative Inquiry, the first three phases (of Discover, Dream, and Design) are joined by the fourth phase of Deliver and the human system focus is squarely on the Community of Interest. Practical outcomes include identifying Best Practices (from research in other communities and related projects) and adding those to the Gaiaspace archives (while tracking its growing connections and nodes).

In the fifth course, the Capstone project is developed and delivered. This course is typically prepared before reconvening in a final residency to present to the Community of Interest stakeholders and faculty, the prototype for addressing the challenge that has been the raison d'etre or theme throughout the whole program. The Integral quadrants are all engaged and Appreciative Inquiry moves beyond the Design and Deliver phase to the Debrief phase where analysis and synthesis enable students to evaluate their prototype and their performance. The human system embraces both the students as practitioners and the Community of Interest stakeholders who receive the prototype as the reward for sharing their challenge and acting as resources throughout the program. The practical application culminates in a presentation of the prototype and an evaluation by stakeholders and faculty on its success.

Table 17: Summary of Sustainable Community Development Program Elements

Course Name	Program Elements	Integral Quadrant	Appreciative Inquiry Phase	Human System Scale	Practical Applications
Pre-Residency	Introduction SCD	_x_/_x_ /	Discover	Self, Other	·Identifying Practitioner Nodes ·Values Assessment ·Team Charter
Residency	Development	___/___ x / x	Discover & Dream	Other Community of Interest	·Map Networks ·Develop Gaiaspace Meshwork ·Large Group Process
DL1 Building Sustainable Community	Community	_x_/___ x /	D, D & Design	Community of Interest	·Community Engagement Practices ·Communities of Practice ·Community of Research Practice ·Profiles of Tools ·Grow Gaiaspace Meshwork
DL2 Sustainable Development	Sustainability	___/_x_ / x	D, D, D, Deliver	Community of Interest	·Identify Cases, Best Practices ·Grow Gaiaspace Archives
Capstone	Sustainable Community Development	_x_/_x_ x / x	Deliver & Debrief	Community of Interest Practitioners, Stakeholders	·Presentation ·Evaluation

COURSE DESCRIPTIONS—KEY POINTS

Working with faculty and Community of Interest stakeholders, program designers develop curriculum for each of the courses. It is beyond the scope of this chapter to provide detailed curricula, but Table 18 presents a summary of the key content points that the design incorporates. (In addition, examples of the Capstone Reports are available as PDF documents to download from http://integralcity.com/resources/resources-research/)

Each course moves along a trajectory that includes: Context, Capacity Building, and Strategies. This effectively also describes the process for building a prototype—first, understand the habitat or context where action is required; next, identify and/or develop the capacities required to effectively adapt, mitigate, or transform the environment in which the challenge occurs; and finally, develop strategies for responding to, implementing, and sustaining the intended changes.

Over the delivery time of the Sustainable Community Development program (generally 6 months), courses are delivered and opportunities are designed in for students to work as individuals, in triad learning partnerships, in teams (of two triads = 6), as a cohort, and with the Community of Interest. Table 19 shows a typical schedule relating to course hours and duration (in an academic environment, translated into credits).

Table 18: Summary of Sustainable Community Development Course Key Content Scheduling Student/Stakeholder Interactions and Course Delivery

Trajectory	Course >>>> Learning Units ∨∧	Pre-Residency	Residency	DL1 Community Engagement	DL2 Exploring Foundations	Capstone
Context	Focus	Personal Definitions of Sustainability Community Development	Local Community of Interest	Local Community of Interest	Local Community of Interest	Local Community of Interest
Context	Themes for SCD Challenge – researched by faculty with Community of Interest and presented to cohort for Res1 proposal devt. This Community of Interest is then the focus of DL1 and DL2 and the Capstone Project. Intention is to link Community of Interest Burning Q's and Official Community Plan, Sustainable Community Plan and Strategic Plan		· Faculty selects with Community; Cohort explores with community · Possibilities: · Environment & Economy · Learning & Culture · Health & Community · Food · Eco-Village · Bridging Solitudes	· Possibilities: · Environment & Economy · Learning & Culture · Health & Community · Food · Eco-Village · Bridging Solitudes	· Possibilities: · Environment & Economy · Learning & Culture · Health & Community · Food · Eco-Village · Bridging Solitudes	· Community Presentation · Links Community BQ and OCP, SCP and Strat Plan
Context	Overview	What are my Burning Questions re SCD?	How does a village raise a child?	How does a village develop?	How does a village sustain itself?	How does a village survive, develop, sustain itself?
Context	Urgency vs Importance	Why Here? Now? Us?	Why Here? Now? Us?	Tensions – Community (Intention & Culture) & Sustainability	Tensions – Sustainability (Environmental & Economic) & Community	Living in Tension with Intention Integrally
Context	Design		Learners develop Assignment & Assessments for SCD Integral Template	Community Development	Sustainability Issues	Test design with stakeholders
Capacity Building	Governance	Explore Team Roles, Team Charter Develop Framework	Select Team Members Team Charter Practice	Team/Cohort/Community Agreement	Team/Cohort/Sustainability Experts tbd	Team performance in producing Capstone
Capacity Building	Communication		Listening Integral Awareness Dialogue	Communicating with teams and community online	Analysing Cases	Written and verbal presentation

Capacity Building	Assessment	Values Assessment - Self	Values Assessment – Team	Values Assessment – Community	Assessment – Sustainability	Assessment Summary: Practitioners, Team and Community
Capacity Building	Practices & Tools	Awareness – Self Portfolio	Awareness – Self, Other, Culture Group PPT Portfolio	Awareness - Self, Other, Culture CultureSCAN and MeshSCANLite	Awareness – Self, Other, Culture, Social Economy	Effective presentation brings COI and Cohort system together
Capacity Building	Sustainability	Self	Collectives in community	Community stakeholders	Infrastructure & Ecology in Community	Whole system
Strategies	6 P's: Purpose Profit People Principles Processes Praxis	Overview	Purpose Profit People Principles Processes Praxis	Purpose Profit People Principles Processes Praxis	Purpose Profit People Principles Processes Praxis	Framing 6 P's
Strategies	Decision Making	Overview	· Integral/spiral framework · Polarity Management · Eco-Footprint · Appreciative Inquiry	· Integral/spiral framework · Polarity Management · Appreciative Inquiry	· Integral / spiral framework · Eco-Footprint	Recommen-dations
Strategies	Scale & Measurement	Overview	6 months - 10 yr time/space/ morality	6 months - 10 yr time/space/ morality	6 months - 10 yr time/space/ morality	Recommen-dations
Strategies	Boundaries	Overview	Boundaries - integral	Boundaries - subjective & intersubjective	Boundaries - objective & interobjective	Recommendation
Strategies	Paradigms	Overview	Gross Commty Product Vs Gross Commty Happiness	pre-modern-post-integral	empirical-post-modern-integral methodological pluralism	Recommendations

Table 19: SCD Typical Program Schedule

SCD Program is typically scheduled in units, hours and duration as follows:		
Pre-Residency	33 hours	3 weeks
Residency	33 hours	1 week
Distance Learning	1–99 hours	10 weeks
Distance Learning	2–99 hours	10 weeks
Capstone	33 hours	3 days

COMPETENCIES & LEARNING OUTCOMES

Competencies

The program learning competencies are listed below. The definition for each competency may be defined by the institution or framed by the faculty. (It is assumed that each competency can be demonstrated within an integral learning frame similar to the format used in the Impact Questions at the end of each chapter of this book.)

- Learning
- Collective Capacity Building
- Evaluation—Process
- Evaluation—Output
- Assessment—Individual
- Assessment—Collective
- Paradigms, Worldviews, & Ethics
- Change Catalyst
- Systems Thinking
- Evolution and Development
- Critical and Creative Thinking
- Communications
- Research & Inquiry
- Leadership

Learning Outcomes

Each competency is more completely defined and supported by Learning Outcomes in each course (and are adapted and documented separately for each Community of Interest Challenge). The comprehensive learning outcomes for this course and the assessment criteria for evaluating whether a learner has achieved the learning outcomes are summarized in Table 20.

Table 20: Summary of Learning Competency Outcomes

Trajectory	Learning Competency	Pre-Res Outcomes	Residency Outcomes	DL1 Community Engagement Outcomes	DL2 Exploring Foundations Outcomes	Capstone Outcomes
Capacity Building	Learning	Personal Learning Plan for SCD Res1	• Respond in community learning container • Integral Listening • Kolb Learning Assessment • How do I commit to learn?	Kolb & Collective Learning	Contextual Learning	
Capacity Building	Leadership		• Leading Development in self, others related to SCD Challenge	Leading Community	Leading Sustainability	
Capacity Building	Collective Capacity Building	Identify and explore team roles (Belbin)	• Team Learning & Building • Build the SCD Network • Team Assessments • Cohort Network Map	Team & Community Building	Team Community of Research Practise	
Capacity Building	Evaluation - Process		• Learner Teams, Cohort, Triads • Integral Reflective Feedback	Teams, Cohort, Community Integral Reflective Feedback	Teams, Cohort, Experts Integral Reflective Feedback	Community of Interest & Faculty Feedback to Cohort
Context	Assessment - Individual	Team & Cohort Discovery Process	• What is your passion? • What do you do? • Where is your hope? • Blog into Gaiaspace on Self Reflection, combine Values Assess & Kolb	Online Participation	Online Participation	• What is your passion? • What do you do? • Where is your hope? • Blog into Gaiaspace on Learnings throughout SCD
Context	Assessment - Collective		• Why Here? Now? Us? • Cohort Vision • World Café	Community Vision	Sustainability Principles for Community	Sustainability Mission for Community

Trajectory	Learning Competency	Pre-Res Outcomes	Residency Outcomes	DL1 Community Engagement Outcomes	DL2 Exploring Foundations Outcomes	Capstone Outcomes
Context	Paradigms, Worldviews, & Ethics	(RRU) Ethical Guidelines – consent, justice, no harm	· Integral Framework (AQAL) · 4 key Worldviews · Sustainability Paradigms · Research Ethics · Team Ethics Guidelines for R&I	Appreciative & Integral Inquiry Ethics Guidelines	Case Study Taxonomy	Integral framing of paradigms, worldviews, ethics related to SCD Challenge
Strategies	Change Catalyst	Integral Change from what to what?	· Demonstrate change in local organizations · Action Research in Community - Proposal	Demonstrate relationships in local sectors Action Research in Community - Relationships	Demonstrate change in local infrastructure Case Studies applied	Change Potential Catalyzed thru Integral, AI, Cases
Context & Strategies	Systems	Register in online platform (e.g. Gaiaspace)	· Systems Seeing, Thinking & Disturbing · Complexity Game · Contribute Best Practices and/or Docs to online platform	Community Systems Model	Sustainability Logic Model Systems Model	Community Systems Integrally Mapped
Context & Strategies	Evolution		· Identify: evolution/ development/ · sustainability · @ Pre-modern, modern, post-modern, integral · Evidence in Community for evolutionary frameworks	· Identify: evolution/ development/ · sustainability · @ Pre-modern, modern, post-modern, integral · Evidence in Community for capacity building: Education, Health, Civil Society, Business, · City Governance	Research in teams: AI for: · Tobacco stop · Seat Belts · Recycling · Y2K · Non-Violence Research for cases related to infrastructure and environment	Adapt and present Best Practices from AI success research for community

Trajectory	Learning Competency	Pre-Res Outcomes	Residency Outcomes	DL1 Community Engagement Outcomes	DL2 Exploring Foundations Outcomes	Capstone Outcomes
Strategies	Critical & Creative Thinking		• Self • Other • Organization • Sustainability • Discovering Creative Capacity Meshwork	Innovation and Creative Analysis	Case Study Analysis applied to Community	Design & Format of Presentation
Strategies	Communica-tions		• Communicating with Team, Network • Communication re SCD Research & Inquiry for community audiences in 4 paradigms	Communi-cating with Community stakeholders	Communi-cating with Experts and Practitioners	Communi-cating with Reps for Community
Strategies	Research & Inquiry		• Appreciative Integral Inquiry in community • Discover, Dream, Design, Deliver Debrief Integrally	Building Community of Research Practise and Relationships with Community	Collecting Archive of Case Studies	Recommen-dations COI
Strategies	Evaluation - Output		• PPT Program Portfolio – Learners & Faculty	PPT Program Portfolio – Learners & Community Leaders, Policy Makers	PPT Program Portfolio – Learners & Sustainability Practitioners, Experts	PPT Program Portfolio – Learners, Community & Sustainability Practitioners, Experts

UNDERSTAND HOW THE 4 VOICES OF THE CITY SPONSOR, REVIEW, AND CONTRIBUTE TO THE PROTOTYPE.

How is a Community Selected for the Sustainable Community Development Challenge?

The 4 Voices of the city (explored in *Chapter 9*) play an integral role in how the Community of Interest contributes to Sustainable Community Development. We have found that a careful selection process ensures the best match between a community and the Sustainable Community Development program participants. In order to evaluate the readiness of each Community of Interest, we recommend reviewing a number of requirements, including responses to the following questions:

1. What opportunity or threat related to sustainability capacity could a Sustainable Community Development proposal address?

2. Does your community have a current Official Community Plan and/or Strategic Plan and or Sustainability Plan? If so, can the Sustainable Community Development students have access to these plan(s)?

3. How is/are the plan(s) linked to your most pressing sustainability priorities?

4. What part of the plan(s) and priorities are related to the sustainable community development needs of your community?

5. Describe what you see as the sustainable community development need/opportunity that the Sustainable Community Development program candidates can address in a 6-month timeframe?

6. Have there been past attempts to address this need/opportunity (either internally or using an outside firm)? If so, please describe these attempts—when were they addressed, what was successful, and what was not?

7. What stakeholders should be identified and/or contacted related to addressing this need/opportunity? How could we select stakeholders from the 4 Voices of the city?

8. *Optional question:* What is the hypothetical budget and timeline for addressing the Sustainable Community Development need/opportunity? (Note: we recommend omitting a question about budget. In many cases, if they knew exactly what they needed, it would not be the kind of challenge the Sustainable Community Development program can best respond to.)

Why Should a Community Share its Sustainable Development Challenge?

By sharing a Sustainable Community Development challenge with Sustainable Community Development program participants, the community gains a fresh perspective from innovative mid-career professionals with a broad spectrum of experience and knowledge and from many different sectors of the economy.

The Sustainable Community Development program provides all organizational and instructional requirements. The faculty assists with identification, framing, and development of the Sustainable Community Development Challenge and its exploration with the participants and the Community of Interest. Program participants collaborate to apply their considerable personal leadership experience, along with their new knowledge, skills, and abilities to develop real-time solutions to the Sustainable Community Development challenge. During the Capstone Residency, the presentation time is scheduled in conjunction with the Community of Interest stakeholders, who will have an opportunity to ask questions and to engage in dialogue with the team(s).

The Role of the Community of Interest

When a community decides to pursue this opportunity, it provides Sustainable Community Development program faculty and students with the information needed to frame and document the Sustainable Community Development challenge. This process typically unfolds over a 2- to 3-week period starting with an initial meeting to discuss possible zones of inquiry and to gather background material to provide context for the challenge. Faculty will draft the Sustainable Community Development challenge document and forward it for review. A second meeting may be held to finalize revisions and to give final approval of the challenge. The challenge is then presented on the second day of the program to the participants by a member of the Community of Interest and/or the faculty, and a tour of the Community of Interest is organized for that day and/or subsequent days so that participants gain first-hand experience of the Community of Interest.

Access to a Community of Interest resource person throughout the First Residency week is beneficial to the participants. The Community of Interest organizes a pre-arranged check-in with a Community of Interest resource person to answer questions or clarify issues. A mutually agreeable timeslot is established for this—typically by email and/or telephone—where participants put forward their questions and issues. At the end of the first Residency week, the participant team(s) present their proposal to a panel made up of 2–3 senior representatives from the sponsoring Community of Interest and/or other external coresearchers. Panel members should be of a senior level, able to accept the Proposal as adding value to the Community of Interest, and at the Capstone presentation, review the recommendations that will result from it, comment on their feasibility and viability and, if accepted, then take them forward for implementation.

EVALUATE THE PROTOTYPE FOR PRACTICAL IMPLEMENTATION

Community of Interest Commitment

In order to optimize the learning opportunity for participants and to offer the Community of Interest the greatest value for its involvement, faculty ask each Community of Interest to meet the following commitments:

1. Provide an overview of the Community of Interest , including vision, values, official community plan, and strategic goals.

2. Provide required supporting background material including any requested reports.

3. Participate in pre-seminar planning and review of materials related to the Sustainable Community Development challenge in order to ensure accuracy.

4. Participate in an in-depth discovery process of the Community of Interest exploring the zones of research interest in order to assist the students in selecting a focus for study in the following 6 months. This can be coordinated with key Community of Interest stakeholders (e.g., staff, elected officials, businesses, NFP, and residents) over significant time slots in 1–2 days.

5. Be available for up to 90 minutes for Question and Answer session(s) during the first residency week.

6. Be available for one, 90-minute Question and Answer Proposal Presentation during the first residency week.

7. Provide a contact person(s) for the cohort to connect with during the program.

8. Provide 2–3 senior members of your Community of Interest to attend the Capstone presentation at the end of 6 months and provide feedback to participants.

9. Provide a progress report to faculty 6 months following the seminar.

What the Community Receives

The Sustainable Community Development students each have a depth of career experience and are leaders in their organizations throughout the world. The Community of Interest will receive an integrated Sustainable Community Development plan that addresses its community's sustainability objectives. This plan will be created by teams of 6–10 participants under the guidance of multi-disciplinary faculty and expert leadership.

The students are required to address the key elements of a Sustainable Community Development proposal while they consider the community's objectives. At the end of the course they will prepare a professional report and presentation (which may be PowerPoint, video, website, animation, or some combination of these modes) to the stakeholders that will include these elements:

- Executive Summary.
- A review of Community of Interest sustainability need(s) and community engagement environment.
- An assessment of the 4 Voices in the stakeholder audience(s) and how their characteristics (including values and worldviews) will contribute to the plan.
- Proposed sustainability goals and an evaluation plan.
- Recommendations and suggestions for implementation. This may include budget recommendations if financial information is provided.
- Evaluation framework, including concrete measures and qualitative indicators.
- References and Appendices.

While the development of the plan is an academic exercise designed to challenge the students' creativity and teamwork, it is also an exercise designed to provide significant value to the community through the collective brain trust of the world's leading sustainability researchers and practitioners. (Examples of reports can be downloaded from http://integralcity.com/resources/resources-research/.)

It is also important to note that the plans presented to the Community of Interest will be created within the time restraints related to the course outlines and may require further refinement by the Community of Interest after presentation. That is the nature of prototypes—they offer rapid research of an experimental nature and typically require revisions and refinement for final implementation.

(Note: A more formal exploration of Integral City project evaluation is discussed in *Chapter* 15).

CONCLUSION: WHY2

The students in the Sustainable Community Development program generally each have a depth of career experience and may be leaders in their organizations throughout the world. The Community of Interest is invited to share with the class, a challenge that it would like to solve and receives in return a prototype that is an integrated Sustainable Community Development plan that addresses its community's sustainability objectives. This plan has been created by teams of 6–10 participants under the guidance of Integral City-informed multi-disciplinary leadership.

The students are required to both frame a proposal (to test the doability and acceptability of their offer by the Community of Interest) and then build a prototype that meets the needs addressed in the proposal.

While the development of the prototype is an (academic) exercise designed to challenge the students' creativity and teamwork, it is also an exercise designed to provide significant value to the Community of Interest through the collective brain trust of the world's leading sustainability researchers and practitioners as interpreted by the prototyping team.

As already noted, the plans presented to the Community of Interest are typically created within the 6-month time restraints related to the course outline and may require further refinement by the Community of Interest.

All that being said, the development of a workable prototype involves the students in the perspectives of the Integral City's 4 quadrants and multiple levels of development. The prototyping process thus develops the designer (student), the design team (learning cohort), the object of the design (sustainability challenge), and the system/habitat within which the design process operates (Community of Interest). Thus the prototyping exercise (deriving intelligence and input from all the other chapters of this book) is a powerful process that has the potential to bring together and apply inquiry, action, and impact in service to the well-being of the emerging Integral City.

REITERATION OF INQUIRY OBJECTIVES

The objectives of this chapter were to:

1. Frame prototyping as a practical informal and/or formal academic process and outcome.
2. Apply Integral City frameworks to the design of a sustainable community development course.
3. Outline a course design and key curriculum.
4. Describe how students work together as a prototyping team.
5. Understand how the 4 Voices of the City can sponsor, review and contribute to the prototype.
6. Evaluate the prototype for practical implementation.

ACTION PLAN FOR PRACTITIONER, CATALYST, MESHWORKER

Review this chapter and make notes below of your impressions, insights, and questions. Locate yourself on the Integral City practice scaffolding. Notice what you have observed, thought, felt, and what you now want to do in any of the three possible practice configurations: as a Practitioner, as a Catalyst, as a Meshworker.

After you have made these notes, consider some of the Impact Questions (below). They also might help you reflect on how to generate impact through inquiry and action. Finally check out the Resources and Links suggested for this practice at the end of the chapter.

IMPACT QUESTIONS: DEEP, WIDE, CLEAR, HIGH

UL DEEP: What might motivate me to develop a prototype that could address sustainability issues? What are my curiosities about prototyping? What dreams and fantasies do I have to build something greater than my own resources might allow?

LL WIDE: How would working with a learning cohort support my own development in service to sustainable community development? What value does a Team Charter add to teamwork on any kind of project? (See format in *Appendix I*) How could a Team Charter contribute to a working prototype?

UR CLEAR: What actions have I taken in the past that could be useful in prototyping? What actions have I taken related to sustainability issues? What experiments or rehearsals have I tried out in any area of interest, in the past? What would I like to do/make/create more of to test out ideas related to sustainability?

LR HIGH: Who would we like to teach us how to design or prototype? Whom do we respect in the field of sustainability? community? development? What qualities do the best teams have who produce project or prototyping results? How could studying the systems used by inventors and innovators like Steve Jobs' Apple or Elon Musk's Tesla help us learn to work effectively as a prototyping team? What guidelines would we develop for managing and learning from failures as well as successes?

CHAPTER RESOURCES AND/OR LINKS

Appendix B: Integral City Maps (1–5): 1, 2, 3, 4

Appendix C1: Definitions of 12 Intelligences: Eco, Emergent, Integral, Inner, Outer, Social, Cultural, Inquiry, Meshworking, Navigating

Appendix C3: Integral City GPS Locator: Resilient, Integral

Reflective Question for Whom /Where/ What I Could Use as:	Practitioner	Catalyst	Meshworker
What do I observe as I read?			
What do I think?			
What do I feel?			
What do I want to do next?			

SECTION VII — *Meshwork Purpose, People, Place, and Planet*

This section on Meshworking describes the most complex Integral City applications of inquiry and action in the book. It integrates all of the stages of inquiry and action described in the previous chapters. With both the complexity and integration challenges in mind, it is easy to see that meshworkers, meshworks, and meshworking are not for the faint of heart and call on advanced skills from Integral City activators.

Chapter 13 sets out the basics of meshworks, meshworking, and meshworkers and how they work together to align intentions and develop and evolve the cities we want to realize.

Chapter 14 offers a case study that illustrates why (and how) the most advanced level of Integral City practice is called "Meshworker"—and why the annual award of "Meshworker of the Year" (won by this case study's practicing meshworkers) recognizes individuals and organizations who have demonstrated these practices in order to reflect and amplify their Deep, Wide, Clear, and High accomplishments.

REALIZE MESHWORKING CAPACITIES IN THE HUMAN HIVE

This chapter is adapted from 2 conference papers and presentations: one was prepared for Integral Theory Conference 2010, titled **Meshworking Integral Intelligences for Resilient Environments; Enabling Order and Creativity in the Human Hive** (*Hamilton, 2010b; Hamilton, 2012b*).

INQUIRY OBJECTIVES

The Inquiry Objectives of this chapter are:

1. Define and differentiate the meanings of meshworks, meshworking, and meshworkers.
2. Learn how the practice of meshworking expands Integral intelligences for the human hive (aka city).
3. Show how meshworks integrate the self-organizing network of city relationships with hierarchies of structural organization.
4. Learn the basic design for a meshwork.
5. Understand how meshworks recalibrate networks and communities into holarchies of practice.
6. Link the intelligence of Meshworking to the intelligence of Navigating with Integral vital signs monitors.

7. Learn how the practical application of meshworking stimulates life conditions where Integral capacities can naturally evolve and enable resilience in the human hive.

INTRODUCTION TO INQUIRY, ACTION, AND IMPACT FOR MESHWORKING IN THE HUMAN HIVE

It may be... that our minds are a kludge (or bricollage) of different kinds of intelligence: some intelligent abilities arise out of decentralized and parallel processes, others from centralized and sequential ones.

— (De Landa, 1995)

James Lovelock proposed that humans are Gaia's most advanced "organ of reflection" (Lovelock, 2009). He says it is our job to improve that reflective capacity in the interests of our species' survival and evolution. The collective life of the human hive provides enormous opportunities to create the conditions to accelerate our reflective capacity. At this time of seemingly continuous world crises, developing practices that grow our consciousness is a matter of life or death.

Meshworking is a natural capacity-building process that enables effective and efficient use of energy in progressively more complex integrations. It appears that the Universe creates complexity using meshworking processes. The process of creating a meshwork enables complex adaptive systems to emerge. This chapter explores the characteristics of meshworking, meshworks, and meshworkers and how the city or human hive integrally emerges from these processes, practices, and people.

If we look at the city as a whole living system, the 4-quadrant integral model, developed by Ken Wilber, gives us a picture of the whole because, it embraces both the visible and the invisible aspects of the city (Wilber, 1995, 2000b, 2006). It allows us to see the city in terms of different views of reality, how each of the quadrants relates to one another—how the subjective (Upper Left) and the intersubjective (Lower Left) realities are interlinked to the objective (Upper Right) and interobjective (Lower Right) realities.

Integral City: Evolutionary Intelligences for the Human Hive (Hamilton, 2008a) uses four versions of the Integral Map and a subsequent article

(Hamilton, 2012a) sets out the fifth map of spirituality in the city (all repro-duced in *Appendix* B). This chapter builds on Maps 1 and 2 but primarily references Maps 3 and 4 which reveal the relationships that we can see in the self-organizing elements of Map 3 and the structural elements of Map 4.

Integral thinking allows the use of some fuzzy logic to compare the different metrics that one uses to see reality from each quadrant and gain insights about how they might be influencing one another. This provides a platform to see how the reflective capacity of the individual (Upper Left) relates to the shared worldviews of their culture (Lower Left) and connects to the structures in the brain (Upper Right), which in turn become translated into structures and systems in our physical environment (Lower Right).

The basis of complex adaptive systems applied by Spiral Dynamics (D. Beck & Cowan, 1996) to the emergence of human capacities (related to values, leadership, organization) suggests that we can measure intelligence as it becomes more complex. The integral parsing of the Spiral Dynamics framework reveals that the different quadrants arise from different qualities present in the system and can be known through different epistemologies and metrics. We can locate the qualitative measurements of Placecaring in the left-hand quadrants (subjective and intersubjective) and quantita-tive metrics of Placemaking in the right-hand quadrants (objective and interobjective). Integral City research (Hamilton, 2003b) has proposed that the descriptors of developmental emergence in each quadrant reveal the connections between the metrics in consciousness capacity (Upper Left), values (Lower Left), brain-body development (Upper Right), and asset development (Lower Right).

Responding to Lovelock's injunction to evolve our reflective capacity, the integral and spiral models offer maps to notice or design feedback loops and measure our evolutionary progress. The use of meshworks to explain how integral developmental capacities emerge offers us a view of the city that explains what is working, what is not working, and what may emerge (see *Chapter* 10).

One of the ways that Don Beck (D. Beck, 2000a, 2004, 2007b) designs organizational systems that work (i.e., fit the people, purpose and habitat) is by using MeshWORKS™ or Meshwork Solutions™. In order for the organi-zation to coherently operate, he proposes the alignment of the X template (for functional flow), Y template (for resource fitness), and Z template (for vision integration), all working to achieve a superordinate goal. At the organizational level, his definition for a MeshWORK™ is realized when these templates emerge in a system. This is one of a series of explanations that he uses, applying Meshwork Solutions™ at different levels of scale up to nation and global systems (D. Beck, 2004, 2007a, 2010). Beck's design mirrors Adizes' (Adizes, 1999) proposition that organizational effectiveness depends on the functioning of PAEI—Producers and Entrepreneurs (X template), Administrators (Y template), and Integrators (Z template). As discussed earlier (*Chapter* 4), these patterns seem to be the human equivalent of the beehive's 4 roles of Conformity Enforcers and Diversity Generators (X), Resource Allocators (Y), and Integrators (Z). Thus, the Human Hive makes use of fractal patterns that arise in other living systems.

The term "meshworks" itself emerges from living systems. It was originally coined by brain scientists. Images of meshworks from the microscope include descriptions that the brain builds itself by "Laying down large synaptic highways which [create] scaffolds of communication corridors—these in turn then [create] secondary and tertiary corridors—and eventually we end up with a kind of hairnet of axons" (Bleys, Cowen, Groen, Hillen, & Ibrahim, 1996, p. 1038).

Manuel DeLanda (1995, 1997, 2006) describes meshworks in terms of how the brain builds a mind and how a mind builds the brain. He reveals the process of emergence where the self-organizing connections among synapses eventually emerge into habitual patterns that create the conditions for the sudden emergence of a new brain structure that enables learned capacity to be locked into the brain.[48] More recent brain research is revealing the role that even microscopic brain structures (called microtubulin) may have in processing the information pathways that become reinforced at the micro-spatial and nano-second time structures that govern the brain and consciousness, and in fact, the energy field in which they exist (Hameroff, Huston, & Pitney, 2010).

---

48 Readers familiar with the functioning of Holosync entrainment recordings will recognize the principles that this technology uses to accelerate the brain's capacity to develop more complex structures (IntegralLife, 2010).

Field theory (McTaggart, 2001) itself offers intriguing explanations that potentially explain the sudden, unexpected emergence of new capacities in the system, by suggesting that living systems have morphogenic fields (Sheldrake, 1988, 1999, 2003) that exist in the zero point energy field (Laszlo, 2004; Mitchell & Williams, 2001) and which hold species-related information such as these learned habits, structures, and patterns. This field (as we explored as the Knowing Field in *Chapter 1* and *Chapter 2*) may be where the meshworks are accumulated, stored, accessed, and built-on by the species.

At the micro level, it appears that the energies and dynamics of meshworks develop the mind/brain's natural potential by using a combination of self-organizing processes and hierarchical structures. Meshworks have an intriguing both/and nature that seems to take the best of two processes that appear to be dynamically opposed. But when they are married into an iterative cycle (supported by a field of remembered habits), each contributes to expanding the influence of the opposite process—a self-organizing process that expands structural complexity and a structural complexity that locks in energy-efficient habits and expands self-organizing potential.

This is a dynamic that lies at the heart of the resilience model described by the multi-disciplinary research team who mapped out the 4-stage resilience cycle of Panarchy (Gunderson & Holling, 2002): exploitation (of unaligned resources), conservation (and structuring of aligned resources), destruction (of alignment and relationships), and redistribution (of resources to a self-organizing field). This same cycle is the one explored by Howard Bloom (Bloom, 2010)—formulator of the beehive roles—who calls it the pendulum of re-purposing. He suggests that the cycle explains the alternating fortunes of resources and people in the boom/bust, integrate and differentiate swings of ever emerging economic complexity, using principles that the Universe has developed from deep time.

This cycle also seems to lie at the heart of the dynamics in Graves' (Graves, 1974) developmental learning model (which underlies the framework of Spiral Dynamics) and the ways humans are naturally created to be complex adaptive systems who relate to one another (and environmental life conditions). Graves' 6-stage learning model proposes that a person:

1. must have potential in the brain
2. have solved current life conditions
3. experience dissonance, such that a problem cannot be solved using existing solutions
4. experience an "aha" insight
5. integrate the insight into prior learning (transcend and include the insight so that previous behaviors, psychology, culture, and systems make new sense)
6. consolidate the integration into all sectors of their life.

Beck (2006) elaborates further on these conditions at the organizational and/or societal scale, adding four more that enable large scale change: inserting energy into the system; mapping change from what to what; leveraging tipping points; and anticipating the next set of problems that will emerge from new solutions.

So, we can see that meshworks apply at the microscopic level, the individual, and collective human level. They also occur at the macro scales of the Universe and the meso scale of the city.[49]

It appears then, that the human hive exists at the mid-size of human systems (between the individual and the nation)—a location that suggests cities have a critical role to play in humans becoming Gaia's organ of reflection. In considering the energy, matter, and information that our special case of intelligent stardust has evolved to, an examination of aerial images of cities (particularly the ones taken at night where you can see the energy patterns in the city, and not just the built structure),

---

49 In 2008, EnlightenNext re-published photographs from Science Times (Constantine, 2006) taken by the powerful Hubble telescope space shots that showed galaxies in formation and microscopic images of brain synapses with their long axons spidering out from the neuron. The fractal nature of these patterns was so unmistakable that the images of the galactic scale were virtually interchangeable with the images of the microscopic scale. A critical contribution of alignment relating these widely separated scales of the micro and the macro, was offered in the observations of the authors of "The View from the Center of the Universe" (Abrams & Primack, 2006). They proposed that in all the manifest universe, the human was at the mid-size of all things—what they called the "Midgard." Thus, human systems, being in that size zone had a peculiar opportunity to adapt its functions as "intelligent stardust."

the more it seems that the same patterns reveal themselves through the telescope and the microscope. Perhaps the city is the same fractal pattern we can see at the macro scale at the galactic level, and the micro scale at the neuronal and microtubulin level? We can justifiably ask, "Is the human hive the meso scale of this pattern and how does this pattern emerge?"

The weaving together of fractal patterns that use the capacity to learn and reflect in a cycle of learning called meshworking seems to explain the patterns of connectivity and thus patterns of relationships in the city (and galaxies and brain cells). Wheatley and Frieze (2006) proposed that connections in the meshworking process, like the hairnet mesh (described above) enable an infinite number of self-organizing pathways that span thoughts, ideas, innovations, feelings *and* emerge into directed, dependable, learned behaviors. They identify the progressive complexity of networks, communities of practice, and centers of influence. Without naming it as such, they describe the behaviors of a meshwork, the practices of meshworking, and the skills of a meshworker.

Thus, we have identified the context and elements of a framework that might explain the capacities and behaviors of cities as human systems. Is it possible that cities are nothing more or less than a meshwork of the relationships of the people who live in them, the outcomes of the minds/brains that created them, and the fields that contain them? Moreover, can meshworks explain the functioning of collectives, communities, and the social intelligence that create Gaia's organ of reflection?

Integral City thinking proposes that meshworks explain how the city emerges from the interconnected patterns of matter, energy, and information that make up the city. A meshwork, or meshwork of meshworks, enables capacity to arise from the integration of relationships, embedded in ideas, behaviors, cultures, and systems that results in order and creativity in the human hive. And being aware of and acting on/with/as these patterns that integrate process and structure lies at the heart of the basic definition of Meshworking Intelligence (see *Appendix C1*).

Now let us understand how meshworkers can intentionally use inquiry and action to stimulate and manifest a meshwork.

FRAMING INQUIRY FOR MESHWORKING IN THE HUMAN HIVE: WHO, WHY1

WHO

- Integral City Facilitators/Meshweavers
- Meshworkers
- Stakeholders from the 4 Voices
- Thought Leaders, Designers, Practitioners
- X Template (P, E): workers/producers, diversity generators
- Y Template (A): resource allocators
- Z Template (I): integrators, leaders

Those who meshwork in the city work most effectively when they organize themselves using the roles from the beehive (described in *Chapter* 4), or Beck's XYZ Template (D. Beck & Cowan, 1996) or Adizes' PAEI roles (Adizes, 1999).

Holding the **Integrator** role (of the Z Template or I) is a team with advanced meshworking skills, that we call **Meshweavers**.

Resource Allocators act as **Meshworkers** (at the Y Template or A), organizing and allocating needed resources. They may include other integrally-informed system consultants who act as Integral City Catalysts and Practitioners as defined in the *Introduction* chapter (and who work at the city, community, and organization scales).

The **Producers and Diversity Generators** (X Template or P and E) include stakeholders from the city's 4 Voices, as well as purposely invited Thought Leaders, Designers, Practitioners, and administrators from various disciplines and sectors.

WHY1

Meshworking is a core Strategic Intelligence in the Integral City (see *Appendix* Cl). As noted above, meshworking intelligence creates a meshwork by weaving together the best of two operating systems—one that self-organizes, and one that replicates hierarchical structures that lock in learning. The resulting meshwork creates and aligns complex responsive structures and systems that flex and flow.

Meshworking intelligences are triggered by dissonance (or constraints) in the environment. Dissonance creates blocks, barriers, and problems in the system that require a new solution. Dissonance is actually necessary for change, as it motivates the desire to change and triggers the self-organizing responses that enable us to adapt. It is the source of our constant creativity, resilience, and very evolution.

At the same time, meshworking intelligence utilizes hierarchical structures and capacities to sort and select that allow the humans in the hive to make sustainability survival choices. As structural capacities emerge, new values systems emerge as well, creating a level of complexity that develops where both our individual and hive-minds can meshwork hierarchies and make hierarchies out of meshworks.

Meshworking works by connecting individuals into a collective; a collective into a network; then a network into a community of practice (COP); then a COP into a sphere of influence; and finally a global meshwork of human-hives. Some examples from our recent past include: the activism related to seatbelts, no smoking, and recycling—all once individual beliefs and practices that have become institutionalized forms of security, well-being, and sustainability.

The unique capacity of the meshworking intelligence is that it continues—through diversity generation—to produce self-organizing responses that eventually the hive mind weaves into complex hive structures.

Meshworking as an intentional social act catalyzes a shift in the human hive system to cause new capacities to emerge, and catalyzes the city system to reorganize itself into something more internally resonant and externally coherent. When this occurs, a new level of capacity emerges in the complex hierarchy of city systems and we may then be able to solve problems that we never could before at the city, regional, national, and even global scales.

Process of Meshworking

The process of meshworking applies meshworking principles as a design strategy that capitalizes on the ordering aspect of a meshwork to produce a desired end. Meshwork designs create conditions, practices, and processes that move a heap of disconnected individuals and/or organizations into a network, then a community of practice, then spheres of influence. For example, at the global level, a Netherlands team developed a practice (the health of mothers and newborns) that served Millennium Development Goal 5 (Bets, Fourman, Merry, & Voorhoeve, 2008) and the climate change summit in Brazil (Fourman & Merry, 2009a). These pioneers have become meshworkers or meshweavers on a national and international scale. In working together on these different projects they have developed a formative meshworking community of practice (based on practices described below).

This kind of skillful facilitation requires a maturity of development that embraces more than inquiry and leadership practices. It requires the processes of capacity building (for self, others, organization, and system) and the catalyzing alignment process embedded in meshworking hierarchies and self-organizing systems. The people who meshwork as Resource Allocators within the system act as meshworkers. Those who take the role of Integrators often do it as system outsiders acting as meshweavers (because these advanced skills are still limited to a small group of master practitioners who can work at the level of complexity of the city scale).

INQUIRY PRACTICE FOR MESHWORKING IN THE HUMAN HIVE: WHAT / HOW

WHAT

All meshworking processes start with a question formatted in a classic change equation[50] : **How does who, do what to whom, for what purpose, under what life conditions, where?**

For example: **How does an integrally-informed research team (who) design a program (what) for youth (whom) that builds life-giving capacities in youth, to replace gang-style behaviors (purpose) that have cost youth lives (life condition), in this city (where)?**

HOW

Integral City Book 1 (Hamilton, 2008a) describes the work of a number of meshworkers: for sustainable environments, learning communities, and

---

50   This equation originates with Dr. Don Beck and the Spiral Dynamics (1996) change methodology.

community engagement. Wheatley and Frieze (2006) propose four steps in using innovation to take projects to scale: Name (the issue, challenge, intention); Connect (people in the system); Nourish (the relationships); and Illuminate (what emerges).

A meshwork starts with a **vision** that is clearly stated—to solve a problem, invent a product, achieve new outcomes. In an emergency this may be clear and easy to formulate and accomplish because the urgency is so high. In non-acute situations, stating the vision may take months or even years to formulate—for example, agreeing on a long-term vision for a city, or the purpose for city redevelopment strategies.

Once the vision is clarified as an intended goal (and it effectively becomes the superordinate goal for the meshwork), then it is possible to backcast from the desired end and identify the strategic actions necessary to achieve it. However, although this can be drawn as a linear process (see Figure 22), in fact it is a non-linear, iterative, process of growth and emergence in a living system—the core characteristics of meshworking. Keeping this in mind, effective meshworking follows the criteria used by living systems to create value (through Placecaring) and realize that Value (through Placemaking).

Among other criteria, Beck (2010) proposes no meshwork exists until the XYZ templates emerge: X connects the pathway to realize a vision; Y provides the support; Z integrates resources to achieve the vision. He suggests that you must design from the integral paradigm, so that a natural structure can achieve the vision the system desires.

Integral City experience shows that it is important to create the conditions so that self-organizing and structuring can alternate their contribution to co-create evolutionary complexity. To do this effectively requires the understanding, experience, and reflection on the Inquiry and Action practices described in earlier chapters of this book. When we observe those practices in action we see that skilled meshworkers (in all the human hive roles) appear to interact and follow these rules:

1. Integrators (Z, I): **Catalyze fractal connections** in the human hive. (Early Integral City research showed these connections should link all quadrants and multiple levels (Hamilton, 1999).)

Imagine Durant City Process Overview

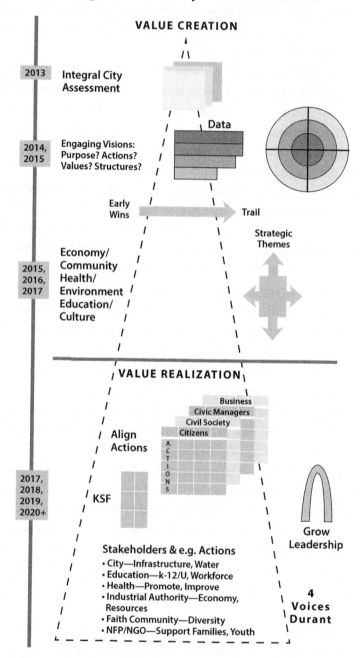

Figure 22: Meshworking as a Simplified Linear Process

2. Resource Allocators (Y, A): **Bring diverse individuals together** who would not usually encounter one another (unlikely allies).

3. Resource Allocators (Y, A): **Provide the resources and support** so that individuals can link together in a network for ongoing communication and learning.

4. Integrators and Resource Allocators (Z/Y, A): **Build bridges** across silos, stovepipes, and solitudes (Dale, 2001) that normally separate individuals and networks, and facilitate participants to create a community of practice.

5. Resource Allocators (Y, A): **Recognize the depth of capacity** in the meshwork—that not all people and organizations are working from the same worldviews, structures, or values.

6. Integrators and Resource Allocators (Z/Y, A): **Enable the multiplication of networks** and communities of practice (COP) and keep them linked in a natural integral alignment, through technologies that are appropriate to the people and situations involved.

7. Resource Allocators (Y, A): **Assist the COP to connect** across geographies so that they mesh their learning, levels, and lifecycles and develop the principles that underlie their structures and hierarchies.

8. Integrators and Resource Allocators (Z/Y, A): **Enable these structures to transform**, transcend, and transmute capacities to serve the world, by shifting into Spheres of Influence that offer new ways to make a difference.

9. Producers and Diversity Generators (X, P): **Need others to get out of the way and let people do the work** at which, they are naturally skilled and talented.

From the experience of the transnational meshworkers in Europe and the national meshworkers in Canada, it appears that the practice of meshworking enables the design of:

- Intentional Large-Scale Change
- Citizen Involvement
- Sustainable Plans

- Resourceful Management
- Resilient Evolution
- Integral Cities[51]

A City Learning Lhabitat for Meshworks in Action

Integral City's experience in one location provides an example to observe meshworks, meshworkers, and meshworking in a smaller container over a decade. This example has revealed the challenges faced by all who start out "just" to change the city, but end up in discovering that by acting on their intention they also increase the reflective capacity within the human hive. From this experience, it appears that the span of time that each of the stages of meshworking can take is often much longer than original expectations anticipate. Because these expectations are usually based on people's experience with organizational change, they also embrace assumptions about a relatively linear process for achieving a meshwork of functions within a single organization. However, the kind of commitment required to hold the space long enough for emergence to happen at the city scale demands a long-term, multi-year dedication (and even trust). Nevertheless, the observations of Wheatley and Frieze (2006) support the proposition that the "natural conditions" of meshworking—even at the city scale—can be noticeably accelerated with skillful facilitation in the roles of Integrator (Z, I) and Resource Allocators (Y, A).

The city-scale Learning Lhabitat for our study of meshworking has been the city of Abbotsford, located 100 km east of Vancouver, British Columbia, Canada (site of the Winter Olympics, 2010). The early beginnings of Integral City thinking have germinated in Abbotsford since 1984, witnessing its evolution from two predecessor municipalities to an amalgamated city; from a population of 80,000 to 140,000; from a small town

---

51   In looking at the application of meshworks to cities, a recent history of the city of New York provides an apocryphal example (Burns, 2004) of the marriage of how meshworks emerge from the combination of self-organizing and structuring capacities. Robert Moses, the powerful New York City Planner was a hierarchy structuralist, while Jane Jacobs, a new breed of community activist, became his self-appointed protagonist using a novel self-organizing approach to activism. Though neither was able to admit the merits of the other, together they brought elements of a meshwork to the city and increased its capacity for resilience because the city was forced to build infrastructure (by Moses) and engage citizens (by Jacobs).

with minimal infrastructure to the fifth largest city in British Columbia and the fastest growing city in Canada for a decade, with a university, regional hospital, and cancer agency, and recreational facilities for all ages. Integral City teams have also witnessed its reputation shift from that of a strong faith-based "City in the Country" attractive to families, to be labeled the "murder capital of Canada" (after the murders of four youth, in gang and drug related circumstances, in the first six months of 2009)—and then back again to be recognized as a youth "City of Character," to develop a strategy for "Abbotsforward" in 2015–16.

With this context of our Learning Lhab, we will share three cycles of meshworking that have enabled Integral City to experiment, develop processes, and identify principles that reveal how the elements of meshworking build on one another and the outcomes of each cycle, enabling order and creativity to emerge more complexity in this human hive. The three cycles are called: Values Mapping; Visioning for the Future; and Engaging Multiple Generations at Home and Work.

Values Mapping: What do we know about our Community anyway?

When Hamilton joined the Board of Directors for the Abbotsford Community Foundation (ACF), the first opportunity for meshworking came in 2002. The Board of Directors asked, "If we want to be an effective community foundation, what do we know about our Community anyway?" In attempting to define its purpose, ACF's big dissonance was that City Hall (and thus the City) did not have an articulated vision for itself. As a result, ACF was operating in somewhat of a vacuum. It did not have a clear context in which to be of service. By naming that undiscussable, the Board of Directors released the tension that prevented it from exploring what it was we did know about the city—and in pursuing that inquiry, discover ACF's purpose for the study.

Thus was born the conditions for mapping the values of Abbotsford's citizens using the values analysis framework that had been developed by studying the Berkana Community of Conversations using an integral lens (Hamilton, 1999).

Once the inquiry began, a series of unexpected connections emerged in a totally unplanned and self-organizing way. Partners emerged in the form of the City Recreation Department, another member of the Board of Directors who operated a Research Firm, and the community newspaper. The early integrally-informed research methodology provided some order and the city agreed to include research on Abbotsford's values in a city-wide general purpose survey. From those survey responses, an integral map of Abbotsford values emerged that showed that its key values were Family/Friends, Order/Good Management, and Community Caring. By contrast, the city's main difficulties (shadows) were unhealthy expressions of personal energy in crime, drugs, prostitution, and inappropriate boundary management. The data also showed that the community valued most the family relationships in the lower left quadrant. The data was translated into an AQAL graphical display (the Flower Map in *Appendix* K) published by the community newspaper, and shared with the Board of Directors and committees, the City management staff, and many civil society groups over the years.

From what started as a stage of exploratory self-organizing, the Values Map framed the answer to the question *"What do we know about our community?"* and became the trigger for a new stage of order in the ACF. The Foundation applied the AQAL filter to examine its granting process to ensure that it was fair and balanced. A new grants application was developed asking respondents to report on intentions. Later, ACF also used a similar framework to evaluate the quality of the granting outcomes so that it could improve its input into decision-making (see discussion in *Chapter* 7).

In summarizing the meshwork process that emerged from the values inquiry, we can identify an early stage of highly generative self-organizing and several subsequent stages of progressively greater order as new connections were made amongst stakeholders, decision-making processes and feedback loops.

Visioning for the Future: How do we imagine Abbotsford in 30 years?

Four years after the values mapping process, ACF became a catalyst for a different form of meshworking. In 2006, ACF was invited to become a regional node in the Imagine BC Dialogues. This invitation invoked a conjecture expressed by Beck (2003; D. Beck, 2004, 2007b), that in order for an applied meshwork to be effective, a vision must be shared by people working together to achieve an inspiring outcome. Such a vision embraces people's differences and aligns their motivations and goals, effectively creating an ecology of diverse agents (rather than a container of homogenous players).

The Imagine BC invitation asked, "What do we imagine Abbotsford 's future to be in thirty years?" It launched a self-organizing exploration for ACF to find partners in this new inquiry. It reached out to three other not-for-profit co-partners. ACF advanced the self-organizing process by creating a steering committee composed of skilled professionals, who volunteered their time because they wanted to live in a successful and thriving city.

Their first step was to engage more self-organization by opening a dialogue with Thought Leaders in the city through storytelling. Next, they found a new partner in the community newspaper who published the report of the dialogue in a special section and distributed it to 33,000 households in the city. This produced an ordering picture of a possible new future and launched a second stage of self-organizing. The steering committee opened their inquiry to the public and began a new cycle of self-organizing discovery and connections, which culminated in another community news publication distributed to 33,000 households. Finally, building on the two prior images of possible order, the steering committee selected a key group of policy makers to complete their self-organizing inquiry. From this third dialogue a final community news report was published and distributed to 33,000 households.

At the end of this first year of Imagine Abbotsford Dialogues, some citizens and activist groups suggested that the steering committee was a new political party, because the commitment and interaction of the group did not have a precedent. This provoked a subsequent round of dialogues in the following year that included the very people challenging the process. Over 3 years, the artful cycling between self-organizing engagement and ordering reports, enabled the emergence of a new vision for the City of Abbotsford 30 years into the future. The meshworking process engaged as much diversity in the city as possible to contribute to critical themes (which acted as strange attractors to the agents who participated and the order that emerged). The themes were:

Year 1: Economy & Environment
Year 2: Culture & Learning
Year 3: Health & Community

Imagine Abbotsford was designed as an action research and action learning process that meshworked intelligences from all sectors, ages, genders, and interests across the city. The Steering Committee estimated that over 400 different people participated (many multiple times). 33,000 households received the news reports three times per year for 3 years. Each year, the three different dialogues embraced a progression of perspectives and respondents, that started with thought leaders, then included members of the public and concluded with policy makers. The nine dialogues were published in the Abbotsford News.

The same process was honed and repeated for 3 consecutive years, and resulted in the Steering Committee proposing to the city and its three committees that serve its sustainability initiatives (Economic, Social, and Environment), that the insights and outcomes from the dialogues be integrated into the Strategic Planning Process. The City of Abbotsford agreed and subsequently went on to design a new Values Realization process that it called *Abbotsforward* (with a new mayor and a new group of stakeholders serving in the 4 roles and 4 Voices in the human hive.)

In addition, the ACF applied the recommendations (which had been analyzed using an Integral lens into Placecaring (subjective and intersubjective initiatives) and Placemaking (objective and interobjective initiatives) to create proactive endowments committed to the well-being of the city. On ACF's first event in support of the endowments, it raised $100,000 towards solutions for affordable housing and homelessness.

Imagine Abbotsford demonstrated how creating a container where civic engagement using self-organizing connections can shift the system into an order that builds dialogue bridges across silos, stovepipes, and solitudes. These bridges can then produce strategic outcomes. From the earlier meshwork associated with ACF, Imagine Abbotsford Dialogues built on the order of ACF's internal resources (people and information) that emerged from the prior meshwork and created new capacities through an inquiry that invited in multiple organizations and individuals. A core group of these people shifted into an integral worldview, which offered new ordering principles and new possibilities for applying meshworking principles in many other ways throughout the city.

Engaging Multiple Generations at Home and Work: How can youth be supported to discover options for a healthy, vibrant life in Abbotsford?

In 2009, the last year of Imagine Abbotsford, a shocking reminder of how a lack of vision and a failure to think in whole systems can undermine a city's well-being made an unwelcome headline in the news. Four young men (two just ready to graduate from high school) were murdered in the clash of gangs and drug culture.

In response to this dissonance, key meshweavers and meshworkers from the Imagine Abbotsford Dialogues formed a new collaboration for an 18-month project in 2009–2011, sponsored by SUCCESS and the province of BC's Welcoming and Inclusive Communities and Work Places initiative (WICWP). Supported by collaborative community partners, the project was designed to develop the assets of youth aged 13–34 in the city of Abbotsford. The project, named Food for Thought (FFT), was born out of the intention to create positive and proactive youth connections to businesses in the agricultural sector of the community as a means of moving them away from gang-related and antisocial behaviors.

This project had many resources to draw on because of the previous meshworking experiences—integrally informed people, paradigms, research, and intentions. Members from the Imagine Abbotsford Steering Committee joined with the BC Healthy Communities who used an integral capacity-building framework as a guiding philosophy. This project used the ordering principles of a developmental perspective on capacity-building and framed the challenge to youth within asset development, inter-sectoral partnerships, healthy public policy, and interconnected determinants of health while at the same time addressing the issues of environmental sustainability, community economic and enterprise development, and climate change (Abbotsford Team, 2009a).

Nested into the FFT Demonstration Project were two supporting projects—one for Public Education and the other for Knowledge Development and Exchange (Abbotsford Team, 2009b). The Knowledge Development and Exchange provided integrally ordering research methodology, which developed and presented updated knowledge about Abbotsford's values base. The project built on the 2003 Values Map of Abbotsford. It injected self-organizing diversity into its design by utilizing student interns to conduct a survey of values in four language groups significant to Abbotsford: English, Punjabi, Korean, and Mandarin. A random sample telephone survey was also conducted. Together, both collection methods produced data from 460 respondents. The following questions were asked: What is important in this place? What is working? What is not working? What vision of the city do people hope for? With special focus on youth and visible minorities, the map provided the values base necessary to create context for the larger Demonstration Project and to create a prototype of an Integral Vital Signs Monitor, tracking progress in creating a welcoming and inclusive Abbotsford community (see discussion of values mapping in Chapter 7 and IVSM in Chapter 8).

This project built on the information and values patterns that had emerged from the 2003 and 2010 values surveys and identified values-based vital signs that included biological, psychological, cultural, and social dimensions. The project cycled self-organizing connections among youth and food system business owners with the ordering processes of digital storytelling and entrepreneurial boot camps. The intention was to create the conditions for youth to discover and/or create linkages in our food system so that it can be sustained into the future. This challenge was framed as a leadership development exercise and community development initiative that would translate to less crime, healthier neighbourhoods, and higher personal incomes—all attractors of increased purchasing and new employees to Abbotsford.

The 2009–2011 FFT and Knowledge Development and Exchange projects arose from the self-organizing connections that had started with the 2003 Abbotsford Values Map and the insights about Abbotsford relationships and order that emerged during the 2006–2009 Imagine Abbotsford Dialogues. As it progressed, FFT moved beyond the stage of network affiliations and catalyzed diverse connections in the community into a community of practice in service to the well-being of the city's youth (and thus the well-being of the city as a whole).

All these are indicators of maturing meshworks, which the Integral Vital Signs Monitor can use to provide feedback loops that affirm life-giving directions and allow for corrective feedback to both the systems of order and systems of self-organizing in the city.

CONCLUSION: WHY2

Meshworks in Principle

When we examine the three examples of meshworking in Abbotsford, we can see the progress from values mapping to dialogic engagement to action demonstration that has emerged complexity over a decade and beyond (and incorporates many of the Inquiry and Action practices described in prior chapters).

Each of the projects has built upon the capacities that have emerged from the outcomes of prior projects. As Wheatley suggests (Wheately & Frieze, 2006), the properties of the emergent system are not simply the sum of the individual contributions. Something much greater has emerged through the mapping of values which revealed worldview patterns and relationships; through Imagining Abbotsford, which revealed a shared vision for the future which people are willing to work towards; and for the inspired community of practice that is working together to build youth capacity.

The continuity of key participants has enabled structural complexity and the interaction of new contributors has released creativity and attracted real resources into the community. It is as if the key actors in the city (Resource Allocators) are aligning passion, purpose, priorities, people, place, and planet (without necessarily being aware of the catalyzing actions seeded by the initiating change agents and Integrators).

When we look back over the three cycles, here are the steps that contributed to completing each meshworking cycle.

1. Create a system container by asking a burning question. Let finding the answer to that become the Purpose for your container's life.

2. Recognize and name the dissonance in the system—overcoming that dissonance provides the impetus or catalyst to change.

3. Identify the purpose for change—create the vision for changing from what to what?

4. Find the agents for change—enable leadership to emerge from those who have the passion for solving the catalyzing dilemma and/or attaining the vision.

5. Amplify the dissonance/catalyst/impetus for change, so others can see it.

6. Identify the resources needed to facilitate the process of change and invite others to contribute them so they can become involved.

7. Co-design a process for change that self-organizes passion, purpose, priorities, people, and planet. Expect it to be messy and enjoy the mess.

8. Engage as many stakeholders in the process as possible—actively seek out diversity and make room for difference. Ask, who else should be here?

9. Create reflective feedback loops into the system so that participants can self-correct and develop operational structures that work.

10. Make the feedback accessible to all by publication and display: community newspapers, online media, real time intelligence display systems.

11. Develop a real-time Integral Vital Signs Monitor (IVSM) so that the system can be accountable to all.

12. Celebrate goals attained, publish the results, and pay forward your learnings so that other groups, projects, networks, and communities of practice can build on your creative responses to changing life conditions and keep your environment resilient.

Meshworks in the Human Hive

Behind Integral City's understanding of the meshworking intelligence, years of local civic activism was inspired by the global and transnational inquiry of others. The work of Margaret Wheatley (Wheatley & Frieze, 2006), Peter Merry (Fourman & Merry, 2009a, 2009b), Morel Fourman (Fourman, Reynolds, Firus, & D'Ulizia, 2008), Don Beck (D. Beck, 2000a, 2004, 2010), the

Ginger Group Collaborative, and many others have inspired Integral City to adapt others' designs and insights for "glocal" outcomes. These examples are intended to demonstrate how meshworking is an emergent process that arises from partnering, collaborating, togethering, and collectively learning (now called creating "We-space" as we explored in *Chapter 2*) in the human hive. These experiments with the engagement through multi-year public dialogues, developing the capacity of civil society boards and connecting nodes of integral capacity in specific city sectors, could not have been tried without the contributions of many others from a variety of communities of practice and meshworks. These pioneers have blazed a trail (i.e., energized and created patterns in the energy field) that inspires our ability to create conditions for evolutionary intelligences in the human hive. We can enable integral capacities to naturally evolve through cycles of self-organization and ordering, and in this way expand our resilience in service to Gaia as her highest organs of reflection.

Can't you imagine that as cities mature into utilizing conscious mesh-working, a global meshwork of human hives will emerge and we will wake up one day to discover that we have meshed Integral Cities into a glocal field of a Planet of Integral Cities?

Integral City Meshworking Intelligences offer many advantages for thriving in the human hive. As we align the intelligences of governments, civil society, organizations, students, and leaders (our 4+1 Voices), together we can imagine entirely new operating systems for sustainability and resilience that enable economic, environmental, social, and cultural recovery.

With a meshworking design, we can cocreate habitats for sustainable communities, so that our human hives become healthy because our actions:

- Align capacities along a purpose-driven trajectory.
- Enhance our city and community self-images and reputations because we become effectively aligned for both Placecaring and Placemaking.
- Secure supply chains in and around Integral Cities that strategically nurture a metabolic flow of resources.
- Mitigate risk through discovering and reinforcing shared values with proximate peers.

- Attract and retain high-performers who are motivated to be effective, efficient, caring, sustainable, and resilient.
- Create opportunities for sustainable energy efficiencies as we learn how to competitively recycle energy and effort in our eco-region.
- Redefine value-added profitability for organizations, city, eco-region, and Gaia.

When multiple stakeholders mesh resources and diversity for a purpose, we create community sustainability systems that become regenerative—where we naturally align roles, intelligences, principles, and strategies that transform entire cities into living, exceptional, sustainable human hives.[52]

Meshworking is one of Integral City's key strategic intelligences. The Integral City GPS gives a reckoning to meshweavers and meshworkers that naturally points to the Integral City Master Code: To take care of yourself, each other, this Place, and this Planet.

REITERATION OF INQUIRY OBJECTIVES

The Inquiry Objectives of this chapter were:

1. Define and differentiate the meanings of meshworks, meshworking, and meshworkers.

2. Learn how the practice of meshworking expands integral intelligences for the human hive (aka city).

3. Show how meshworks integrate the self-organizing network of city relationships with hierarchies of structural organization.

4. Learn the basic design for a meshwork.

5. Understand how meshworks recalibrate networks and communities into holarchies of practice.

6. Link the intelligence of Meshworking to the intelligence of Navigating with Integral Vital Signs Monitors (IVSM).

---

52 It is interesting to note that conferences offer natural prototyping habitats for gaining meshworking skills. Conferences tend to connect some of the brightest and most advanced leaders on this planet. Conference designs can incorporate meshworking practices that will potentially expand capacities of participants and pay forward strategies into many communities and cities before, during, and after the conference.

7. Learn how the practical application of meshworking stimulates life conditions where integral capacities can naturally evolve and enable resilience in the human hive.

ACTION PLAN FOR PRACTITIONER, CATALYST, MESHWORKER

Review this chapter and make notes below of your impressions, insights, and questions. Locate yourself on the Integral City practice scaffolding. Notice what you have observed, thought, felt, and what you now want to do in any of the three possible practice configurations: as a Practitioner, as a Catalyst, as a Meshworker.

After you have made these notes, consider some of the Impact Questions (below). They also might help you reflect on how to generate impact through inquiry and action. Finally check out the Resources and Links suggested for this practice at the end of the chapter.

IMPACT QUESTIONS: DEEP, WIDE, CLEAR, HIGH

UL DEEP: How do my natural interests, talents, and values fit into the 4 roles of the Integral City (Integrator, Resource Allocator, Producer, Diversity Generator)? How do my passions contribute to the work I do? What insights might they bring to creating a meshwork?

LL WIDE: What aspects of our organizational culture could contribute to a meshwork? Where could we best serve the 4 roles of the Integral City (Integrator, Resource Allocator, Producer, Diversity Generator)? Who else should be at the meshworking table/community/network? How can we invite others to join us in a meshwork initiative?

UR CLEAR: What do I observe in the community/city systems related to some issue that matters to me? How effectively do those city systems perform? How aligned are they in their actions? How could my observations and actions make them more aligned and effective?

LR HIGH: How could our organization contribute to the network of the 4 roles of an Integral City meshwork (Integrator, Resource Allocator, Producer, Diversity Generator)? What vision energizes our organization? How does our organizational purpose align with the city's vision (and purpose)? Who else in our supply chain needs to be involved as stakeholders in a meshwork for creating city values and realizing city visions?

CHAPTER RESOURCES AND/OR LINKS

Appendix B: Integral City Maps (1–5): 2, 3, 4

Appendix C1: Definitions of 12 Intelligences: Integral, Cultural, Structural, Meshworking, Inquiry, Navigating

Appendix C3: Integral City GPS Locator: Smart, Resilient, Integral

Reflective Question for Whom /Where/ What I Could Use as:	Practitioner	Catalyst	Meshworker
What do I observe as I read?			
What do I think?			
What do I feel?			
What do I want to do next?			

MESHWORK A NEIGHBORHOOD DEVELOPMENT STRATEGY

The case study in this chapter was initiated, designed, delivered, and documented by a team working under Beth Sanders and Dynanesh Deshpande. The original document was published as Strathcona County Mature Neighbourhood Strategy, Preliminary Consultation Program: Summary Report *(anon, 2013). All quotations and page numbers in this chapter refer to that report.*

INQUIRY OBJECTIVES

The Inquiry Objectives of this chapter are:

1. Learn from a case study how to design a meshwork.

2. Describe the role of the process designers as meshweavers.

3. Understand how the 4 Voices contributed to the meshwork.

4. Identify processes, roles, and tools used in facilitating a meshwork.

5. Map out the stages used in the case study meshwork.

6. Summarize a process for evaluating a meshwork.

INTRODUCTION TO INQUIRY, ACTION, AND IMPACT FOR MESHWORKING A MATURE NEIGHBORHOOD STRATEGY

This chapter uses a case study to understand a real meshworking application based on a project completed in 2012–2013, in Strathcona County, near Edmonton, Alberta, Canada. The consultants who undertook this research were both Integral City-informed city planners (Beth Sanders, in fact, styles herself as a "civic meshworker"). They acted as designers of this study as well as the principle facilitators or "meshweavers" and harvest reporters.

The client, Strathcona County, on behalf of the city of Sherwood Park (that is situated within its boundaries), faced a challenge that is common to many cities. Sherwood Park had a number of mature neighborhoods where landowners were submitting requests to redevelop, developers were asking for re-zoning to introduce new forms of residential development, and Sherwood Park was nearing build-out within its boundaries. All of these issues and circumstances created life conditions that called for reviewing and updating existing development guidelines and planning policies. The client wanted a review of mature neighborhoods that would address: public realm improvements, infrastructure and servicing upgrades, and criteria to clarify the appropriate location, scope, scale, and aesthetics of redevelopment and infill initiatives. They intended such a review to become the first phase of a Mature Neighborhood Strategy (MNS).

FRAMING INQUIRY FOR MESHWORKING A MATURE NEIGHBORHOOD STRATEGY: WHO, WHY1

WHO

- Consultant Process Designers
- Meshweavers (Team Leaders)
- Meshworkers (Team and key stakeholders)
- City Planner
- Harvest Scribes
- Data Collectors, Surveyors, and Data Analysts
- Publisher

- Stakeholders:
  ◦ City Client
  ◦ 4 Voices of the City

When designing a meshwork, to begin with, the meshweavers do not always know who are the specific, appropriate participants. However, using Integral City frameworks they do know the stakeholders will be drawn from the 4 Voices of the city. So, the first questions to ask are: *Who are the stakeholders for this issue? Who represents the 4 Voices of the city?* Once they discover the breadth of the stakeholder boundaries, they then can determine who should be on the meshworking team.

In this case, the two designers started with their own multi-disciplinary capabilities (as city planners with strong people engagement skills) and added team members for specific processes and events. With the input of the client as civic manager, they identified candidates for the 4 Voices and moved the inquiry so they could engage the stakeholders in the city spaces in which the 4 Voices were invested and/or belonged (see Figure 23 below):

- Citizens in the Community Centre
- Business at the Chamber of Commerce
- Civil Society in their field offices
- Civic Managers at City Hall

After the selection of methods to engage the stakeholders (as discussed below) the engagement facilitators (for large and small groups), data collectors, and harvest team acted as meshworkers who perform the functions of Resource Allocation and Administration throughout the project.

WHY1

In defining the scope of any city project—and particularly a meshwork—the consultant needs to be very clear about the boundaries of the meshwork project they are undertaking. Setting these boundaries effectively delineates the intention of the meshwork. The boundaries can be defined in terms of three scopes:

- Timeline: How long is the project from initiation to final presentation and how might it be one phase of a larger project?
- Space: What is the geography of the city that will be included?
- Moral: Who will participate in the project and what are the assumptions and expectations about how people will be engaged to participate?

The Strathcona County MNS project set out its intentions this way: *Review opportunities in older neighbourhoods of Sherwood Park to redevelop, intensify and create complete and sustainable communities with the support of the local residents.* (Strathcona County Mature Neighbourhood Strategy, 2013, p.3)

The consulting team framed their study within the context of 3 phases needed to achieve the desired strategy. They clarified with the client and the meshworking team that their project was Phase 1 of a 3-phase program:

- Phase 1 was the Inquiry Phase.
- Phase 2 was the Designing Strategy Phase.
- Phase 3 was the Implementing Strategy Phase.

The team set out the timeline and identified the space locations and people engagement scope in their timeline (see Figure 23).

The team also located the mature neighborhoods on geo-spatial maps, which they referenced frequently throughout the project and in their final report.

INQUIRY PRACTICE FOR MESHWORKING A MATURE NEIGHBORHOOD STRATEGY: WHAT / HOW

WHAT

The inquiry question for a meshwork design acts as a superordinate goal itself, while the issue that it addresses seeks an answer that also becomes a superordinate goal.[53] As will become clear in the discussion below, the superordinate goal acts as a "strange attractor" to bring people to the

---

53   A superordinate goal is a goal that transcends and includes other goals in a way that everyone supports because they see that their own interests are addressed by pursuing it.

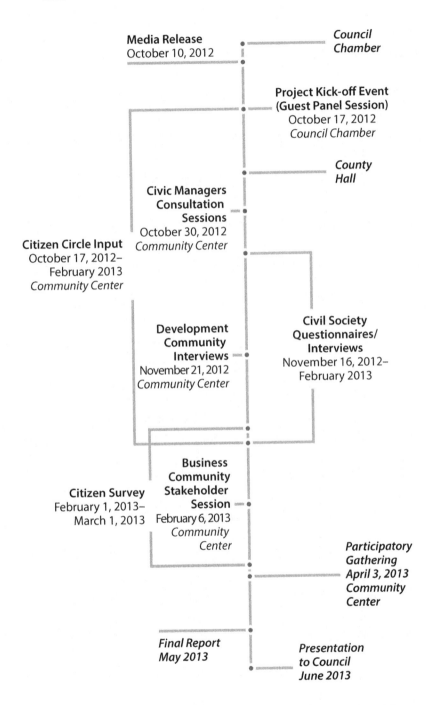

Figure 23: Sherwood Park Project Timeline, 4 Voices, Locations (MNS, p. 18)

table to achieve it. It also becomes the energizing point towards which the meshwork aligns.

The inquiry question for this project followed the classic meshworking question set out in *Chapter 13*: **How does who, do what to whom, for what purpose, under what life conditions, where?**[54]

The inquiry question for designing and facilitating a meshwork for Phase I of the MNS was:

How does the consulting team develop a multi-modal process for Sherwood Park to engage the 4 Voices of the city about concerns and issues related to developing mature neighborhoods, locating the engagements in or close to their mature neighborhood locations?

HOW

Define the Consultation Framework and Methods

The Integrator meshweavers (design consultants and project team leaders), organized the meshworkers (team and key stakeholders) to perform the various resource allocating and administrative tasks as required by their design.

The team started by planning the project within the Integral City framework of the 4 Voices. They set out to learn for each of these differing groups, their priorities, business models, and aspirations. They customized a variety of engagement methods to adapt to the needs of each Voice and optimize their contribution.

After engaging separately with the 4 Voices, they concluded their research with a Participatory Gathering of all 4 Voices together. All of the data gathered from these engagements was then analyzed and synthesized into key themes that were geo-physically mapped and/or charted in various ways. At the end of the project, the analysis was incorporated into a report using the 4 Voices framework, which was organized aesthetically using an iconic graphic of the 4 Voices that they called the stakeholder wheel (see Figure 24).

---

54 The concept of the superordinate goal and this equation originates with Dr. Don Beck and the Spiral Dynamics (1996) change methodology.

The team selected appropriate methods (e.g., survey questionnaires, interviews, and focus groups) to address a variety of qualitative questions to which all participants responded. In addition, each participant group received customized questions to identify their specific challenges. This design ensured that stakeholder input avoided personal biases and identified what they really valued in mature neighborhoods, as well as what issues had direct impact on their quality of life and services that were provided in any business models. Quantitative questions identified citizen demographics to provide context for further interpretation of results (based on age, gender, postal code, etc.).

The methods used for each of the 4 Voices are described next.

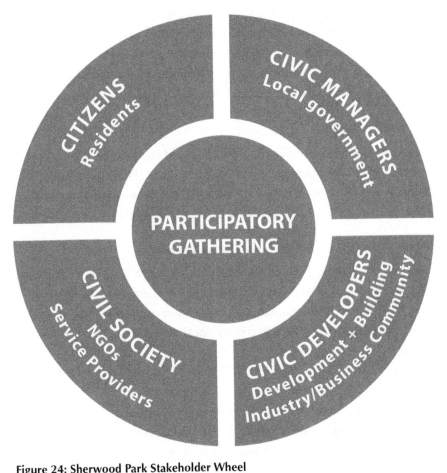

Figure 24: Sherwood Park Stakeholder Wheel

Citizens: Methods for Engagement

Citizen Circles

The team selected **Citizen Circles** as the primary method of engagement for people who have a vested interest in and knowledge of the Mature Neighborhood where they live. The circles gave citizens an opportunity to gather when and where they chose at their own convenience. The team prepared a workbook to guide discussion and record and submit input. The workbooks were designed to obtain information from residents on demographic trends and quality of life. The workbooks were widely and conveniently accessible both online and in paper format at project events and the County offices.

This method was designed to be convenient, accessible, and exploratory but not exhaustive. Citizen Circles commenced in October 2012 and continued through February 2013. Completed workbooks were personally delivered to a County address, mailed, electronically mailed, and also faxed.

Data collection produced 62 workbooks, representing 216 citizens.

Social Media

In addition to the Citizen Circles, citizens could contribute via social media to the County's Facebook page and Twitter account. They could also receive periodic updates via these channels when the team issued information, invitations to participate, or points of interest related to the project.

Civic Managers: Methods for Engagement

The Civic Managers (CM) as a group were characterized by their professional training, knowledge, and interests in the issues of the Mature Neighborhoods. Civic Managers included municipal planners, infrastructure specialists, councilors, and other local government representatives.

Civic Manager Workshop Day: Circles, Small Groups, World Cafés, Mapping

A one-day session to convene the multi-disciplinary expertise of the Civic Managers used a series of methods, starting and ending with a **plenary circle**. The plenary circles allowed participants to identify their perspectives (first circle) and to share their learnings (final circle).

After the opening circle, the Civic Managers were divided into **small groups of mixed professionals** where they were given a **mapping** exercise to geo-spatially identify and locate all the challenges related to MNS.

The next method introduced a **World Café** process where small groups were asked to identify issues and challenges that could *not* be mapped. In this process, the Civic Managers started in one small group and then moved to multiple tables to cross-pollinate the exploration. Ultimately, this people-weaving process produced a set of themes that were captured in a **Wordle** in the final report.

The last method was an **Interdepartmental Charting** activity. Civic Managers identified the roles they might play to improve quality of life in a MNS. Each Civic Manager identified tasks they might perform during the project timeline. These were then summarized into the rows and columns of a matrix that clearly identified interdepartmental connections. This revealed the degree of cooperation and collaboration that would be needed to achieve a MNS.

Civil Society: Methods for Engagement

Civil Society included organizations such as school boards, housing agencies, health systems, faith communities, not-for-profits (NFPs), advocacy groups, and both public and private organizations. Civil Society organizations provided vital services for discovering, sustaining, and developing quality of life. Because these groups represented communities both broadly or specifically, it was critical to design methods that could tap their city intelligences.

The Civil Society groups who provided data for this project were:

- Clubs and Common Interest Groups
- County Initiatives and Advisory Boards
- Education Organizations
- NFP Organizations
- Faith-based Organizations.

Targeted customized telephone interviews were used to gather specific input from a wide range of organizations. Prior to the interview, participants received background information on the project. Each interview was customized to gather organization-specific information.

Questionnaire Surveys were also sent to 30 Civil Society organizations serving the Mature Neighborhood in Strathcona.

Data collected from the Civil Society groups was analyzed by organizational source (as noted above) and summarized under the headings:

- Impacts of infill, redevelopment, and increased population density
- Challenges facing Civil Society and the people they serve
- Specific issues or impacts the County should address

Civic Developers: Methods for Engagement

Civic Developers (CD) build the community through the physical environment and the services they provide. In this project they were both individuals and organizations and were divided into two groups:

- Development/Building Industry (DBI)
- Business Community

In-Person Interviews were used to collect data from the Development/Building Industry (DBI). The DBI included architects, developers, builders, housing foundations and co-ops, professional DBI organizations, and County boards and groups involved in regulating development in the County. Each interview included one or two people and lasted 30 to 45 minutes.

The interviews focused on current and future development plans, existing opportunities and barriers to infill and redevelopment, appropriate types of infill and redevelopment, the County's role in facilitating appropriate scale of infill and redevelopment projects and current land use policy and regulations.

Themes gathered from this data were summarized in a table by Organizational Source under the headings:

- Most Appropriate Types of Infill and Redevelopment
- Barriers and Opportunities for Infill and Redevelopment
- County Role and Changes Needed to Clarify Current Land Use Policy and Regulations.

A Focus Group/World Café session was designed for the Business Community stakeholders. These stakeholders included a variety of businesses from small to large, located in many business types from free-standing to strip malls to indoor shopping malls. This was organized with the local Chamber of Commerce for a small group of 12 representatives for a two-hour session.

The World Café small groups considered the questions:

- What is great about your neighborhoods?
- What would you like your future relationship with these Mature Neighborhoods to be?
- For business success what investments need to be made in your Mature Neighborhood?

The data collected (under the headings: Existing community assets, Changes necessary to local businesses, and Necessary investments for business success) was shared as a Wordle in the final report.

4 Voices, Multi-Stakeholders: Methods for Engagement

To bring the 4 Voices together, the designers created an afternoon session for participants to gather and an evening session for the public to view an exhibit of the results of the process.

A **Participatory Gathering** was designed to bring together all the 4 Voices so that they could hear their own and other Voices' emerging themes and share them with the County. In addition, this gathering added value to the project because it created an interactive platform where all Voices could work together and collectively discuss issues affecting them and establish a path for moving forward. This gathering included 54 participants: 25 Citizens from 11 Mature Neighborhoods (minimum 2 from each Mature Neighborhood), 8 Civil Society Agencies, 8 Civic Developers, and 13 Civic Managers (both staff and elected officials).

Working in a series of **Small Groups**, participants were asked to review the data from each group and offer opinions on what was *Most Important* to each group. Then in new groups participants looked for what was *Consistent* in the feedback that was similar across all stakeholder groups. Then the groups identified what was *Inconsistent* or different in stakeholder groups. In new groups again, participants then identified what *Needed the Collective Attention* of all stakeholders.

A **World Café** was the penultimate process used to ask the participants how important developing a strategy was to the future of Mature Neighborhoods and how to engage the 4 Voices.

The **Final Circle** brought the large group back together to summarize the learnings from the months-long process and the discoveries of the day.

A **Public Open House** followed the afternoon Participatory Gathering. This presented an exhibit of the data collected and analysis generated to date. Citizens were invited to review the exhibit and provide further feedback (on both information provided and the processes used).

Aligning, Integrating, Harvesting, and Reporting

For a meshwork to be successful, the designers and meshweavers must align the 4 Voices so that they can optimize their functions in the city from the perspective of the 12 Intelligences and 4 Voices (see *Chapters 5, 6,* and *9*). In this MNS example we can see how the 4 Voices were aligned to recognize time, space, and moral contributions (see Figure 23).

Before the project team commences its interaction with stakeholders, the designer/meshweavers must assign tasks to team members to ensure methodical practices for data collection (at each interaction), analysis (during and after interaction), and synthesis of themes (during and after interactions and between stakeholder groups).[55]

The design team can optimize "simple" data collection by reframing it within the context of "harvesting." Harvesting transcends and includes data into a reflective meaning-making container that anticipates how outcomes and impacts will be most effectively conveyed by combining narrative with visual and auditory (and sometimes performing) arts. Considerable added value is contributed by non-verbal harvesting processes such as

---

55 These practices are not detailed here because they are well-documented elsewhere in methodologies for Action Research (Coghlan & Brannick, 2007; Stringer, 1999), Action Inquiry (W. Torbert & Associates, 2004; William R. Torbert, Livne-Tarandach, Herdman-Barker, Nicolaides, & McCallum, 2008) and Qualitative Research (Berg, 2004; Creswell, 1998; Merriam, 2002; Palys, 1997).

graphic facilitation, photography, videography, and audio recording. These contributions can then be woven into the final report distribution channels to illustrate with images, color, and enlivening ideas.

A very important integrating task of the design team is to agree with the client on the process of reporting the results. This involves decisions about the format, distribution channels, and of course the budget for communicating the results of the study. Attention to this final step of any phase of a project can ensure its success. However, for a first phase, like this example of the MNS illustrates, attention to reporting can amplify the investment in the whole multi-phase meshworking endeavor. The reporting activity provides a feedback loop back to the multiple stakeholders—both those who participated and those who did not. In this way, the harvest informs the city system and expands its interconnections—and thereby its health or well-being. Remember: **If you want to improve the health of a system, connect it to more of itself** (as noted in Chapter 10).

Sharing the harvest strategically can mean the difference between the first phase of a longer-term project being stillborn or surviving so that momentum is generated for Phases 2 and 3 to complete the whole cycle.

Recognizing the importance of communicating the harvest outcomes of the whole meshwork design is strategically critical, especially if the report is to be delivered on multiple platforms: as a printed document, as a PDF downloadable from a website, as an executive summary recorded for YouTube; as key points on Facebook, or as eblasts via Twitter.

Communicating the Harvest

Keeping in mind the vital reasons for designing an effective report, the MNS design team organized the summaries of their data analysis and synthesis into chapters based on the 4 Voices. Their Table of Contents reflects all the principles that they used for the meshwork design and implementation organized around the 4 Voices:

- Project Outline
- Citizens
- Civic Managers
- Civil Society

- Civic Developers
- Participatory Gathering
- Conclusions
- Appendices

Each chapter provided an Introduction, Description of Engagement Methods, Summary Results, and Emerging themes.

Lastly, the Conclusion integrated the results from all the engagements and presented a framework for evaluation of the original intent through the Summary of the Emerging Themes, Recommendations, Next Steps, and an Evaluation of the Process.

CONCLUSION: WHY2

This case study reveals the core design differences between **traditional development experts** providing a professional consultation to city hall on the issue of a Mature Neighborhood Strategy and a **meshworking design team** cocreating a habitat for discovery for, with, and as the 4 Voices of the city. In the spirit of Action Learning and Action Research, the meshweavers and meshworkers in this case study were co-researchers. Their role was to create the life conditions (habitat) that catalyzed the people who made up the city systems to express their knowing (individually and collectively), enable learning, align intelligences, and discover the purpose, priorities, and praxis (operational functions) of the strategy that naturally fits the people and place (and planet).

This case study provides a self-documenting evaluation of a design built on attaining a superordinate goal by engaging the two major systems required for the emergence of a meshwork namely:

- The integrating organization of hierarchies and holarchies embedded in the time, space, and moral boundaries and methodologies of the project design.
- The self-organizing opportunities for interconnections built into the methods for engaging the 4 Voices homogenously (in separate groups) and heterogeneously (in combined groups).

The hierarchical systems of organizing frameworks (sequencing, timelines, locations, participant selection) enabled learning to surface as the project unfolded. This became especially important in its concluding stages of synthesis and generation of recommendations and next steps.

The second system of self-organizing people engagements and interactions allowed for unexpected discoveries, surprises, continuous learning, new combinations, and innovation to occur throughout the project.

It is the interplay between these two systems that generates capacities for sustainability through using a framework of useful practices (which can be replicated and eventually institutionalized in the city) and capacities for resilience through imagination, adaptation, playing around, and inventing (which generate the art and energy of creativity and innovation in the city).

Understanding the importance of both systems also reveals the importance of the roles of the meshworking team. The designers/meshweavers act as Integrators who guide the whole process while paying attention that the hierarchical methodology supports the self-organizing engagement methods and that the self-organizing data collection engagements feed the hierarchical systems. The engagement facilitators, harvesters, and other team members act as Resource Allocators and Administrators who ensure outcomes and impacts happen at each engagement level.

The 4 Voices themselves are the meshwork's Producers, generating the data, insights, ideas, and opportunities that the meshweavers and the meshworkers gather and align into the emerging meshwork—whose purpose is to answer the question that originally started the whole project.

In the end, the meshworking team evaluated the success of the meshwork (and project) by returning to their superordinate goal. The MNS study examined the responses that emerged from asking the question that precipitated the meshworking process (set out in WHAT above).

The MNS meshworking team offered an excellent Concluding Summary in their report that evaluated the effectiveness of the meshworking approach that they designed—including "speed bumps" as well as highlights. The last line in the report captured the core value of designing a meshwork process: "**Such an approach enabled the stakeholders to take leadership and provide clear direction about what is valuable for them.**" (Strathcona County Mature Neighbourhood Strategy, 2013, p. 89)

Here is the full text of the MNS Conclusion:

The consultation program provided a unique opportunity for citizens, the business community, the development community, civil agencies and County staff to provide their input on issues related to mature neighbourhoods at a very early stage of the project. The Guest Panel Session provided initial push to generate interest about mature neighbourhoods. The Citizen Circles enabled informal group discussions and an opportunity to provide collective opinions. The informal nature of the Citizen Circle format received a mixed response. Citizens who got involved in the process were looking for more clarity in terms of project purpose, overall mandate and the actual trigger that might have initiated the project. The issues of infill housing dominated discussions. The ongoing project updates and additional informal citizen circle meetings organized by the County sought to provide additional clarity to ensure citizens that the project scope will address all aspects of mature neighbourhoods such as servicing, ongoing maintenance, public realm improvements and potential new developments. In addition, a Citizen Survey was also mailed to all households in 11 mature neighbourhoods. These efforts received a good response from citizens for both Citizen Circle and Citizen Survey questionnaires. The qualitative and quantitative responses ensured that key issues and opportunities were properly documented. The focus group sessions, one on one interviews and telephonic questionnaires ensured targeted input from civil agencies, civic developers and municipal staff. The Participatory Gathering event provided an opportunity to all stakeholders to review each other's feedback and finally summarize key emerging themes relevant to the future of mature neighbourhoods. Such an approach enabled the stakeholders to take leadership and provide clear direction about what is valuable for them.

REITERATION OF INQUIRY OBJECTIVES

The Inquiry Objectives of this chapter were:

1. Learn from a case study how to design a meshwork.
2. Describe the role of the process designers as meshweavers.
3. Understand how the 4 Voices contributed to the meshwork.
4. Identify processes, roles and tools used in facilitating a meshwork.
5. Map out the stages used in the case study meshwork.
6. Summarize a process for evaluating a meshwork.

ACTION PLAN FOR PRACTITIONER, CATALYST, MESHWORKER

Review this chapter and make notes below of your impressions, insights, and questions. Locate yourself on the Integral City practice scaffolding. Notice what you have observed, thought, felt, and what you now want to do in any of the three possible practice configurations: as a Practitioner, as a Catalyst, as a Meshworker.

After you have made these notes, consider some of the Impact Questions (below). They also might help you reflect on how to generate impact through inquiry and action. Finally check out the Resources and Links suggested for this practice at the end of the chapter.

IMPACT QUESTIONS: DEEP, WIDE, CLEAR, HIGH

UL DEEP: What level of skill do I consider my Integral City activator capacities—Practitioner, Catalyst, Meshworker? How could I most effectively bring my highest good to contribute to a meshwork? What challenges might I encounter in the process of meshworking?

LL WIDE: What organizational or sectoral relationships in our community or city are aligned? Misaligned? How do we see our organization as part of the 4 Voices of the city? How could our collaborations improve with the process of meshworking? Who else should we invite to a meshworking table that we might jointly assemble? How can our interests attract others to join us in a meshwork initiative? How would they benefit?

UR CLEAR: What city issues matter to the success of my organization in the city? What is my role in the organization in relation to those issues? How could the process of meshworking improve my organizational effectiveness? How could a change in organizational effectiveness impact our sector? The 4 Voices? The city as a whole?

LR HIGH: How can our city's Civic Managers initiate a meshworking process to align stakeholders around a key issue? Why is it important that stakeholders from all 4 Voices contribute to solving this key issue? In the city's key supply chains (metabolic economy) who are the Integrators, Resource Allocators, Producers, Diversity Generators? What question might act as a superordinate goal to attract the 4 Voices to align in a meshwork to discover a workable answer/approach?

CHAPTER RESOURCES AND/OR LINKS

Appendix B: Integral City Maps (1–5): 1, 2, 3, 4

Appendix C1: Definitions of 12 Intelligences: **Integral, Structural, Cultural, Inquiry, Meshworking, Navigating**

Appendix C3: Integral City GPS Locator: **Integral**

Reflective Question for Whom /Where/ What I Could Use as:	Practitioner	Catalyst	Meshworker
What do I observe as I read?			
What do I think?			
What do I feel?			
What do I want to do next?			

SECTION VIII — *Evaluate Impact*

These last two chapters consider the challenge of evaluating the success of Integral City interventions. They are designed to reflect the action learning and action research spiral of inquiry that progresses through the classic action research stages of: observe, plan, act, review, learn, repeat. They unpack the reflective questions that underpin the design of each of our chapters of:

What (do we observe)?
So What (does this mean?)
Now What (are we going to do as a result)?

This cycle of reflection can take us right back to where we began in the Knowing Field. We could easily return to *Chapter 1* to complete the journey of Placecaring and Placemaking and we encourage readers to do that because you will discover deep insights about the patterns embedded in your inquiry, action, and impact.

However, we also ground the cycle of Placecaring and Placemaking with an evaluation process that is itself a fractal of the cycle. In order to be coherent with our many propositions that an Integral City is a meta-system, our approach to evaluation is based on a systems view of life. This view

(Capra, 1996) considers that a system is alive when it can survive, adapt to its environment, and reproduce or regenerate. Research indicates those life processes are only possible because the system utilizes feedback to inform it of its success in surviving, adapting, and regenerating. This feedback is the most basic form of evaluation—on the life-giving level. Deriving from these basic premises, we suggest that a living, learning, systems frame is required to design an evaluation process that is sufficient to the task of providing feedback (i.e., measuring) the success of Integral City processes for the benefit of all stakeholders, including both those who participated in any formal research and those who were part of the larger city system that is always the container for the research. In striving to map out that evaluative and reflective feedback loop, we have borrowed from aspects of the qualitative approaches of Patton's utilization evaluation (Patton, 2013), the circular flow of the Kellogg Logic Model (anon, 2004, nd) and the complexity scales of Thrivability (Wood & Bruitzman, 2016).

In Chapter 15, we keep in mind these basic tenets and influences, and describe a basic evaluation process that can be applied to any of the processes outlined in previous chapters. Chapter 16 summarizes key elements of the basic structure of the entire book: Inquiry (what are the questions we have asked to start each area of research); Action (what are the processes we have undertaken to learn about our Human Hive; and Impact (to what path do we commit in pursuing our journey to well-being in the city)?

EVALUATE INTEGRAL CITY IMPACT WITH INTEGRATIVE EVALUATION PROCESS

INQUIRY OBJECTIVES

The Inquiry Objectives of this chapter are:

1. Differentiate between monitoring vital signs and evaluating.

2. Consider the reasons to evaluate.

3. Outline the steps in designing an evaluation.

4. Learn the basics of logic modeling.

5. Apply a logic model to a city change process.

6. Evaluate the evaluation process.

INTRODUCTION TO INQUIRY, ACTION AND IMPACT WITH INTEGRATIVE EVALUATION PROCESS

In Chapter 8, we explored the value of developing an Integral Vital Signs Monitor. Vital signs are designed and intended for monitoring the ongoing aliveness and well-being of a system. They are the pulses we take to measure if the city systems are performing against predetermined targets for well-being. We suggested there were nine clusters of vital signs to monitor on an ongoing basis. These metrics become the indicators on the dashboard of city hall who monitors their readings on behalf of all 4 Voices and the stakeholders of the city.

An evaluation, on the other hand, is an assessment of a particular project, program, or process whose boundaries have been scoped out by the research team and in an Integral City consulting process, also with the client. The systemic form of evaluation that we use is quite fractal—it can be used at any scale—individual, group, organization, community, city. In fact it could be used not only for evaluating any of the Integral City processes or projects addressed in the chapters of this book (such as implementing an Integral Vital Signs Monitor) but it could be used to conduct a meta-evaluation of the whole Inquiry-Action-Impact process—exploring systemic constellations, implementing the Master Code, assessing the 12 Intelligences, mapping city values, designing an integral vital signs monitor, convening the 4 Voices, prototyping learning habitats, and meshworking stakeholders.

The evaluation process also aligns with core principles of the Integral City Action Research/Learning methodology that we have described in previous chapters. It assumes that the evaluation team integrates the spirit and action of co-researchers, including both the Integral City members and the city/client stakeholders as designers and implementers of the evaluation process.

Where a contract has been drafted with the client, integrative evaluation processes (which may be included as Appendices to the contract) summarize the evidence that demonstrates the contract has progressed as intended (formative feedback) and/or has been completed (summative feedback). This developmental/learning approach to evaluation is therefore a form of reality check (see Figure 25) to discover did we accomplish:

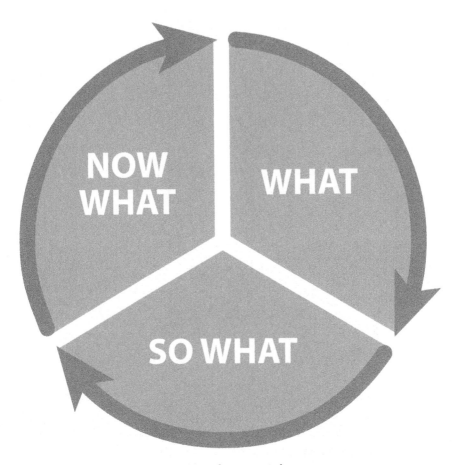

Figure 25: Reality Check—What, So What, Now What

- **What** we set out to do?
- **So What** do we do/think/relate/create as a result of using the inputs to produce the outputs?
- **Now What** are the next steps we take as a result of the outcomes producing the intended impacts?

Our integrative evaluation is clearly a completion of a cyclic process (as in Figure 26) that sets out to answer a research question and confirms with evidence what answer we discovered and then suggests with recommendations a new learning platform to move us forward to the next opportunity.

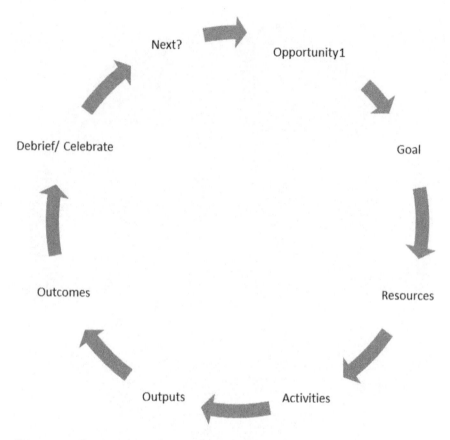

Figure 26: Kellogg Logic Model Cycle

The systems approach that Integral City uses to design evaluation borrows a simple methodology to document the design and map the elements of the evaluation process. The classical design of the Kellogg Logic Model (anon, 2004) provides a simple format to set out the factors we can use to measure the formative and summative stages of our project goals (see Figure 27). The key elements that the model identifies and tracks are:

- **Opportunity Statement**: What life conditions provide the context for embarking on the project?
- **Goal Description**: How do we define the goal we intend to achieve as the overriding outcome of the project?

- **Assumptions**: How do we scope the project in terms of time, space, and moral constraints? What are the limitations and delimitations of the project?
- **Resources/Inputs**: What assets, capacities, and resources do we bring as inputs to energize and fuel the project?
- **Activities**: Who does what, with whom, when, and where?
- **Outputs**: What tangible, quantitative deliverables will be produced by the project? How can we measure them using SMART[56] metrics?
- **Impacts Measured as Outcomes** (short-term, mid-term, long-term): What quantitative and qualitative outcomes will produce impact in 1-year, 3-year, 5-year time frames?

These factors can often be displayed on a one-page document that crystallizes the intentions and flow of work into a graphical flow (as illustrated in Figure 27).

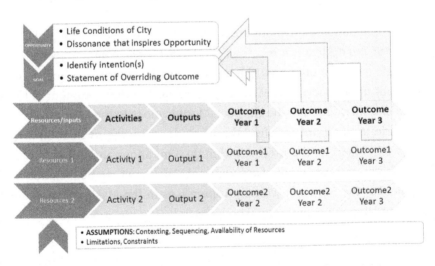

Figure 27: Logic Model Overview

One of the reasons that this form of evaluation modeling is very powerful is that it works for many audiences (coming from all quadrants and all levels), multiple purposes, various implementation strategies, and a

---

56   Specific, Measurable, Accountable, Relevant, Trackable ("SMART criteria," n.d.)

range of evaluation scopes. It is both visual in the sequencing of the elements and textual in briefly describing them. The Logic Model can be very succinctly summarized in templates and tables, but also unpacked into longer narratives or high-appeal visual and/or graphical presentations, if required.

(An example of a logic model from a generic contract is presented in *Appendix J*).

FRAMING INQUIRY WITH INTEGRATIVE EVALUATION PROCESS: WHO, WHY1

WHO

- Integral City Contractor
- Client
- Project Team

The evaluation logic model may be first drafted by the Integral City contractor, but optimally it is co-designed with the client and project team. The logic model(s) unpack(s) the deliverables for the project and helps the client understand how each stage is related to the statement of the scope of work defined in the contract. Modifications to the logic model(s) are made until all are satisfied that they describe the evaluation map that will be used for the project within the limitations and delimitations identified in the statement of assumptions. They can then be included as outlines for the Scope of Work in Appendices in the Master Agreement between client and contractor (see *Appendix J*).

WHY1

The purpose of an Integral City evaluation is to confirm that the work that was proposed was completed within the scope of time, space, and moral influence—basically when, where, and with whom the project commits to generating deliverables in its written and/or verbal contract.

In a complex, multi-year project a series of logic models may be required to track the series of goals identified within the various subsystems of the city. For example, a long-term city development contract might have these major Project Goals (each with its own deliverables):

Placecaring

- Coach and develop an executive team/board.
- Train and coach staff and volunteers.
- Develop a city vision and communicate it to city stakeholders.
- Map the values of the city and develop an Integral Vital Signs Monitor.

Placemaking

- Conduct core sustainability and service reviews of city functions and service departments.
- Develop master city sustainability plan.
- Develop plans for (re)development of specific geo-spatial areas of the city.
- Develop strategies for implementation of plans.

Each of these goals would have a logic model mapped out to track its progress and completion. In addition, a project management platform may also be used such as Microsoft Project or Gaiasoft™. As a minimum, a Gantt graph matrix will identify the estimated timeline for key activities (as shown in Table 21).

Table 21: Project Timeline

Activity	Year 1	Year 2	Year 3	Year 4	Year 5
1	X	X			
2		X	X		
3		X	X		
4			X	X	
5				X	X
6					X

INQUIRY PRACTICE WITH INTEGRATIVE EVALUATION PROCESS: WHAT / HOW

WHAT

The inquiry question for integrative evaluation centers around: **How did we achieve the goal that the opportunity presented and that we set out to accomplish?**

The opportunity and goal are stated as the opening statements of the logic model. All the other elements of the logic model are set out on the circular path designed to achieve the goal (as shown above in Figure 26).

HOW

The process of evaluation may be undertaken at any time during the project and at its conclusion. Using logic models allows for the mapping of deliverables that are both Outputs (generally, quantitative visible material artefacts) and Outcomes (quantitative and qualitative artefacts that are categorized into short-, medium-, and long-term time frames). Thus, the logic model can be revisited multiple times throughout the project by the project team and the client for formative feedback (work in progress) and summative feedback (completion of work).

With an Action Research/Learning perspective the co-researchers can review the logic model and consider progress with these questions:

- Are we managing to stay on course of the scheduled timeline?
- Are all our resources available and performing as planned?
- Have we undertaken the sequence of activities identified on the logic model?
- Are we producing the intended outputs? On time? At the level of quality intended?
- Are we achieving the intended outcomes in the short, medium, long term?

In all cases, if the answers are positive, the team can affirm progress and continue on course. On the other hand, if any response is negative, then the team needs to review the situation and agree what steps to take to correct their course.

The project manager may utilize a number of project management platforms/applications and team management decision-making models to manage the project. Those will unpack the logic models into trackable tasks that are assigned to specific team members.

Formative evaluation should be scheduled into project work on a recurring basis (weekly, bi-weekly, or monthly) so that the team maintains a continuous overview of the progress of the whole project, at the same time keeping each other informed about specific activities, accountabilities, and achievements.

One project management system that we find especially useful for Integral City work and evaluation is the integrative decision-making process developed by Holacracy™. Holacracy is a purpose driven, leadership process that assumes that the complexities of life will *prevent* a direct, unaltered progression from start to finish. Instead it assumes that what is needed is "dynamic steering" like the process used in riding a bicycle—which requires a series of course corrections as the rider moves along the intended route (which we have mapped out into a logic model). In order to make those course corrections with a team, the integrative decision-making process enables team members to *optimize* individual contributions within a container of collective intelligence that makes the best possible decisions for course direction and correction at any given time while expecting that changes will continue to happen. This creative process resolves tensions and conflicts that can undermine intentions and plans. It enables optimization of project activities and prevents misutilization of resources while keeping the project moving forward logically. The process thus replaces the constraints of rigid linearity and hierarchy with flexibility and flow that invites innovation and creativity from all the co-researchers. The basics of the integrative decision-making process are summarized in *Appendix L* and are more fully explained on Holacracy's website: http://www.holacracy.org/

The final stage of integrative evaluation is to debrief and celebrate the achievement of the first stage of achieving outcomes. This is an important part of the development cycle because it is the time for co-researchers to reflect, recognize, and renew their energy, since they have completed the work that they set out to do. In integrative evaluation, even if a project is redefined, cut short, or abandoned, we recommend this step be maintained.

The opportunity for learning is always available—and as we noted in *Chapter* 11, when prototyping—sometimes the most powerful learning arises from failure. But with integrative evaluation, if that is the apparent outcome, the attitude must be the same as the great inventors (Edison, Bell, Musk) who knew the value of discovering how *not* to do something was a vital step on the road to achieving the goal they ultimately sought.

CONCLUSION: WHY2

Integrative evaluation is a form of harvesting for any Integral City project. Integrative evaluation is a process of formal reflection on the work we have designed—whether that be Placecaring or Placemaking or both.

Large cities will no doubt have whole departments that manage projects, along with professional project managers. However, smaller cities may not have any of these resources and will depend on the Integral City contractor to make sense of the goals, the process to achieve them, and the model to track progress.

Integral City contractors should be interested in the formative evaluations that occur during the progress of the project as well as the summative evaluation at the end of the project. Because both experiences should bring together the co-researchers (client and project team) they offer opportunities to develop and deepen the relationship with the client stakeholders. Therefore, this form of integrative evaluation, instead of causing conflicts or being punitive, is a creative, problem-solving, capacity-building process.

With both formative and summative evaluation, the Integral City team should be practicing the reflection of their own personal performance, their performance as a team, and the performance of the client/city relationship. This approach to integrative evaluation enacts the Master Code of caring for self, others, and place. The team must also ensure ongoing evaluation of the project achievements over the mid- to long-term so that the evidence of the project work can be clearly tracked with deliverables in the form of outputs and outcomes. It is the combination of the qualitative Placecaring practices along with the quantitative Placemaking practices that integrates into the developmental learning that characterizes the cycle of Integral City work. As each project team evaluates their success they model the impacts of growing Gaia's reflective city organ—and the organelles and cells within it.

REITERATION OF INQUIRY OBJECTIVES

The Inquiry Objectives of this chapter were:

1. Differentiate between monitoring vital signs and evaluating.
2. Consider the reasons to evaluate.
3. Outline the steps in designing an evaluation.
4. Learn the basics of logic modeling.
5. Apply a logic model to a city change process.
6. Evaluate the evaluation process.

ACTION PLAN FOR PRACTITIONER, CATALYST, MESHWORKER

Review this chapter and make notes below of your impressions, insights, and questions. Locate yourself on the Integral City practice scaffolding. Notice what you have observed, thought, felt, and what you now want to do in any of the three possible practice configurations: as a Practitioner, as a Catalyst, as a Meshworker.

After you have made these notes, consider some of the Impact Questions (below). They also might help you reflect on how to generate impact through inquiry and action. Finally check out the Resources and Links suggested for this practice at the end of the chapter.

IMPACT QUESTIONS: DEEP, WIDE, CLEAR, HIGH

UL DEEP: What is my experience with evaluation at a personal level? How has formative evaluation helped me to optimize my performance in various situations and/or projects? How did summative evaluation contribute to my learning process throughout my career?

LL WIDE: How does our organization practice evaluation? Who is responsible for designing the evaluation process? Who participates in the implementation of the evaluation? In what ways do we use formative evaluation to improve quality control, develop relationships, and improve service? How is formative evaluation a form of organizational learning for our organization?

UR CLEAR: What actions or behaviors have I had evaluated in my life? In sports? In performing arts? In professional practice? How did evaluation change my behaviors in positive ways? In negative ways?

LR HIGH: How does our organization design into our functions and systems feedback processes that help us improve performance? How does our organization value team learning? Team evaluation? How do we set goals and performance targets that contribute to evaluation processes? How do evaluation processes contribute to institutionalizing standards of performance? What other organizations, professions, or cities present positive models for optimizing the use of evaluation? How is our city/organizational performance evaluated and reported to the public?

CHAPTER RESOURCES AND/OR LINKS

Appendix B: Integral City Maps (1–5): 1, 2, 4

Appendix C1: Definitions of 12 Intelligences: Integral, Structural, Inquiry, Navigating

Appendix C3: Integral City GPS Locator: Smart, Resilient, Integral

Reflective Question for Whom /Where/ What I Could Use as:	Practitioner	Catalyst	Meshworker
What do I observe as I read?			
What do I think?			
What do I feel?			
What do I want to do next?			

16

CONCLUSION—INQUIRY AND ACTION FOR IMPACT IN THE HUMAN HIVE

INQUIRY OBJECTIVES

The Inquiry Objectives of this chapter are:

1. Recapitulate the purpose of the design cycle of the book.
2. Summarize the inquiry intentions of the book:
   - Identify the audiences.
   - Summarize the sections.
3. Summarize the action practices of the book.
   - Identify the research questions.
4. Summarize the impact outcomes of the book.
   - Identify the impact questions.
5. Affirm continuous learning for Placecaring and Placemaking as the double helix of whole learning for an Integral City.

RECAPITULATING THE PURPOSE FOR INQUIRY, ACTION, AND IMPACT IN THE HUMAN HIVE

It is time to recapitulate the value of this book. To do so, we will let the book's design guide the recapitulation. We will review the intentions, action practices, and impacts in our methodology cycle by asking a classic meshworking question: **How does the book offer to readers an Inquiry, Action, and Impact Cycle for Placecaring and Placemaking?**

This book intended to focus on the emergent practices that reveal the patterns of city development practice in the Integral City. We set out to describe a methodology for enacting the 12 Intelligences of the Human Hive (Hamilton, 2008a) by describing a cycle of inquiries that enabled Placecaring and Placemaking.

We aimed our methodology design at two audiences:

1. The first audience comes from the pioneers of the Integral movement who want to know how to take the Integral paradigm to scale at the city level.

2. The second audience comes from the practitioners of city, urban, and eco-regional professions who want to know how to evolve their city-regional design, engineering, and operational practices to incorporate the Integral paradigm.

Both audiences may see themselves as "activators" of the human hive, who have gained the qualities to facilitate this work through a combination of education, on-the-job knowledge, and experience at different scales of human systems and at different levels of complexity. We described the profiles of the Practitioner, Catalyst, and Meshwork in Table 1 and noted that all three activators need to be active to support the emergence of an Integral City.

With its approach towards seeing reality in terms of consciousness, the Integral audience may have a bias to the Placecaring methodologies we describe, whereas with its intention to design livable cities, the city-professional audience may have a bias to the Placemaking methodologies we describe. In any case, we propose that an Integral City requires both

Placecaring and Placemaking practices to optimize the performance of the Human Hive.

Our metaphor of the Human Hive is an image of wholeness (like the beehive) that helps us bio-mimic and imagine the city as a whole living system without getting lost in the enormous scale and complexity of the actual city. We borrow from the bees the need for a superordinate goal—our 40 pounds of honey needed for annual hive survival—that helps us align the functions of the city—the most complex system yet created by humans.

We propose that well-being is the superordinate goal of the city that aligns each stage in the grand cycle of city emergence. We have identified those stages in the two parts of the book—Placecaring and Placemaking. Within each of the parts we explore 4 sections. In Placecaring, we progress from the Knowing Field of consciousness, through the Master Code of caring, into the 12 Intelligences of evolving and finish with the spiral of Values and Vital Signs that mark our unfolding development. In Placemaking, we build capacity with the 4+1 Voices and Roles, prototype possibilities to accelerate emergence, align stakeholders into self-organizing Meshworks, and dynamically steer evaluation of the outcomes of our intentions.

Within each of the sections, two chapters draw from aspects of Action Research/Inquiry/Learning by describing case studies and/or templates with the pattern of Inquiry, Action, and Impact.

The chapters are organized into this standard design so that readers can use the sets of Integral City intelligences for each stage to be able to: understand **Context**, employ **Integrally** informed individual and collective input, prototype **Strategies**, and contribute to the **Evolution** of continuous learning for the city.

Inquiry sets out the research question and describes the discovery process.

Action invites the reader, as an Integral City leader, to synthesize their learnings from each chapter into observations, thoughts, feelings, and intentions across the spectrum of Integral City practice.

Impact frames a final set of reflective questions from each quadrant to provide ground for realizing the influence and outcomes that the cycle of action research generates.

At the end of each chapter we identified Resources for drawing on the foundations of the Integral City paradigm and understanding and applying the method described in the chapter. We pointed to *Appendix B*, which includes the five Integral City maps and *Appendix C1*, which defines the 12 Intelligences. We also referred to the *Appendix C3*, which locates the Smart, Resilient, and Integral City types positioned within the 12 Intelligences.

We discovered that the Integral City position on the Integral City GPS locator points especially to the Caring Capacities of our cities—the ones that emerge from our attention to living the Master Code and expanding the circles of care in our lives.

We have learned that as we expand our capacity to **embrace greater circles of care**—from self, to others, to place, to planet—we **expand our capacity to develop habitats that carry** and support the life conditions that we most need to be Smart, Resilient, and Integral.

For as much as we struggle to locate right direction, right action, and right cities, with our strategic Smart City approaches and systemic Resilient City adaptations, it is not until the Integral City GPS adds Care and Evolution to the equation that we can really sustain and grow all the capacities that make our cities Integral. We explored the depth of this evolving circle of care in the section on embracing the Master Code of caring for self, others, place and planet (see *Chapter 3*).

The value proposition of Integral Intelligences is that they add the evolutionary caring capacities (of the left-hand quadrants) to implement the carrying capacities of (the right-hand quadrants) in Smart and Resilient City Plans and Strategies. This is core to the Pope's spiritual call for activating an Integral Ecology (Francis, 2015) and it may be the missing link in enabling the IPCC's scientific call for a global strategy to address climate change (Adger, Aggarwal, Argawala, Alcamo, & etal, 2007; Alley, Bernsten, Bindoff, Chen, & etal, 2007; Barker, Bashmakov, Bernstein, Bogner, & etal, 2007; Bernstein, Bosch, Canziana, Chen, & etal, 2007; Francis, 2015).

The Evolutionary Power source lies at the centre of our Integral City Locator. All cities of any stripe draw on energy sources to power functioning. Smart Cities and Resilient Cities source their energy externally. To build Smart Cities, we drew on fossil fuels. To develop Resilient Cities, we are drawing on renewable energy. To energize Integral Cities, we access the interior energy source of Evolutionary Intelligence.

The constancy and persistence of Evolution's driving force across 14 billion years (of the emergence of the universe), now explored by both scientific and spiritual communities begs us to discover the next evolutionary step of inter-city and intra-city collaboration.

Business Innovators tap its mysteries to leap ahead of what Citizens and Civic Managers sustain as the status quo. Civil Society Integrators observe its evolutionary patterns to discern alignment and rebalancing of systems.

Evolutionary intelligence as a Human Hive Mind emerges when we convene the 4+1 Voices (as explored in *Chapter* 9) within each city and multiple cities.

Working together as 4+1 Voices of many Cities, we have the intelligence to go beyond the Smart City, beyond the Resilient City, into the Knowing Field of the Integral City.

The Integral City GPS aligns Master Coded performance that produces well-being and recalibrates our intentions, expectations and outcomes for cities.

With these caveats in place, now let us review what we have learned about Inquiry Intentions, Action Questions, and Impacts.

SUMMARIZING INQUIRY INTENTIONS: WHO, WHY1

WHO

The audiences for this book are both integrally informed and/or city professionals. Whether we classify them into the 4+1 Voices or simply identify them as stakeholders in the well-being of our cities, the Integral City paradigm recognizes that any of them can initiate change in the city. While Smart and Resilient cities depend primarily on Civic Managers to provide the fulcrum for change, the kinds of processes that we have described in this book can be implemented by Citizens, Civil Society, or Business, as well as Civic Managers. Moreover, we propose that transformative and lasting change can only happen when all 4 Voices work together.

WHY1

The Inquiry, Action, and Impact process was described in two parts in the book: Placecaring and Placemaking. Each Part had four sections. Each section had two chapters. We bring together the following overview of the parts and sections to gain a summary of the methodology design process of the book.

Part 1: Placecaring

Part 1 of the book started with the left-hand quadrants of the Integral City model and explored how to enact Placecaring through inquiry and action. This was a vital sequence to recognize and respect because it completely underpinned the effective practice we explored in Part 2—namely inquiry and action for Placemaking. In Part 1 we explored the fields of systemic constellation and values creation in the Integral City which is foundational to the values realization that we explored in Part 2.

The four sections that we covered in Part 1 included: Inquiry in the Knowing Field, Embracing the Master Code, Assessing the 12 Intelligences of the City, and Discovering and Mapping Values and Vital Signs.

Activate Inquiry in the Knowing Field

These two chapters introduced readers to a discovery that has profoundly impacted Integral City inquiry and practice—namely inviting in the Knowing Field (aka morphic field). *Chapter 1: Activate Inquiry for Knowing Cities* situates the Integral City work knowingly in the realm of consciousness. We have found this to be vital in making accessible the energetic qualities of the city as a whole at all scales of human systems within it. Working, playing, and recreating in the Knowing Field gives us insights into the invisible aspects of the city that we believe are continuously impacting it through stored energy, habits, lineages, traumas, and wisdom in the Knowing Field. In *Chapter 2: Cultivate We-Space Inquiry for Human Hive Mind* we explained also how the Knowing Field opens the Integral City practices from those engaged in by individual I's to those embraced by a collective We. It is our belief that our practices have uncovered the early stages of what we call the Human Hive Mind. By starting here, Integral City believes it is opening the doors to a unique inquiry and action practice that distinguishes its approach from other advanced but more technological or environmental frameworks (like Smart City and Resilient City).

Embrace the Master Code

These two chapters explored the Master Code that is another hallmark of Integral City inquiry and action practice. *Chapter 3: Amplify Caring Capacity with Master Code* explained what the Master Code is, and *Chapter 4: Inspire Spiritual Communities to Serve Evolution of the Human Hive* gave a specific example how spiritual communities (as a Voice of the Civil Society) have a particular role to play in modeling, sharing, and practicing the Master Code with the other Voices of the city.

The Master Code is a whole systems meta-intelligence that coalesces the energies and intentions of all scales of human systems in the city.

Assess the 12 Intelligences of the Integral City

These two chapters explored the 12 Intelligences of the city—first in *Chapter 5: Find the 12 Intelligences in the City* by demonstrating how to assess them, and secondly in *Chapter 6: Use the 12 Intelligences to Assess Business Opportunities* by sharing a case study that shows how the intelligences can be applied to assessing practical business ventures or city-scale prototypes of any kind. Exploring the 12 Intelligences of the city effectively translates the Master Code into inquiry and action practices that bring awareness to what it means to act, experience, relate and create in the Human Hive.

Discover and Map City Values & Vital Signs

These two chapters shared some of Integral City's applications that have been longest practiced. They are based on Hamilton's original dissertation research into learning and leadership in self-organizing systems (Hamilton, 1999) and weave in the multi-source paradigms from the Integral and Spiral Dynamics integral authors (Wilber, Beck, Laszlo, Hubbard) and communities.

Chapter 7: Discover Integral City Values focused on Values Mapping and revealed how this process profiles the city not just in psychological terms (as used by Richard Florida, (2008)) but also in developmental terms. This reveals city patterns that map bio-psycho-cultural-social qualities at 4 major stages of complexity (reflecting the Master Code) that are GIS mappable. Such data becomes integral to effective implementation of any change in the city because it reveals how to communicate what to whom in a values-based language they understand. In today's "mongrel" cities that contain all the cultures of the world living cheek by jowl with one another, this is necessary intelligence to have for effectively implementing security, sustainability, and resilience strategies.

Chapter 8: Map & Monitor Vital Signs in the Integral City explored the possibilities of Integral Vital Signs Monitoring (IVSM). This inquiry and action practice suggests a possible platform on which the complex tracking of data could be organized. But the key value of this chapter is to demonstrate how to use the Integral City values assessment to seek out and choose relevant vital signs data (most of which already exist in organizational databases spread throughout the city). Examples were offered of how to assemble a dashboard and maintain it and how to attract stakeholders and how to collect their data for a pilot project or prototype IVSM dashboard.

Part 2: Placemaking

Part 2 of the book moved into the right-hand quadrants of the Integral City model and explored how to translate the Placecaring inquiry and action research from earlier chapters into Placemaking inquiry and action. We effectively moved from values creation into values realization by describing how we: Engage the 4+1 Voices of the City; Prototype with Learning Lhabitats, Pop-Ups and Sustainable Community Development; Meshwork Purpose, People, Place, and Planet; and Evaluate Impact.

Engage the 4 Voices of the City

These two chapters explored the 4+1 Voices of the City: Citizens, Civil Society, Civic Managers, and Business (and the +1 Voices of other Cities).

Chapter 9: Attract the 4 Voices of the City started with the practical question of: How do you bring the 4+1 Voices to the table? *Chapter 10: Dialogue with the 4 Voices of the City* laid out the elegant process of how to design a dialogue where the 4+1 Voices can respectfully listen to one another and take effective action.

Prototype Design for Learning Lhabitats, Pop-ups and Sustainable Community Development

These two chapters built strongly on all the foregoing chapters in the book. They offered advanced applications of working with multiple stakeholders

(4+1 Voices of the City) to prototype possible solutions without having to commit huge investments.

Chapter 11: Empower People with Learning Lhabitats and Pop-Ups described 2 ways to engage the 4 Voices to learn together in full scale Learning Lhabitats and spontaneous Pop-Ups. *Chapter 12: Prototype Sustainable Community Development* described how to prototype Sustainable Community Development through a longer term (6 month) course—where a cohort of students can work with a real community to bring collective wisdom to a real issue.

Meshwork Purpose, People, Place, and Planet

This section on Meshworking described the most complex Integral City applications of inquiry and action in the book. It integrated all of the stages of inquiry and action described in the previous chapters. With both the complexity and integration challenges in mind, it is easy to see that meshworkers, meshworks, and meshworking are not for the faint of heart and call on advanced skills from Integral City activators.

Chapter 13: Realize Meshworking Capacities in the Human Hive set out the basics of meshworks, meshworking, and meshworkers and how they work together to align intentions, and develop and evolve the cities we want.

Chapter 14: Meshwork a Neighborhood Development Strategy offered a case study that illustrates why (and how) the most advanced level of Integral City practice is called "Meshworker"—and why the annual award of "Meshworker of the Year" (won by this case study's practicing meshworkers) recognizes individuals and organizations who have demonstrated these practices, reflecting and amplifying their Deep, Wide, Clear, and High accomplishments.

Evaluate Impact

These last two chapters considered the challenge of evaluating the success of Integral City interventions. They are designed to reflect the action learning, and action research spiral of inquiry that progresses through the classic action research stages of: observe, plan, act, review, learn, repeat. They unpacked the reflective questions that underpin the design of each of our chapters:

What (do we observe)?
So What (does this mean?)
Now What (are we going to do as a result)?

This cycle of reflection can take us right back to where we began in the Knowing Field. We could easily return to *Chapter 1* to complete the journey of Placecaring and Placemaking and we encourage readers to do that because you will discover deep insights about the patterns embedded in your inquiry, action, and impact.

However, we also grounded the cycle of Placecaring and Placemaking with an evaluation process that is itself a fractal of the cycle. In order to be coherent with our many propositions that an Integral City is a meta-system, our approach to evaluation is based on a systems view of life. This view (Capra, 1996) considers that a system is alive when it can survive, adapt to its environment, and reproduce or regenerate. Research indicates those life processes are only possible because the system utilizes feedback to inform it of its success in surviving, adapting, and regenerating. This feedback is the most basic form of evaluation—on the life-giving level. Deriving from these basic premises, we suggested that a living, learning, systems framework is required to design an evaluation process that is sufficient to the task of providing feedback that measures the success of Integral City processes for the benefit of all stakeholders. We included in the evaluation process both those who participated in any formal research and those who were part of the larger city system that is always the container for the research. In striving to map out that evaluative and reflective feedback loop, we borrowed from aspects of the qualitative approaches of Patton's (Patton, 2013) utilization evaluation, the circular flow of the Kellogg Logic Model (anon, 2004, nd), and the complexity scales of Thrivability (Wood & Bruitzman, 2016).

Chapter 15: Evaluate Integral City Impact with Integrative Evaluation Process kept in mind these basic tenets and influences, and described a basic evaluation process that can be applied to any and all of the processes outlined in previous chapters. *Chapter 16: Conclusion—Inquiry and Action for Impact in the Human Hive* summarizes key elements of the basic structure of the entire book: **Inquiry** (what are the questions we have asked to start each area of research); **Action** (what are the processes we have undertaken to learn about our Human Hive; and **Impact** (to what path do we commit in pursuing our journey to well-being in the city)?

SUMMARIZING ACTION PRACTICES: WHAT/HOW

WHAT

Each chapter described an inquiry that started with a generative question. This research question framed the "What" that we intended to inquire about. The series of Inquiry Questions used in our chapters became a progression that built on discoveries revealed in preceding chapters. The progression of WHAT questions were these.

C1: How can I catalyze the city's field of well-being?

C2: How can we develop a process for exploring Integral City insights at the ITC Conference?

C3: How do I and We practice the Master Code?

C4: How can Spiritual Communities serve the evolution of the Human Hive as Gaia's Reflective Organ?

C5: For this city [name], how strong are and what is the evidence for the 12 Integral City Intelligences? The subquestion is: How do the Intelligences suggest recommendations for action and impact?

C6: How does our design add value to the daily lives of citizens?
- Would this Project adapt to different cities (geographies, cultures, economies)?
- Should this Project become part of my (client's) investment portfolio?
- How could our organization partner with the Project developer?
- In what ways might marginalized citizens resist the Project?

C7: How do people experience city Quality of Life (QOL) in bio-psycho-cultural-structural realities?
- What values support people in city life conditions? What is working around here?

- What values impede people in city life conditions? What does not work around here?
- What values do people aspire to change in the city? What do you imagine is possible?
- How do you describe yourself?

C8: What salutogenic indicators can you suggest that are already being collected for the following 9 scales of human systems:
- Individual Human Health (Internal/External)
- Families (Internal/External)
- Workplaces (Internal/External)
- Education System (Internal/External)
- Healthcare System (Internal/External)
- Civil Society (Internal/External)
- Recreation/Faith (Internal/External)
- City Hall/Infrastructure (Internal/External)
- Environment

Who is the potential source and/or owner of the data?

What is the appropriate metric for each data set?

How frequently should the data be updated?

What agreements exist for privacy of information and how might new agreements need to be drafted to share the data in an Integral Vital Signs Monitor?

C9: How can the 4 Voices of the city discover the conditions that enable caring for and making a place that provides well-being for all?

C10: How can the 4 Voices of the city work together to create the conditions to improve the well-being of the city? We invite you to dialogue on the theme of (x) in exploring this question.

C11: How do practitioners attract, strengthen, and engage the Citizen Voice?

C11a: *What happens when we speak as Mother Earth?*

C12: *How can city hall improve the participation rates of a solar panel installation program for residential homes?* or *How can the regional transportation system attract citizen engagement from multiple municipalities to improve and expand the pedestrian and bicycle path network?*

C13: *How does who, do what to whom, for what purpose, under what life conditions, where? For example: How does an integrally-informed research team (who) design a program (what) for youth (whom) that builds life-giving capacities in youth, to replace gang-style behaviors (purpose) that have cost youth lives (life condition), in this city (where)?*

C14: *How does the consulting team develop a multi-modal process for Sherwood Park to engage the 4 Voices of the city about concerns and issues related to developing mature neighborhoods, locating the engagements in or close to their mature neighborhood locations?*

C15: *How did we achieve the goal that the opportunity presented and that we set out to accomplish?*

HOW

Each chapter not only set out to answer a question, it necessarily described a change process. At the conclusion of the change process, the reader as co-researcher, returned to the 4 quadrants with a personal inquiry to reflect on the impact they could make as an individual through intention (Upper Left) and behaviors (Upper Right), and collectively within their cultures (Lower Left) and organizations (Lower Right). The panorama of questions is summarized below with all 15 Impact Question sets agglomerated by quadrant. Each question implies an action that the reader could take. Each action opens the door to impact that can ensue.

The question sets within each quadrant reveal a progression of practice capacities that naturally unfold in the Integral City activator as they engage in increasingly more complex inquiries at the city scale.

The question sets as a whole, unpack the power of the Master Code through the quadrants and they palpably remind us of Margaret Mead's oft-quoted injunction that a small group of committed people can make significant change in the world. Integral City proposes that every change starts with a question—an inquiry—moves into action—and results in impact. It is our experience that this practice of Action Research/Inquiry/Learning initiates the ripples of change the moment the researcher involves the system in exploring the question. Thus, it is important to realize that engaging with any city system—even just to ask a "simple" or "innocent" question (never mind the burning questions) has profound ethical implications, whether the processes we have described are completed or not. Impact always happens. Consider the Impact Questions we asked.

SUMMARIZING IMPACT QUESTIONS BY QUADRANT AND CHAPTER

Impact Questions: Upper Left (UL) Deep

CI UL DEEP: As a coach, facilitator, catalyst, or meshworker with cities, how do I prepare myself to participate by using practices to clear my bio-psy-cho-cultural-social field? Consider: 1-2-3 Shadow work (Wilber et al., 2008); Tonglen meditation[57]; embodied field clearing (a practice of "sweeping" the subtle energy field; and Huebl Presencing[58]. As a Client, how do I come to the systemic constellation with a "draft" question and remain open to the Constellator helping me to improve it for deeper access to the Knowing Field? How willing am I to let go of control and trust the Constellator to guide me in the gross realm and the subtle/Knowing Field realm?

C2 UL DEEP: How does my development as an "I" bootstrap development of others and together how do we bootstrap a "We-space"? How does developing "We-space in turn bootstrap my own development?

C3 UL DEEP: What personal development practices support my appreciation for the Master Code. How do I care for my Self?

C4 UL DEEP: How can I practice the Master Code—taking care of self, taking care of others, taking care of this place?

C5 UL DEEP: How do I rate my leadership in the indicators of Integral City's 12 Intelligences (latent, aware, active, advanced)?

---

57   Tonglen: http://en.wikipedia.org/wiki/Tonglen
58   Transparent Communication: http://www.thomashuebl.com/en/approach-methods/transparent-communication.html

C6 UL DEEP: As Project Leader how do I rate my level of being integrally informed in relation to the 12 Intelligences in this Project (rate each intelligence -/0/+)?

C7 UL DEEP: As researcher, how do I describe my values on the sample survey in *Appendix* D? What filters do they set up to my collection and interpretation of data?

C8 UL DEEP: How can I lead, collaborate, or contribute to the creation of a city Integral Vital Signs Monitor? What does well-being mean to me? What metrics do I use?

C9 UL DEEP: How can I lead, initiate, or convene the 4+1 Voices of the city? What might I consider as a superordinate goal of the city? How could the superordinate goal motivate the 4 Voices to work together?

C10 UL DEEP: How can I lead, initiate, or convene a Discovery Dialogue or a Dialogue Series for the City? What might I consider as triggering event for such a dialogue? How could the dialogue introduce me to other perspectives?

C11 UL DEEP: How can I influence, lead, initiate, or convene a prototyping process for my community or city? What design questions am I curious about prototyping? How might I explore the value of a Learning Lhabitat or Pop-Up?

C12 UL DEEP: What might motivate me to develop a prototype that could address sustainability issues? What are my curiosities about prototyping? What dreams and fantasies do I have to build something greater than my own resources might allow?

C13 UL DEEP: How do my natural interests, talents, and values fit to the 4 roles of the Integral City (Integrator, Resource Allocator, Producer, Diversity Generator)? How do my passions contribute to the work I do? What insights might they bring to creating a meshwork?

C14 UL DEEP: What level of skill do I consider my Integral City capacities—Practitioner, Catalyst, Meshworker? How could I most effectively bring my highest good to contribute to a meshwork? What challenges might I encounter in the process of meshworking?

C15 UL DEEP: What is my experience with evaluation at a personal level? How has formative evaluation helped me to optimize my performance in various situations and/or projects? How did summative evaluation contribute to my learning process throughout my career?

IMPACT QUESTIONS: LOWER LEFT (LL) WIDE

C1 LL WIDE: Are we open to the Constellator clearing the space before starting and how can we work with her/him to do so? Have we thought about what Elements we can propose and who our Representatives might be? Are we open to the Constellator suggesting others?

C2 LL WIDE: What feelings emerge when we contemplate moving beyond our individual "I," beyond participating as an aggregate of "I's" into a We-space where we share a consciousness as a Human Hive Mind? How do we tell the story about the "Space Between"? How does that story reflect the Human Hive Mind? How does the Human Hive Mind make possible deeper inquiry, action, and impact in the city?

C3 LL WIDE: What family practices have modeled how we care for Others? Who and how in our families is a good model for caring for Others? Who has cared for us outside the family? How has that helped us learn how to care for Place and Planet?

C4 LL WIDE: How can you engage with all the 4 Voices of the city within your spiritual community and discover your beliefs about city well-being, sustainability, and resilience as Gaia's Reflective Organ? How can you attract, convene, intend, pray, and play with and as the 4 Voices of the Human Hive?

C5 LL WIDE: How can our organization reach out to other organizations in the city to explore the stories we tell about our city? How can we make those stories more positive, generative, and hopeful—and therefore attractive?

C6 LL WIDE: How does our Project team relate internally? What partners might we need to collaborate with for Project success? What city Voices have we involved (or are missing) in our design process? How can we communicate about this Project to all 4 Voices for multiple wins in the city?

C7 LL WIDE: What is the Center of Gravity (COG) of the values of our research team? How does that impact how we relate to participants, and collect and interpret data? What are the key language/culture groups in the city?

C8 LL WIDE: How can our organization lead, collaborate, or contribute to the creation of a city Integral Vital Signs Monitor? What does well-being mean to our organization? What metrics do we use that could connect with indicators/metrics from other organizations?

C9 LL WIDE: How can our organization lead, initiate, or convene the 4+1 Voices of the city? What Gateway of the city does our organization serve? What might our organization consider to be a superordinate goal of the city? How could the superordinate goal motivate other stakeholders in the 4 Voices to work together?

C10 LL WIDE: How can our organization lead, initiate, or convene a Discovery Dialogue or a Dialogue Series for the city? What strengths, opportunities, assets, or resources do we see emerging in the city that call us to take a wider view of the city's future possibilities? How might our organization catalyze a conversation for change? How could we attract other organizations to join us in the conversation?

C11 LL WIDE: How can our organization use prototyping to discover how we contribute to city success? How might prototyping give us a deeper and/or wider view of the city's future possibilities? How could prototyping invite other organizations into the process for change? How could we attract other organizations to participate in a Learning Lhabitat? When and where might we surprise others with the fun of a Pop-Up?

C12 LL WIDE: How would working with a learning cohort support my own development in service to sustainable community development? What value does a Team Charter add to teamwork on any kind of project? How could a Team Charter contribute to a working prototype?

C13 LL WIDE: What aspects of our organizational culture could contribute to a meshwork? Where could we best serve the 4 roles of the Integral City (Integrator, Resource Allocator, Producer, Diversity Generator)? Who else should be at the meshworking table/community/network? How can we invite others to join us in a meshwork initiative?

C14 LL WIDE: What organizational or sectoral relationships in our community or city are aligned? Misaligned? How do we see our organization as part of the 4 Voices of the city? How could our collaborations improve with the process of meshworking? Who else should we invite to a meshworking table that we might jointly assemble? How can our interests attract others to join us in a meshwork initiative? How would they benefit?

C15 LL WIDE: How does our organization practice evaluation? Who is responsible for designing the evaluation process? Who participates in the implementation of the evaluation? In what ways do we use formative evaluation to improve quality control, develop relationships, and improve service? How is formative evaluation a form of organizational learning for our organization?

IMPACT QUESTIONS: UPPER RIGHT (UR) CLEAR

C1 UR CLEAR: How comfortable am I—or what tensions do I carry (in my body) with my choice/need for the mode of constellation work: face-to-face; online; Skype; etc.? How have I prepared myself through contemplation, meditation, bio-psycho-active material (like reading, video, audio), to be in the Unknown?

C2 UR CLEAR: What qualities attract me to a We-space as a container? What energy does it offer me? What energy do I offer the We-space container? What qualities do I notice about my personal boundaries? About group boundaries, where I am active in the city? How do I sense the "Space Between" me and others; between me and the group? How does this "Space Between" have its own energy?

C3 UR CLEAR: In the next 3 months what will I do to live into the Master Code? What behaviors, actions, and service can I offer to learn and/or expand my practicing the Master Code? What is a stretch goal I set myself in the next 3 months to practice the Master Code?

C4 UR CLEAR: How can I expand my individual practices to model the Master Code as an exemplar for others in the city—in small ways to begin with, and then grow them as I am able?

C5 UR CLEAR: What measures do I use to give myself feedback about personal well-being? What actions do I take that support (or undermine) that well-being? What burning questions do I have about improving my well-being?

C6 UR CLEAR: What metrics have I identified to measure project success? How does project success contribute to city well-being? What actions will link measures of project success to city success?

C7 UR CLEAR: What behaviors in the city have motivated the research? What measures do the Quality of Life (QOL) quadrants reveal about tensions in the city between the 4 bio-psycho-cultural-social realities?

C8 UR CLEAR: What behaviors in the city are important to track? What metrics from the 4 quadrants of bio-psycho-cultural-social realities contribute to city well-being?

C9 UR CLEAR: What values-based actions in the city are important to its energy flow and well-being? How do the core values from the 4 quadrants of bio-psycho-cultural-social realities reveal themselves as behaviors practiced by the 4 Voices?

C10 UR CLEAR: What supply-chain issues and impacts in or around the city are important to its energy flow and well-being? How do the threats and fears that threaten the workforce require a conversation that can support positive change?

C11 UR CLEAR: How could prototyping with Learning Lhabitats engage the city's supply chains that contribute to its metabolic flow and well-being? How could a Pop-Up break down barriers within my organization to new solutions for one of our intractable problems?

C12 UR CLEAR: What actions have I taken in the past that could be useful in prototyping? What actions have I taken related to sustainability issues? What experiments or rehearsals have I tried out in any area of interest, in the past? What would I like to do/make/create more of to test out ideas related to sustainability?

C13 UR CLEAR: What do I observe in the community/city systems related to some issue that matters to me? How effectively do those city systems perform? How aligned are they in their actions? How could my observations and actions make them more aligned and effective?

C14 UR CLEAR: What city issues matter to the success of my organization in the city? What is my role in the organization in relation to those issues? How could the process of meshworking improve my organizational effectiveness? How could a change in organizational effectiveness impact our sector? The 4 Voices? The city as a whole?

C15 UR CLEAR: What actions or behaviors have I had evaluated in my life? In sports? In performing arts? In professional practice? How did evaluation change my behaviors in positive ways? In negative ways?

IMPACT QUESTIONS: LOWER RIGHT (LR) HIGH

C1 LR HIGH: How can we hold the results of the systemic constellation with honor, but lightly? How do we remind ourselves that the effect of entering the Knowing Field continues after the constellation? How do we embrace "It is not over until it is over"? How might we adjust our strategies formulated before the constellation to reflect any discoveries we make? How do we remember that entry into the Knowing Field has already changed the Field, accepting that we don't need to do anything and Field effects will unfold on their own? How comfortable are we and how might we prepare to be surprised as the energies continue to play out (over days, weeks, months)?

C2 LR HIGH: What other groups do we know in our city who are shifting from identification with the individual to a more collective sense of identity? How might we experiment together with inquiry, action or impact for the well-being of our city (or other cities)? In what ways, dimensions or senses do we become aware of the energy in a "Space Between" that transcends individual and group boundaries?

C3 LR HIGH: How could we boost the positive impact of taking care of this place? What will it take to move from the current stage of taking care of my Self, taking care of Other(s) and taking care of this Place to the next stage of caring for our City? Caring for our Eco Region? Caring for the Planet?

C4 LR HIGH: How can you go beyond the spiritual community and reach out to all the other Voices of the city? (Start by learning how they live the Master Code.) How can you go on to convene dialogues with the 4 Voices and create the safe and spiritually energized space where you can co-discover your beliefs about city well-being, sustainability and resilience as Gaia's Reflective Organ? How can you invite dialogue and exchange with spiritual communities in Gaia's other Reflective Organs in the eco-region?

C5 LR HIGH: What strategies for sustainability (from City Hall, Healthcare, Education, Justice, Infrastructure Providers) does our business community support or resist? What is one way our organization could contribute to city resilience in the face of disaster?

C6 LR HIGH: How does our Project contribute to city well-being and sustainability? In what ways might our Project invite support or cause resistance to change in the city? How does our Project contribute to city resilience in the next decade? In the next 2 decades (to multiple generations)?

C7 LR HIGH: Where are the neighborhoods and subpopulations of the city that reveal different values patterns? How do these neighborhoods and subpopulations interact with one another?

C8 LR HIGH: Who are the organizational stakeholders who own and maintain indicators important for a city's Integral Vital Signs Monitor (IVSM)? What organization is optimally positioned and/or resourced to call together a city-wide Community of Practice to create, resource, and maintain an IVSM? What online platform could best serve a city Integral Vital Signs Monitor?

C9 LR HIGH: Who are the organizational stakeholders who affirm, influence, and maintain city values and levels of complex development? What organization is optimally positioned and/or resourced to convene the 4 Voices so they can meet, learn about, and develop conditions to work together? What city systems strengthen individual and all Gateways of the city? How can we work together to keep Gateways open and overcome or prevent Gateways that are arrested or closed?

C10 LR HIGH: Who are the organizational stakeholders who act as primary communicators to other organizations in our city's economic ecology? What organization has influence and recognition to invite others to the table so policy makers will listen? What city systems need to be connected to improve the health of the whole system?

C11 LR HIGH: How might a Pop-Up attract unusual or unlikely allies to the table to explore city infrastructure issues? What organizations already use prototyping in design phases? How could we use their experience to design more effectively for the city systems?

C12 LR HIGH: Who would we like to teach us how to design or prototype? Whom do we respect in the field of sustainability? In community? In development? What qualities do the best teams have who produce project or prototyping results? How could studying the systems used by inventors and innovators like Steve Jobs' Apple or Elon Musk's Tesla help us learn to work effectively as a prototyping team? What guidelines would we develop for managing and learning from failures as well as successes?

C13 LR HIGH: How could our organization contribute to the network of the 4 roles of an Integral City meshwork (Integrator, Resource Allocator, Producer, Diversity Generator)? What vision energizes our organization? How does our organizational purpose align with the city's vision (and purpose)? Who else in our supply chain needs to be involved as stakeholders in a meshwork for creating city values and realizing city visions?

C14 LR HIGH: How can our city's Civic Managers initiate a meshworking process to align stakeholders around a key issue? Why is it important that stakeholders from all 4 Voices contribute to solving this key issue? In the city's key supply chains (metabolic economy) who are the Integrators, Resource Allocators, Producers, Diversity Generators? What question might act as a superordinate goal to attract the 4 Voices to align in a meshwork to discover a workable answer/approach?

C15 LR HIGH: How does our organization design into our functions and systems feedback processes that help us improve performance? How does our organization value team learning and team evaluation? How do we set goals and performance targets that contribute to evaluation processes? How do evaluation processes contribute to institutionalizing standards of performance? What other organizations, professions, or cities present positive models for optimizing the use of evaluation? How is our city/organizational performance evaluated and reported to the public?

CONTINUOUS LEARNING FOR PLACECARING AND PLACEMAKING

As noted above, the Integral City GPS aligns Master Coded performance that produces well-being and recalibrates our intentions, expectations, and outcomes for cities. The outcome of living the Master Code is a process of continuous learning that produces a critical indicator of well-being success—namely Happiness.

Happiness as Evidence of Well-being Success

As noted in our Introduction, happiness studies have produced early evidence for the well-being of individuals, cities, cultures, and nations ("(anon; Cummins et al., 2004; Haidt, 2006; Lama & Cutler, 1998; Montgomery, 2014; Wills et al., 2007a, 2007b). This kind of happiness is not merely egoistic or self-centered, nor is it ethno- or regional-centred, nor even merely place- or planet-centred. Instead, this indicator integrates all the scales of possible happiness that arise when our decision sets are aligned. This happens when we live the Master Code, choosing to take care of our Selves, each Other, our Cities/Places and the Planet all at once—simultaneously—an opportunity we have never before experienced in history.

Happiness measures the right relationship between Caring Capacity (in the left-hand quadrants) and Carrying Capacity (in the right-hand quadrants) coexisting and coemerging at the City scale, like the double helix of emergent cyclical human development that Graves (2005) proposed for the individual scale. Thus, happiness as an evolutionary alignment index of Caring and Carrying Capacities supplies the double well-being feedback loop for sustainability and resilience used by the bees.

We must learn to notice when our BEEings are depressed (indicating we are unhappy, misaligned, underperforming, and poorly rewarded) and what we must do to steward the right relationship of all life in our cities, eco-regions, and planet. We must listen and respond to the Evolutionary Intelligence at the center of our GPS, which has offered a path of Caring Capacity (a gold dot to locate us on our GPS maps) and by now also offered many means to move the path of Carrying Capacity beyond traditional cities to Smart Cities to Resilient Cities. Out beyond all these lives a Knowing Field that embraces the city's well-being as a whole—there we will find the Integral City.

As city experts and Integral activators, what roles can you play as Civic Managers and Business Innovators, as Citizens and Civil Societies, to build on the potential of Smart and Resilient Cities and working together to cocreate the Knowing Field of the Integral City?

The promise of this methodology cycle is that when we bring together the 4+1 Voices of many cities, we can cocreate the next generation of IT—the Integral Technology that will enable us to design cities using the Master Code—the Evolutionary Intelligence of Care. This is so needed by our Planet of Cities to create a planet-centric Integral Ecology (Sean Esbjörn-Hargens & Zimmerman, 2009). By aligning our Caring Capacities, we will naturally expand the Carrying Capacity of our Smart and Resilient Cities. We may also take the critical next steps to avoid the human version of Colony Collapse Disorder that our dancing cousins the bees have warned us about. This book offers a design choreography to invent the dance that integrates the intelligences of the Smart, Resilient, and Integral Cities and wake up the Human Hive to its full potential and cocreate the life conditions for city well-being!

This chapter has reiterated our Inquiry Questions, Action Practices, and Impact Reflections. As a concluding act of research in this grand cycle we invite you to make for yourself a meta-action plan (see below *Meta-Action Plan for Practitioner, Catalyst, Meshworker*) to notice what are the next natural steps you are inspired to take.

And we look forward to meeting you—out beyond the Smart City, out beyond the Resilient City, in the Knowing Field of the Integral City.

We invite you to contact us with your questions, experiences, and discoveries (see contact information in Author Profiles).

REITERATION OF INQUIRY OBJECTIVES

The Inquiry Objectives of this chapter were:

1. Recapitulate the purpose of the design cycle of the book.
2. Summarize the inquiry intentions of the book:
   - Identify the audiences.
   - Summarize the sections.
3. Summarize the action practices of the book.
   - Identify the research questions.
4. Summarize the impact outcomes of the book.
   - Identify the impact questions.
5. Affirm continuous learning for Placecaring and Placemaking as the double helix of whole learning for an Integral City.

META-ACTION PLAN FOR PRACTITIONER, CATALYST, MESHWORKER

Review this chapter and make notes below of your impressions, insights, and questions. Locate yourself on the Integral City practice scaffolding. Notice what you have observed, thought, felt, and what you now want to do in any of the three possible practice configurations: as a Practitioner, as a Catalyst, as a Meshworker.

After you have made these notes, consider some of the Impact Questions (summarized by quadrant above). They also might help you reflect on how to generate impact through inquiry and action. Finally check out the Resources and Links offered in the Appendices.

CHAPTER RESOURCES AND/OR LINKS

Appendix B: Integral City Maps (1–5): 1, 2, 3, 4, 5

Appendix C1: Definitions of 12 Intelligences: Ecological, Emergent, Integral, Living, Inner, Outer, Cultural, Social, Inquiry, Meshworking, Navigating, Evolutionary

Appendix C3: Integral City GPS Locator: Smart, Resilient, Integral

Reflective Question for Whom /Where/ What I Could Use as:	Practitioner	Catalyst	Meshworker
What do I observe as I read?			
What do I think?			
What do I feel?			
What do I want to do next?			

PROFILES: AUTHORS & CONTRIBUTORS

Authors and Contributors can be contacted via www.integralcity.com

AUTHOR

Dr. Marilyn Hamilton is author of *Integral City: Evolutionary Intelligences for the Human Hive* and Founder of Integral City Meshworks Inc. and TDG Holdings Inc. Marilyn leads a practice community using Integral City frameworks and practical tools to support multi-stakeholder groups in transforming their whole city and eco-region into habitats that are as sustainable and resilient for humans as the beehive is for bees. She incubates transformation strategies for City Staff, Civic Leaders, Civil Society, Business Entrepreneurs, and Community Participants that integrate their contributions with Purpose, Place, Priorities, People, and Planet. As Thought Leader and Project Leader Marilyn calls herself an "AQtivator," leading teams to develop integrated resilience strategies that optimize official city plans and sustainability goals. She aligns multiple capacities with Environmental, Economic, Social, and Cultural Capitals. She energizes Community Engagement, focuses Decision Making and designs Dashboards for Monitoring City Performance and Managing Risk.

CONTRIBUTORS

Joan Arnott lives in Surrey, BC Canada. Joan "thinks like a planet." She facilitates deep reflective processes for leaders that expand worldviews, consciousness, and community. Joan has collaborated on practical and visionary projects with IONS, UNESCO, UN-Habitat, healthcare, government, crown corporations, community agencies, the forest industry, non-profits, and private business and is known as an adept Listener. A graduate of the Geo-Justice Track, (developed by Brian Swimme and Matthew Fox), Joan integrates spiritual presence and subtle energy awareness to bring the sacred dimension fully alive in her life and work. Joan is part of the *Integral City* Core Team, and was on the *Integral City 2.0 Online Conference 2012* Team. Central in her life is family and community gardening.

Rev. Alia Aurami is located in the Seattle area, USA. She is Head Minister of "Amplifying Divine Light in All" Church. Her primary ministry of fostering humanity's capacity for living in shared higher consciousness includes helping organizational leaders operationalize Turquoise worldview. http://exploringsecondandthirdtier.blogspot.com, http://organizationalintelligences.blogspot.com

Cherie Beck is located in the Washington DC-Baltimore area, USA. She builds on a career as Executive Account Manager architecting technology-based systems to solve business problems. Conference Operations Co-Pilot and Sponsor Liaison for *Integral City Online 2.0 Conference 2012*, Cherie is master practitioner and trainer of Spiral Dynamics integral; an emissary for Strauss and Howe's work on Generations and cyclical change; and a certified executive coach. She contributes to several think tank organizations on human behavior issues and the design of emerging social and governing structures and innovation startups, assisting business and communities in the adaption of innovative and revolutionary technologies in the city.

Diana Claire Douglas, M.Ed., lives in Ottawa, Canada. She is a systemic constellation work facilitator, coach, and trainer (family, organizational, and social issues), social architect, artist, published author, and explorer of the depths. Founder of *Knowing Field Designs: Aligning Human Systems with*

Life, she is internationally certified as an Organizational Constellation Work facilitator through the Bert Hellinger Institute of the Netherlands. She is the lead facilitator for systemic constellation work for *Integral City* and *The Hague Centre for Global Governance, Innovation and Emergence*. She has created a number of adult education programs including: *The Resiliency Project*, *The Imagination Project*, and *The Heart of the Mother Experience*. She facilitates constellations at international conferences such as INFOSYON 2013 in Amsterdam, Integral Theory Conference 2015 in California, and Integral Europe Conference 2016 in Hungary. www.knowingfielddesigns.com

Beth Sanders, MCP, RPP, MCIP, lives in Edmonton, AB, Canada. She is a Civic Meshworker and City Planner. President of POPULUS Community Planning Inc., Beth works as a registered professional planner across Canada with citizens, civic governments, business, and community organizations, striving to create the conditions for cities to serve citizens well—and citizens to serve cities well. Beth's city work serves at every scale: on the boards of her neighborhood community league (as past president), the Alberta Professional Planners Institute (as past president), and the Canadian Institute of Planners. Former general manager of the Brandon and Area Planning District (Manitoba) and general manager of the planning and development department for the Regional Municipality of Wood Buffalo (Fort McMurray, Alberta), Beth is cofounder of the Center for Human Emergence (CHE) Canada, and codesigner and cohost of the global *Integral City 2.0 Online Conference 2012*. Beth is blogging her book in progress, *Nest City: The Human Drive to Thrive in Cities* at http://populus.ca/plan/blog/ from Edmonton, Canada. http://populus.ca/plan/

Linda Shore, MA, lives near Vancouver, Canada. She is a Human Resources and Succession Planner. Linda served as Director of Human Resources for Metro Vancouver, Canada, for 21 years and provided strategic direction and management of the organization's full suite of human resources activities, as well as leadership of the Human Resources department. She is certified with the Justice Institute of British Columbia for Conflict Resolution and was responsible for overseeing collective agreement negotiations with Metro Vancouver's unions. She chaired initiatives to advance the working relationship between management and labor including the Joint Corporate Leadership Strategy. Linda provides executive coaching services.

Alicia Stammer is located in Sacramento, California, USA. Alicia is an organization development consultant, energy healer, and artist who guides people and organizations through change. She previously managed an independent consultancy and is currently the Director of Organization Development for a large healthcare organization.

Ellen van Dongen lives near Utrecht, Netherlands. She is Founder and producer of Lifemaps.NL. She nourishes the self-learning and cre-ational powers in people, using Lifemaps as the intuitive instruments for their self-discovery of a situation, question, or life. Ellen dreams about a vibrant earth, life-wisdom universities, a we-conomy and green cities. As a biologist she looks at reality as a living system. As a Client Executive at IBM she developed large-scale new business in long-term partnerships. As a Strategic Advisor in social security in The Netherlands, she was a change manager. She believes that human beings are personal creators with much (subtle) influence on their lives and that when mind, body, heart, and soul are aligned and people are united, miracles occur. In search of her potential, Ellen's intention is to live the Master Code of Love: taking care of self, others, place, and planet.

Anne-Marie Voorhoeve lives near Amsterdam, Netherlands. She is a strategic connector, synnervator, and meshweaver with the *Center for Human Emergence*, and Director for *The Hague Centre for Global Governance, Innovation and Emergence*, Netherlands. Anne-Marie initiates and participates as 'meshworking' project leader on multi-stakeholder process design, delivery, development, and training. She is a certified trainer in various community development tools and numerous facilitation processes. She encourages people of all ages to make use of their full potential and own creative power to (re)design their work into a meaningful and empowering part of their life. She works internationally with diverse multi-stakeholder groups. She dedicates significant time to the development of youth and employment, such as the international network YES.

GLOSSARY

Caring Capacity: a term coined to describe the capacities of the left-hand quadrants of the Integral Model related to consciousness (Upper Left) and culture (Lower Left). Caring Capacity measures the increasing circles of care embedded in the Master Code, ranging from self-centric to ethno-centric, to global-centric to Kosmos-centric.

Carrying Capacity: a term coined to describe the capacities of the right-hand quadrants of the Integral Model related to behaviors (Upper Right) and systems/infrastructure (Lower Right). Carrying Capacity measures the increasing levels of complexity that materialize as actions, functions, artefacts, systems, and infrastructures that enable and support the expanding circles of care measured in Caring Capacity. In terms of the city carrying capacity, levels are often described as premodern, modern, post-modern, and post-postmodern (or integral, for example in the architecture discourse).

Community of Practice: a community of practitioners who have developed norms and/or agreements about how to replicate a practice in any human sphere—whether that is professional, like accounting; commercial, like insurance claims processing; artistic, like stone sculpture; or agricultural, like growing organic fruits.

Fractal: simple patterns that repeat at all scales, which in living systems, produce complex designs and behaviors.

Holon: a whole system made up of other whole systems. (A term coined by Arthur Koestler, which Ken Wilber made central to his Integral framework.)

Holarchy: a hierarchy of hierarchies or holons; or a hierarchy of whole systems; a higher order system that includes all the lower-order systems in its functioning. (A term coined by Arthur Koestler.)

Homo Sapiens Sapiens: The human who is conscious of his/her consciousness. A term coined by Barbara Marx Hubbard.

Human Hive: a metaphor for the city, applying the concept of the integrated living system to a species' collective habitat; like the beehive is to the honey bee (apis mellifera), the human hive (or city) is to humans (homo sapiens sapiens). The term was popularized and explored in Integral City: Evolutionary Intelligences for the Human Hive (Hamilton, 2008a).

Integral: a term describing a whole system that integrates and synthesizes multiple perspectives, levels of development, lines of development, and types of form. In this discussion I am using the Integral Metamap developed by Ken Wilber (Wilber, 1995, 1996, 2000b, 2007) with major contributions from Beck and Graves (D. Beck, 2000b, 2001, 2002b; D. Beck & Cowan, 1996; D. Beck & Linscott, 2006; Graves, 1974, 2003, 2005) popularized as Spiral Dynamics with influences from other integralists (Gunderson & Holling, 2002; Laszlo, 2004, 2006a, 2006b, 2006c). It has 4 quadrants (upper left for subjective, upper right for objective, lower left for intersubjective, lower right for interobjective) and eight+ levels of development. Spiral Dynamics describes the eight levels of development in terms of emerging levels of complexity. These eight levels are often compressed into the 4 stages of: traditional/pre-modern, modern, post-modern, and integral.

Intelligences: capacities that enable life to adapt, survive, and thrive in any given life conditions. In terms of an Integral City, 12 Intelligences have been identified at the city scale (see Appendix C).

Integral City Activator: the general description for urban professionals who design and implement Integral City principles, processes, and practices. Three levels of competency are described in the *Introduction* as Practitioners, Catalysts, and Meshworkers.

Integral City Assessor: a professional urban practitioner who uses Integral City 12 Intelligences, Values, and/or Voices to assess and report on the levels of evolutionary emergence, complexity of values systems, and participation of the 4+1 Voices of the city.

Integral Intelligences: a cluster of intelligences that are integrated so that they work together to optimize the function of whole systems. In the Integral City they are identified as Contexting, Individual, Collective, Strategic, and Evolutionary intelligences.

Knowing Field Plus Integral Cities:

- Knowing: we can come to know a city, know about it, and be guided around it.
- Knowing: the city itself as an energetic entity has a knowing capacity within it.
- Knowing: a way of perceiving beyond the five senses.
- Cities: are the largest human systems yet created.
- Cities: include all the dynamics of individual, family, organizational, and community systems coexisting in rhythms, cycles, patterns and fields.
- Cities: are collective expressions of the human species, like a Human Hive.

— (Douglas & Hamilton, 2013a)

Master Code: a core principle of the Integral City that describes the increasing circles of care that must be practiced and aligned for whole city system coherence. Practicing the Master Code entails caring for Self, so that you can care for Others, so we can care for this Place (City), so we can all care for the Planet.

Meshwork: the emergence of patterns in the brain, resulting from the neuro-chemical connections of synapses that produce a hairnet-like mesh of axons (Bleys et al., 1996), characterized by major primary connective pathways that produce and intersect secondary, tertiary, and many further levels of connectedness. It appears that the meshwork self-organizes connections and when a certain density and/or repeated use of pathways arises, a hierarchy of complexity emerges that enables the brain to replicate the patterns (and the capacities that arise from them) allowing retention of learning and efficiencies of energy use. This cycle of self-organizing and hierarchical patterning continues throughout a lifetime, allowing the brain to build up a repertoire of learned behavior while continuing its capacity for self-organizing adaptiveness to dynamic environments and never-ending stimuli. While we can map these structures through fMRI scanning, we can also assess the co-related structures of consciousness that emerge in the mind from ego, to ethno, to worldcentric (Beck, 2010).

Meshworking Intelligence: an intelligence that creates a "meshwork" by weaving together the best of two operating systems—one that self-organizes, and one that replicates hierarchical structures. The resulting meshwork creates and aligns complex responsive structures and systems that flex and flow. This occurs in both the conscious mind and physical brain on an individual basis. Collective intelligences also appear to have emerged that can be evolutionarily located in intersubjective and interobjective contexts.

Morphic Field: The concept of morphic or Akashic fields (Laszlo, 2004; Sheldrake, 1988, 1999, 2003, 2012) creates the possibility that we could harness the intelligence that is concentrated in the city to generate much greater (more complex) intelligence capacities than we have ever dreamed of. If we could truly learn how to think together, we could harness the massive leverage of parallel processing that has enabled us to design modern computers and neural networks (like the linking of personal computers for the SETI extraterrestrial life search project). If we can do this, we will see a significant phase shift in human intelligence that will give cities major new incentives to create optimal life conditions to better support human existence. By the same token, in an optimistic spirit, I anticipate that when this intelligence is harnessed we will finally have the power to add value to life on Earth that is both sustainable, not over-using resources, and emergent, always creating new capacities from existing resources (Hamilton, 2008a, p. 73).

Panarchy: is a theory of change described in a book of the same name. The book describes multi-disciplinary research into transformations into human and natural systems (Gunderson & Holling, 2002). As a theory of change, a "Panarchy is a cross-scale, nested set of adaptive cycles, indicating the dynamic nature of structures depicted in the previous plots" (p. 74). Panarchy labels the four phases of creative destruction and renewal within a cycle as: exploitation, conservation, release, and reorganization. Panarchy also describes the connections between cycles and their capacity to reallocate resources by "remembering" accumulated potentials from larger cycles that can influence earlier, (lower in the nest), faster cycles, as well as their capacity to "revolt" and spark change into larger, higher, slower cycles from smaller, faster cycles. For societies these reallocations might result in the three panarchy cycles of: allocation mechanisms, norms, and myths (Westley) as cited in (Gunderson & Holling, 2002, p. 75).

Resilience: the capacity to adapt to changing environments, survive, and thrive.

Resilient Environment: an environment that is a habitat or eco-system for a given species; for example, like a beehive and the eco-region from which the bees collect energy in the form of pollen and nectar, and pollinate the flowers and plants. In this book, the author borrows this analogy to describe the eco-region of a city as the environment for the human hive.

Social Holon: a whole human system made up of multiple individuals. A social holon does not act as an undifferentiated homogenous mass, but is influenced by the internal consciousness and external behaviors of all the individual holons it contains. In terms of Integral City Maps (see *Appendix* B) social holons can be seen in the collective elements of Maps 2, 3, and 4.

Superordinate Goal: a goal that transcends and includes other goals in a way that everyone supports because they see that their own interests are addressed by pursuing it.

Theory U: a theory of learning and change discovered and first described by Senge, Scharmer, Jaworski, and Flowers (Senge, Scharmer, Jaworski, & Flowers, 2004) and since widely developed, popularized, and applied by Scharmer (Scharmer, 2009). Theory U describes a process of change that occurs across a series of activities designed and facilitated to occur in this sequence:

Sensing: Suspending, Redirecting, Letting Go
Presencing: Letting Go, Letting Come, Crystallizing
Realizing: Crystallizing, Prototyping, Institutionalizing

The design of Part 1 and Part 2 of *Integral City Inquiry & Action: Designing Impact for the Human Hive* can be viewed as following a U pattern (down the left-hand quadrants and up the right-hand quadrants).

Voices: a term used in Integral City to describe 4 subpopulations internal to the city (aka Human Hive), in terms of their contribution to a complex living system: Citizens, Civil Society, Civic Managers, Business. The +1 Voice is represented by other cities (Human Hives) in the eco-region.

APPENDICES

APPENDIX A: INTEGRAL QUADRANTS

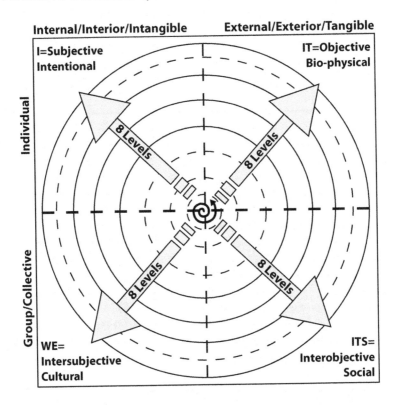

335

APPENDIX B: INTEGRAL CITY MAPS (1–5)

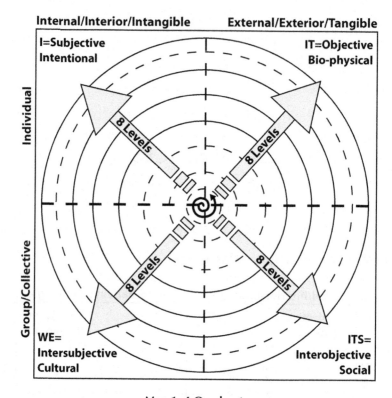

Map 1: 4 Quadrants

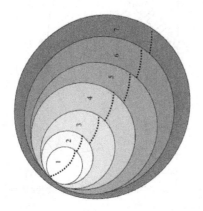

- 1 = individual
- 2 = family/clan
- 3 = group/tribe
- 4 = organizations: workplaces, education, healthcare
- 5 = community(s)
- 6 = city
- 7 = eco-region

Map 2: Nested Holarchy of City Systems

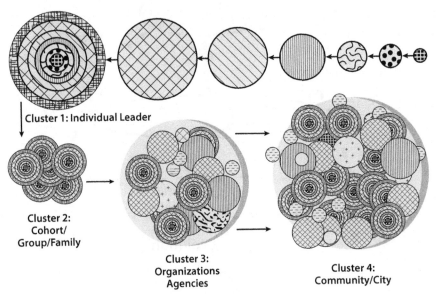

<<<<<<<<<<< Increasing Competencies

Cluster 1: Individual Leader

Cluster 2:
Cohort/
Group/Family

Cluster 3:
Organizations
Agencies

Cluster 4:
Community/City

Map 3: Developmental Sequence of Emerging Scales of Complexity
in the City

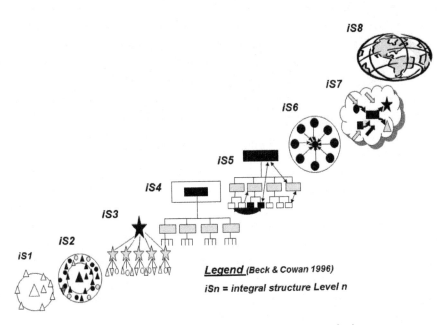

iS8

iS7

iS6

iS5

iS4

iS3

iS2

iS1

Legend (Beck & Cowan 1996)
iSn = integral structure Level n

Map 4: Emerging Levels of Organizational Complexity

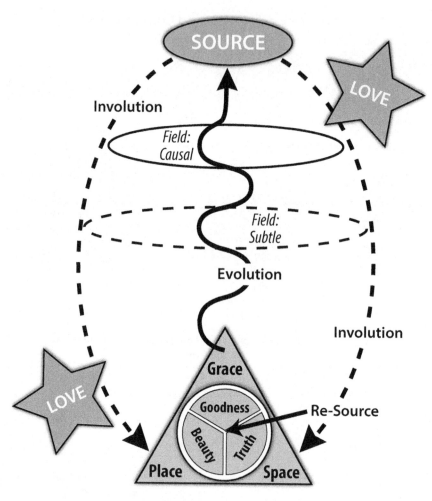

Map 5: Spirituality in the Integral City

APPENDIX C: INTEGRAL CITY 12 INTELLIGENCES

APPENDIX C1: DEFINITIONS OF 12 INTELLIGENCES

Eco

Ecosphere intelligence is an awareness and capacity to respond to the realities of a city's climate and eco-region environment.

Emergent

Emergent intelligence looks at the city as a whole, through the lenses of: aliveness, survival, adaptiveness, regeneration, sustainability, and emergence.

Integral

Integral intelligence uses five essential maps of city life to see the whole city.

Living

Living intelligence relates to the aliveness of each citizen through each of its lifecycle stages and the aliveness of the city through its lifecycle stages.

Inner

Inner intelligence is "I" space of the citizen—the seat of intentional consciousness, attention, interior experience, and lines of development.

Outer

Outer intelligence is the biological "it" space of the citizen—the space where the body acts and behaves.

Social

Social intelligence is the "its" space of the city that gives us the capacity to structure and systemize our environment.

Cultural

Cultural intelligence represents the "we" life of the city—the relationships in the city which transcend boundaries that both contain and separate.

Inquiry

Inquiry intelligence asks key questions that reveal the meta-wisdom of the city.

Meshworking

Meshworking intelligence attracts the best of two operating systems—one that self-organizes, and the other that replicates hierarchal structures—to align systems that flex and flow.

Navigating

Navigating intelligence monitors and discloses the well-being or general condition of the city.

Evo

Evolutionary intelligence is the capacity to transcend and include the intelligences we currently demonstrate, in order to allow new intelligences to emerge.

APPENDIX C2: ASSESSMENT WORKSHEET FOR 12 INTELLIGENCES

(pages 1 and 2)

Integral City: Human Hive Intelligences — Durant 4 Voices

Discoverer: M. Hamilton

Date: Oct. 3, 2013	LATENT	AWARE	ACTIVE	ADVANCED	COMMENTS
CHAPTER 1: ECOSPHERE INTELLIGENCE					
1. Honour the climate and geography of your city.		x			
2. Steward the environment.		x			Concern re Lake Texoma
3. Add value to the earth space.	x				
CHAPTER 2: EMERGING INTELLIGENCE					
1. Survive so holons serve each other's existence.		x			Recognize interdependence
2. Adapt to the environment.		x			See need to learn
3. Create a self-regenerating feedback loop, by interconnecting human regeneration cycles so that they replenish the environment.		x			Seeking ways & means
CHAPTER 3: INTEGRAL INTELLIGENCE					
1. Map the territory integrally (horizontally through four quadrants, vertically through eight plus levels of development, diagonally through its change states, and relationally through its nested holarchies and fractals of complexity).	x				MH Visit = Start
2. Create and sustain an integral mapping system at the highest sustainable level of complexity, that is appropriate to the capacities of city management.	x				
3. Learn from and update the maps annually or more often.	x				
CHAPTER 4: LIVING INTELLIGENCE					
1. Honor the dance of life cycles in the city.		x	x		How to address Senior's needs?
2. Integrate the natural cycles of change within the city.		x	x		How to connect children & Seniors?
3. Learn how to zoom in and out at different scales to dance with the fractal patterns of the city.	x	x			MH Visit
CHAPTER 5: INNER INTELLIGENCE					
1. Show up and be self-aware, present, mindful.		x	x		Engaged 4 Voices
2. Notice the city intelligences and map them integrally.	x	x			MH Report
3. Grow leadership in heart, mind, soul.		x	x		Leadership important value
CHAPTER 6: OUTER INTELLIGENCE					
1. Manage personal energy.		x	x		Fitness, walking, bicycle paths
2. Seek bio-physical wellbeing for self and others.		x	x		Sports Complex
3. Nurture healthy leaders.		x	x		1U training leaders

© Integral City: 12 Intelligences Observations
12 Intelligences: Discovery Tour

Date: Oct. 3, 2013	LATENT	AWARE	ACTIVE	ADVANCED	COMMENTS
CHAPTER 7: BUILDING (STRUCTURE-SYSTEMS) INTELLIGENCE					
1. Manage life sustaining energy for all.		x			Awakening to NG & coal
2. Design from the center, at all scales for all holons.		x			Appreciating City Centre
3. Build structures that integrate self-organizing creativity with hierarchies of order.		x	x		Art Walk
CHAPTER 8: STORYTELLING (CULTURE) INTELLIGENCE					
1. Respect others.		x	x		
2. Listen deeply.		x	x		
3. Speak your story, and enable others to speak theirs, to co-create communities of integral practise.			x		
CHAPTER 9: INQUIRY INTELLIGENCE					
1. Ask what's working (and not) and co-generate a vision for the city's contribution to the planet.		x	x		WIP - MH Visit
2. Create an integral city and community plan.	x				MH Visit +
3. Implement and manage the plan appropriately at all scales in the city.	x				tbd
CHAPTER 10: MESHWORKING INTELLIGENCE					
1. Catalyze fractal connections within the human hive.		x	x		Think organically
2. Build communication bridges across silos, stovepipes and solitudes.		x	x		4 Voices Dialogue = start
3. Enable meshes and hierarchies that transform, transcend and transmute capacities.	x				tbd
CHAPTER 11: NAVIGATING INTELLIGENCE					
1. Select the future destination of the city based on its vision.		x	x		MH Visit+
2. Design and implement integral dashboards, using integral indicators of wellbeing for the city.	x				tbd
3. Notice outcomes and make course corrections to enable progress naturally.	x				tbd
CHAPTER 12: EVOLVING INTELLIGENCES					
1. Expect the unexpected.		x			Change needed
2. Pay attention to the rules.		x	x		Principles, Values important
3. Enable emergence and resilience by transcending and including integral capacities at level 8 and beyond.	x				tbd
MASTER RULE:					
Take care of yourself.		x	x		4 Voices interdependence
Take care of each other.		x	x		4 Voices interdependence
Take care of this place.		x	x		4 Voices interdependence

© Integral City: 12 Intelligences Observations
12 Intelligences: Discovery Tour

APPENDIX C3: INTEGRAL CITY GPS LOCATOR

Homo sapiens has built several types of cities—we focus on three types of cities: the Smart City driven by technology and industry; the Resilient city driven by ecological and eco-regional interdependencies; and the Integral City driven by the Master Code.

The **Integral City GPS** tool locates these 3 city types on 3 bezels that can move both independently and in synchrony.

At the core of the Integral City GPS lies the **Evolutionary Intelligence**, which provides the energetic impulse that drives all the other intelligences. Recognizing that every city emerges along an Evolutionary trajectory is also a core distinction of an Integral City (and explains why we begin the inquiry, action, and impact cycle of the book with an exploration of how to tap into the Evolutionary intelligence in the Knowing Field).

The Smart City Locator is situated on the 2nd bezel. It **uses Logic Models to track the logic** of cities—based on Strategic Rational thinking using the intelligences of Inquiry, Meshworking, and Navigating. It depends on scientific and methodical Inquiry; that is, research and development. It collects big data, maps patterns, tracks vital signs, and navigates the city's neural networks for effectiveness and efficiency. The Smart City Locator organizes the favorite functions used by Civic Managers and Citizens and asks: How are we doing in reaching targets? Do I have the basics of life? Do I have a job? Are the stores open? Do the buses run on time?

The Resilient City Locator is situated on the 3rd bezel. It is like the **Motherboard** of our intelligence system based on the natural systems we have inherited from Mother Earth. The Resilient City Locator locates our Human Hives in the context of their intelligences related to Ecologies and eco-regions; their Emergent responsiveness to local conditions; the basic Integral realities of bio-psycho-culture-systems; and their embedded, recurrent dynamic Lifecycles. It relates the interdependent scales of our cities in terms of their inter-city and intra-city ecologies.

The Resilient City intelligences provide contexts for the Strategies of the Smart City intelligences. It is used by Civic Managers who track the external conditions of the eco-regions of our human hive—asking about climate, water, energy, population densities—to seek feedback that tells us if we are going to be successful at not just reaching our target once, but multiple years into the future. The Resilient City locator alerts Business Innovators to threats and opportunities needing remedies, adaptive strategies, innovations, and inventions. It activates a measure of large-scale systems integration. And working with these impact patterns, it leads us to the third locator.

The Integral City Locator is situated on the 1st bezel. It acts as the **core intelligence chip** that reflects the deepest intelligence of the Human Hive. It offers "Integral Intel Inside." This chip embeds the core intelligences that enable human systems to be the most advanced life systems on earth. The Integral Integrator is built on the very simple architecture of Inner and Outer, Individual and Collective Capacities.

Outer Individual Intelligences include the external objective data elements tracked by the Smart City. The Outer Collective Intelligences include the external inter-objective infrastructural and systemic elements of cities mapped by the Resilient City—like the electric grid, transportation systems, and the built environment.

Inner Individual Intelligences include the internal subjective phenomena of emotions, consciousness, beliefs, mindfulness, and intentions. Inner Collective Intelligences include the internal intersubjective realities of values, worldviews, vision, and culture.

The true distinctiveness of the Integral City locator arises from the power of the Inner Capacities—Individual and Collective Intelligences—that drive city life. These Inner Intelligences in particular enable and constrain all the other intelligences because they define and delimit how we interpret big data, respond to ecological life conditions, and implement the strategies of Smart, Resilient, and Integral Cities. At their best, they add meta-capabilities to patterning, systemizing, evolving, and caring, through the means of collaborative inquiry, action, and impact.

The Integral locator points especially to the **Caring Capacities**—the ones that emerge from our attention to living the Master Code and expanding the circles of care in our lives.

As we expand our capacity to embrace greater circles of care—from self, to others, to place, to planet—we expand our capacity to develop habitats that carry and support the life conditions that we most need to be Smart, Resilient, and Integral.

Note: Traditional Cities are not located with this GPS Locator.

APPENDIX D: SAMPLE VALUES SURVEY FORM (PAGES 1 & 2)

FOR USE ONLY FOR NFP &/OR SAMPLES <60.

Sample survey forms for data collection are available for license under Integral City Protocols for use of Intellectual Property by Profit, NFP and Government organizations.

Thanks for your participation. Please return survey to researcher code: _____
Community/City: _____ **Postal/ZIP Code:** _____ **Date:** _____ , 201__

1. Enjoying a good life in any community comes from many sources. What makes life good for you in your community? Rate how true each statement below is on a scale of 1-10 (1 is not true at all; 10 is totally true).

   ☐ 1. I am happy, ready to learn and willing to change.
   ☐ 2. I behave and live in a healthy way. I drink clean water, and eat a healthy diet. I have lots of energy, or play sports or do performing arts. I don't abuse alcohol or drugs.
   ☐ 3. People care for each other and share beliefs and stories. We know our culture. People speak the same language. We share many of these experiences together—pray, dance, sew, paint, carve or sing.
   ☐ 4. Most people have jobs. Our work places are healthy. We have working water and waste systems. We have useable roads, power and lights and phones. We have good food stores; good housing and furnishings. We have good healthcare, schools and recreation.

2. Communities work well for different reasons. Select the statement that best completes this sentence: I believe the most important reason this community works well is because:

   ☐ 1.B Most people have the basics of life; eg. food, shelter, clothing.
   ☐ 2.P Families are important. People honour the elders. People support family traditions.
   ☐ 3.R Individuals can let off steam in sports, dance, arts and other healthy ways.
   ☐ 4.B Most people respect peace, order and rules at home and play. Many work for the greater good of the community.
   ☐ 5.O People and workplaces use tools, plans and goals to get results that work.
   ☐ 6.G People care for those in need; accept others who are different; and work as partners.
   ☐ 7.Y People use wisdom, work and flex and flow for the health of all.
   ☐ 8.T This community is so balanced and healthy that it adds to the health of the world.

3. Communities do not work well for different reasons. Select the statement that best completes this sentence: I believe the most important reason this community does not work well is because:

   ☐ 1.B Many people don't have the basics of life; eg. food, shelter, clothing.
   ☐ 2.P Families are not important. Families are violent. People don't honour the elders. People don't support family traditions.
   ☐ 3.R Individuals let off steam in unhealthy ways like alcohol, drugs, sex.
   ☐ 4.B Many people don't respect peace, order or rules at home, play or work. Some are criminal. Few people work for the greater good of the community.
   ☐ 5.O People and workplaces don't use the right tools, plans or goals. Often things fail and just don't work.
   ☐ 6.G People don't care for those in need. People who are different can't belong. You don't have partners who help you out.
   ☐ 7.Y People are not wise. People don't, won't or can't work for the health of all.
   ☐ 8.T This community makes the world unhealthy.

4. If you ruled your community for a day, and could do anything you wanted to make your community a better place, what would you do? Select the statement that best completes this sentence: I would make this community a better place, by making sure that:

☐ 1.B Most people have the basics of life; eg. food, shelter, clothing.
☐ 2.P Families are important. People honour the elders. People support family traditions.
☐ 3.R Individuals can let off steam in sports, dance, arts and other healthy ways.
☐ 4.B Most people respect peace, order and rules at home, play and work. People work for the greater good of the community.
☐ 5.O People and workplaces use tools, plans and goals to get results that work.
☐ 6.G People care for those in need; accept others who are different; and work as partners.
☐ 7.Y People use wisdom, work and flex and flow for the health of all.
☐ 8.T The community is so balanced and healthy that it adds to the health of the world.

5. Please rank the three statements that best describe you (1=best description; 2 = 2nd best description; 3=3rd best description):

☐ 1.R Lively, risky, bold, daring, a rebel
☐ 2.Y Loner, look after myself, flexible with lots of interests
☐ 3.B Loyal, others depend on me, strong beliefs
☐ 4.O Go-getter, competitive, a "winner", with high hopes
☐ 5.G Warm, open, friendly, sensitive, look out for others
☐ 6.P Honor elders, cultural ways and family traditions
☐ 7.T World thinker, global links, earth watcher

Tell us about you (anonymous information)

6. Age: Birthdate _____

7. Gender: (Circle) M F

8. First Language _____

Thank you for your time and ideas.

APPENDIX E: SYSTEMIC CONSTELLATION WORK

This Appendix has been written by Diana Claire Douglas (updated Spring 2016) from an article by Diana Claire Douglas & Marilyn Hamilton, first published in The International Constellations Journal; Issue 22, June 2013 as Knowing Cities: The Knowing Field and the Emergence of Integral City Intelligence (Douglas & Hamilton, 2013b). It also formed a presentation at the Infosyon Conference, Amsterdam, April, 2013.

Systemic Constellation Work—originally called Family Constellation Work and founded by Bert Hellinger—can be described in many ways. For Diana, it is *a perspective*—viewing problems, issues, conflicts, entanglements from a systemic perspective, whether it be: individuals, families, organizations, or larger collectives. It is also a *body of knowledge* gathered phenomenologically from trainers and facilitators doing constellations with thousands of people and organizations from around the world. It is an *experiential process*, some would call a *tool* or *method* that has been and can be integrated with many other ways of working. It is a way to *embody energy and information* so that it can be made visible. Systemic Constellation Work is *a change process*. Constellations reveal hidden dynamics—the inner images, behaviors, challenges, and opportunities that exist below our conscious awareness. Once 'what is' is acknowledged, genuine movements (changes) can be made, sometimes immediately and sometimes over time. And finally, Systemic Constellation Work is a growing and evolving *worldwide community of constellators/facilitators* who are applying the experiential process to an infinite number of issues and on multiple scales, including individuals, families, organizations, and collective groups like cities.

Constellator Commentary on doing remote constellations via the internet: phone, Skype, GoToMeeting, or Zoom

Although SCW has historically been done in-person within a group, or in one-on-one sessions, quite recently constellators are finding ways to do this experiential process online. Diana Claire developed with Integral City Community of Practice and others a way to do this non-local, non-linear process via the internet with up to nine members (more participants are possible) simultaneously in different locations in Europe, Egypt, Mexico, and across North America on a monthly or bi-monthly basis.

For distance sessions, each participant prepares their own space – either desktop or floor space – placing a clock chart in the center of the space (see Figure E1). This represents the Knowing Field, the circle or field within which we work. Paper, sticky notes, and ordinary objects are used as place markers on the clock chart. Diana Claire and each participant map the process visually so that all participants are working from the same map. For example, the participant representing the Spirit of Integral City finds her place in the field, and for this constellation, says it is "on the axis between 9 and 3, closer to the center." Everyone marks this on their diagram/space. All the elements to be represented are placed into the field in the same manner. Once the elements are placed, we all look at the visual map that has been created. This map shows time, distance, and direction—the patterns of connection between the elements. It is often different from our conscious mental pictures and begins to allow what has been hidden to emerge.

Representing the Knowing Field

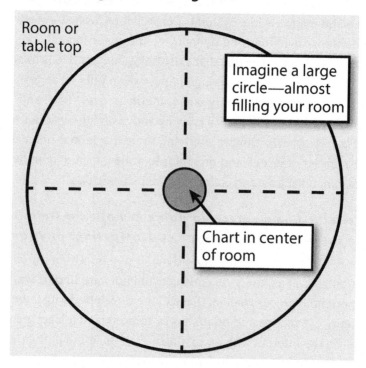

**Figure E1: Clock Face for Distance Systemic Constellation
(diagram by Diana Claire Douglas)**

SCW as a process is done through representing the elements in the constellation. In the ICCOP constellations, each member usually represents one (or sometimes more) elements. Being a representative in the Knowing Field is a unique process. It is not taking on a role. It is allowing the energy and information available through the Knowing Field to move through the human body/mind. For Diana, this is not intuition, although it can be experienced as intuition. The person representing senses this flow through images, words, body sensations, body movements, and/or emotions. The representative then shares what she is experiencing with the group. In addition, we access collective information by having the representatives dialogue with each other.

There are many different kinds of constellations (free, structural, chaos, and more), adapted to many scales (individual, organizational, large-scale collective), used for an extraordinary number of issues, questions, or propositions, by practitioners from all around the world.

For more information, contact: Diana Claire Douglas, Founder of Knowing Field Designs www.knowingfielddesigns.com. Knowing Field Designs is a centre for Systemic Facilitation offered through Coaching, Consulting and Training for Individuals, Organizations + Social Collectives using Systemic Constellation Work.

APPENDIX F: WHOLE SYSTEM METHODOLOGIES

These whole system methodologies have in common the quality of being psycho-active—many are even bio-psycho-cultural-socially active. This makes them all very powerful contributors to systems change and transformation.

Appendix F1: Action Inquiry

Action Inquiry is a term coined by Bill Torbert and associates. They define it as a process to learn leadership in the midst of action, using the "action logics" of adult development. This inquiry method opens eight developmental sequences that enable increasingly more complex strategies and inquiries to unfold both for the individual leader and for the group of co-leaders who may be involved in the inquiry. Action Inquiry enables mutuality in the inquiry process and notices the changes to the collective as well as the individual that ensues from the inquiry.

The "action logics" follow a similar sequence of adult development described by the Integral Framework (Wilber, 1995, 2000a, 2007) and Spiral Dynamics (D. Beck & Cowan, 1996; Graves, 2003, 2005; Wight, 2011).

— (W. Torbert & Associates, 2004; William R. Torbert et al., 2008)

Appendix F2: Action Learning

As used in this book, Action Learning refers to the reflective learning practice that draws on Action Research and Action Inquiry, as outlined in the author's exploration of her own learning applying the Integral Framework and Spiral Dynamics. It traces the impact of life conditions as a habitat for learning (providing the early basis for defining a Learning Habitat or "Lhabitat") and the developmental path traced by Torbert in "Action Logics," Wilber in the Integral Framework, and Beck in Spiral Dynamics. This process was described and presented at the Integral Theory Conference, 2008 as Integral Methods from the Margins: Finding Myself in the Research—A Retrospective of Integral Leadership Development Methods Using Online Dialogue Analysis, a Competency Development Framework and Action Research (Hamilton, 2008b).

Appendix F3: Action Research

This is a term originally coined by Kurt Lewin to describe research that is action-based following a systemic cycle of plan, observe, act, review. Each cycle generates learning that expands the circle of inquiry, allowing succeeding cycles to build on the discoveries of the prior cycles. Action Research incorporates the reflective capacity of the researcher (which was incorporated into the work of Argyris and Schön (1974) with their design students and subsequently into organizational practice, as well into the inter-cultural explorations initiated by Paulo Freire in Brazil (Freire & Horton, 1990).

Action Research typically moves the researcher into the inter-subjective space of the participants, so that they become coresearchers.

Variations of Action Research include Participatory Action Research and Practical Action Research.

— ("Action Research," (anon, 2016a; Coghlan & Brannick, 2007; Stringer, 2014)

Appendix F4: Appreciative Inquiry

Appreciative Inquiry originated at Case Western University where Cooperrider and Srivastva challenged the predominant problem-based approach to developing strategies for change. They turned the model based on overcoming weaknesses, disadvantages, and threats on its head, and asked, "What strengths do we have to co-create a solution?" This asset-based approach builds on a process cycle of group engagement, that was popularized by Diana Whitney, now referred to as the 5 "D's"—Discovery, Dream, Design, Deliver, Debrief.

Like Action Research the cycle expands wider time, space, and moral horizons to continuously learn and grow strengths and assets.

Appreciative Inquiry is frequently coupled with Action Research to discover ways that groups can inquire, research, and act together.

— (Bushe, nd; Cooperrider & Whitney, 1999; Hammond, 1996; Watkins & Mohr, 2001; Whitney & Trosten-Bloom, 2010)

Appendix F5: Integral Inquiry

Integral Inquiry is the general term used by the author to embrace Integral Methodological Pluralism (IMP), as defined by Ken Wilber (Wilber, 2006, p. 33). Wilber says Integral Methodological Pluralism (IMP) "involves... at least 8 fundamental and apparently irreducible methodologies, injunctions, or paradigms for gaining reproducible knowledge (or verifiably repeatable experiences).... the quadrants [with their inside and outside, and individual and collective dimensions]... are often represented as I, you/we, it and its... [as well as] the Good, the True, the Beautiful; or art, morals and science... " (p. 33).

The Integral City Core Team has described Integral Epistemological Pluralism as "the concurrent employment and availability, for the purpose at hand, of all faculties and capacities of consciousness (especially those related to "knowing") available to a given individual or group at a given time, employed in priorities optimal to accomplishment of the purpose" (Hamilton et al., 2015, p. 5).

Appendix F6: Logic Models

Logic Models were popularized by the Kellogg Foundation to introduce systemic and systematic thinking into the planning, development and evaluation of projects. Logic Models make visible the inherent logic of a sequence of tasks involving input, transformation, and output.

As used in this book, the factors we employ to measure the formative and summative stages of project goals (see Figure 27) include the following key elements:

- **Opportunity Statement**: What life conditions provide the context for embarking on the project?
- **Goal Description**: How do we define the goal we intend to achieve as the overriding outcome of the project?
- **Assumptions**: How do we scope the project in terms of time, space, moral constraints? What are the limitations and delimitations of the project?
- **Resources/Inputs**: What assets, capacities, and resources do we bring as inputs to energize and fuel the project?

- **Activities**: Who does what, with whom, when, and where?
- **Outputs**: What tangible, quantitative deliverables will be produced by the project? How can we measure them using SMART[59] metrics?
- **Impacts Measured as Outcomes** (short-term, mid-term, long-term): What quantitative and qualitative outcomes will produce impact in 1-year, 3-year, 5-year time frames?

These factors can often be displayed on a one-page document that crystallizes the intentions and flow of work into a graphical flow (as illustrated in Figure 27: Logic Model Overview).

— (anon, 2004, nd)

Appendix F7: MetaIntegral 4-Quadrant Impacts

At the Integral Theory Conference 2015, MetaIntegral Foundation introduced the framework that their research projects (and researchers) were using to measure the impact of the projects. They used a 4-quadrant framework that measured:

UL Deep Impact—Transforming Mindsets
LL Wide Impact—Transforming Relationships
UR Clear Impact—Transforming Behaviors
LR High Impact—Transforming Systems

In this book we have used this 4-quadrant framework to set out for each chapter, the reflective questions related to the potential impacts generated by the inquiry explored in that chapter. (S. Esbjörn-Hargens, 2015b)

Appendix F8: Polarity Management Examples

Polarity Management (Johnson, 1996) is a process developed to explore intractable problems that can be represented in two dimensions each across a spectrum of possible realities (often represented in terms of intensity expressed by plus or minus). The polarities are typically represented in a 4-quadrant diagram with the issue being examined situated on a trajectory that traces the polarity qualities as the situation changes.

---

59   Specific, Measurable, Accountable, Relevant, Trackable ("S.M.A.R.T Goals," 2016)

This process helps leaders realize that intractable problems cannot be solved with simple solutions—but that by changing one factor in a situation it inevitably causes changes in other factors.

Below is a **diagram and a list** of examples of polarities found in the discovery visit to one city.

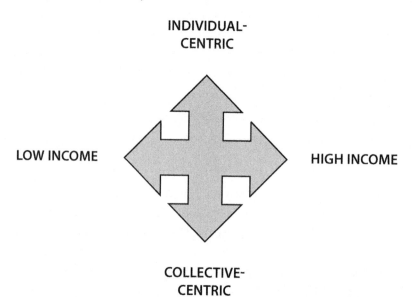

Dimension	Pole A	Pole B
Point of View	Individual Centric	Collective Centric
Ethnicity/Culture	Choctaw Nation	Other OK/American Culture
Economy	Middle & Upper Income	Lower Income
Economic Sectors	Tourism	Industry
Economic Growth	Casino	Other Tourism
Environment	Balanced Development	5 Threats (Climate, Water, Energy, Food, Finance)
Development	Human Development	Sustainable Development
Planning	Local Plans	Regional Plans
City Hall	Status Quo Management	Succession Planning
Government Relations	City Governance	State, Federal Governance

Dimension	Pole A	Pole B
City Layout	Inner Core – Heart of City	Outskirts – Large Footprint
City Building Inventory	Old Town	New Suburbs
Justice Agency	Police Department	Community Civility
Emergency Services	Fire Station(s)	Ambulance/ERT
Healthcare	Population Health Needs	Medical Centre Resources
Organization Relationships	Employer	Employee
Leadership Practice	Leader	Manager
Job Fitness/Opportunities	Many Job Openings	Not Enough Local Workers with appropriate skills
Labor force Skills	Using Local Job Skills	Importing "Away" Job Skills
Labor force Development	Ignoring Local Skill Development Needs	Developing Local Skills
Housing Stock	Middle & Upper Ownership	Lower Income Renters
Property Ownership/Inventory	Absentee Landlords	Home Owners in Residence
Housing Needs	Single Family Units	Condos, Apartments, Townhouses
Education - Elementary	K-8	9–12
Education - Undergrad	High school	SOSU
Citizens	Old Timers	Newcomers
Generations	Seniors	Youth
Recreation	Senior Recreation	Active/Bicycle/Walking
Expressive Energies	Arts (Walk)	Sports Centre
Interests	Whole City	Special Interests
Belief Systems	Churched	Unchurched

APPENDIX G: INTEGRAL VITAL SIGNS MONITOR—COMPOSITE SET OF INDICATORS

Integral Vital Signs Monitor

Key Performance Indicators

Composite for Ecocity Builders 2013

Integral City Vital Signs Monitor: City Sub-Groups

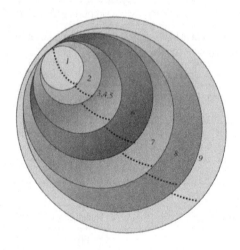

FRACTALS OF HUMAN SYSTEMS

1 = Individual

2 = Family

3,4,5 = Organizations: workplaces, education, healthcare

6 = Civil Society

7 = Recreation/ Faith

8 = City Hall/ Infrastructure

9 = Environment Eco- region

Figure G1: Integral Vital Signs Sub-Groups of Human Systems in Cities

OVERVIEW OF INTEGRAL VITAL SIGNS MONITOR

The prototype for this document was developed over a number of years. First, with the Bowen Island GeoSurvey and Healthy Community Data (in 2003) for Abbotsford Canada; and from the Globe Sustainable Awards Jury; and a Futures project in South Africa. The indicators are organized into an integral framework based on the models of integral perspectives (Wilber, 1995, 1996, 2007), values evolution (D. Beck & Cowan, 1996) and Integral City intelligences (Hamilton, 2008a) as shown above in Figure 1.

The Integral Vital Signs Monitor (IVSM) prototype operates on an online platform developed by Gaiaspace™. The IVSM displays a set of salutogenic (health generating), integral (bio-psycho-social-cultural) indicators and metrics.The indicators are all measured in terms of targets set by the stakeholders of the data. The targets are displayed on a dashboard using a Traffic Light System; Blue = Exceeds Target, Green = On Target; Yellow = Little to Moderate Off-Target; Orange = Moderately to Majorly Off-Target; Red = Danger Zone (see Figure G2 below).

The IVSM offers cities and communities a set of indices to measure overall health and well-being and whether those health indicators are moving towards greater or lesser health. What makes it successful is the premise that community partners distribute the workload of creating and tracking the data because partners contribute the indicators they "own," and a composite picture of the whole community emerges from the integral map. As a result, each community partner has a stake in the success of the IVSM and together the community of partners gains insights of the interconnections that contribute to the well-being of the whole city.

The Key Performance Indicators (KPI) were extracted from the cities who were finalists in the Globe Sustainable City Award, 2010 and 2011; a Futures project in South Africa; and two well-being projects in Canada. These KPIs are a composite selection. In a real situation it would be recommended that KPIs be drawn from existing data, with two to three KPIs per sub-group (Internal and External).

The indicators in the table below are a composite drawn from these cities: Curitiba, Brazil; Sydney, Australia; Songpa, South Korea; Vancouver, Canada; Murcia, Spain; Malmo, Sweden; Ekurhuleni, South Africa; Abbotsford, BC, Canada. One view of the IVSM is displayed below in Figure G2.

INTEGRAL VITAL SIGNS MONITOR		

1. INDIVIDUAL
 	
Internal
HS Graduation Count   95%
 	
External
Reduction Incidents of
  Diabetes   50%
	2. FAMILY & FRIENDS
	
	Internal
	Reduction Incidents
	  Family Violence 10%
	
	External
	Housing 85%
		3. WORK PLACE
		
		Internal
		# Jobs Created for Youth 40%
		
		External
		Farm Gate Revenue $MM $m37

4. HEALTH SYSTEM
 	
Internal
Reductions Youth Mental
  Health Incidents   10%
 	
External
Reduction Youth
  Communicable Disease 30%
	9. ENVIRONMENTAL
	CONTROL
	
	External
	Climate—GHG 90%
	Earth—Soil Quality 65%
	Water Quality 99%
	Air Quality 85%
	Biosphere Diversity 71%
		5. EDUCATION
		
		Internal
		Youth Literacy 72%
		
		External
		Number High School
		  Teachers 370

6. CIVIL SOCIETY/
COMMUNITY
 	
Internal
Youth-to-Youth Volunteer
  Hours   1200
 	
External
NFP & NGO Count   20
	7. RECREATION & SPORT
	
	Internal
	Cross Cultural Events 1
	
	External
	Capital Investment
	  Rec Facilities 0%
		8. CITY HALL, POLICE, FIRE,
		INFRASTRUCTURE
		
		Internal
		Safety Rating City Streets
		  at Night 75%
		
		External
		Ridership Public Transit 55%

Figure G2: Integral Vital Signs Monitor 9 Scales—Municipal Home Page

Gathering the Data

The general indicator data is reported with no Highlighting. The Grey Shading indicates data that can be used for special subpopulations—in this case, Youth. The Gaiasoft Platform is able to report all data, subpopulations, and special interest data.

201x Sub-Group	Composite
1. Individual	
Internal	
	» Happiness » LPRM Learning Processes and Results Monitoring: monthly, this tool evaluates efficiency and efficacy of all activities in course » Social Indicators framework to enable measurement and monitoring of social well-being
	» HS graduation count » Post-Secondary Education Registrations » % of Grade 4 and & students reading below Grade level by cultural group » % readiness for Grade 1 » Vulnerability rate on Early Development Indicator scores » Enrolment Full Day Kindergarten enrolment » Awards Unclaimed as % Unclaimed Community Foundation Scholarships » Crime counts for youth » Youth employment » Youth entrepreneurship » Incidents Youth Mental Health Admissions
External	
	» Resident survey- General satisfaction level: » Homes built in the municipality under bio-climatic and/or sustainable architecture criteria (% of newly built homes).
	» Healthy City Youth Data » Enrolment in recreational activities » Youth Relationships with Adults » Youth Housing Shelter Use » Mental Health Drugs dispensed by Youth age
2. Family & Friends	
Internal	
	» Social indicators framework to monitor social well-being » Number of citizens aware of energy saving; especially immigrants, women, elderly, students

201x Sub-Group	Composite
	» Incidents of family violence as % total families » Trauma from war zones » Family Structure with 2 parent support » Gang Activity » House Parties with alcohol or drug complaints » Crime Recidivism
External	
	» Green home KW » social and affordable housing levels » Relocation of families to healthier areas of city
	» Youth house units » Homeless Rate » Cost of Living » Community Affordability Indicator » Generational differences in cultures » Eldercare to youth care ratio by culture
3. Work Place	
Internal	
	» WEP Work and Evaluation Plan: weekly, every planned activity is evaluated in relation to project's main objectives, and in relation to its specific resources (time and people) » Key supporter of successful bid to host City Innovation Awards » Target audience of business representatives at the Sustainability Dialogues: an increase x%. » All presenters and panelists who volunteer their time to participate in city advisory councils
	» New business start-ups » Number of business licenses in total For-Profit and NFP » Entrepreneurial recognition/ awards » Adult employment vs Youth employment » Corporate Social Responsibility Registrations » Best organizations to work for recognition
External	

201x Sub-Group	Composite
Financial	» Capital Investment in FFE » Capital Investment in physical plant » Key Industry healthy performance » Farm Gate Input/output » Measure manufacture & processing returns » Measure info technology, resource, financial services for support biz returns » Measure restaurant & food supply returns » Measure retail & home food supply returns
	» All of the above
4. Health System	
Internal	
	» Best Practices Capacity of leadership performance » Community relationships - How health system relates to its client base » Mental Health » Measure of how Learning and faith contribute to health prevention and healing » healthy community indicators that are 4Q8L
	» Youth Mental health needs special attention to prevent complications as adults » Healthy Youth indicators that are 4Q8L
External	
	» Hospital power Kw » Nursing home for elderly power Kw » Infectious disease incidents » Capital investment in FFE » Capital Investment in physical plant » Healthy City population strata
	» All of the above for Youth
5. Education	
Internal	

201x Sub-Group	Composite
	» Ethical values (human, social, and cultural capitals) » Number children on daily educational programmes » number mothers and newborns supported » video production on traditional culture masters » community self-esteem enhancement » happiness and harmony within project teams
	» High School Teacher Performance » High school student performance » Measure of literacy & numeracy indicates basic skills needed for career success
External	
	» School Solar power » Schools / academic centers in the municipality with photovoltaic equipment » Capital investment in FFE » Capital Investment in physical plant
	» Number km paths » Number & % schools with bicycle model program
	» Measure quantitative availability of HS teachers per population
6. Civil Society/ Community	
Internal	
	» Projects and programs supported by community participation » Strategic capacity measure of civil society leadership » Volunteer hours
External	
	» Number of civil societies registered » Number of NGO's registered » Number of Employers who invest employee hours as volunteer hours for community » Value Revenues & Investments in NFP » Reliance on Social Safety Net
7. Recreation & Spirit	
Internal	

201x Sub-Group	Composite
	» Awards received by sports athletes, coaches, sponsors » Awards received by artists, art teachers, sponsors » Number of Cross & inter-cultural events » Number of interfaith events » Attendance levels of community events
	» Awards received by sports athletes, coaches, sponsors » Awards received by artists, art teachers, sponsors » Number of Cross & inter-cultural events » Number of interfaith events » Attendance levels of community events » Number of Non-School Events
External	
	» Capital investment in FFE » Capital Investment in physical plant » Sports & Cultural Centre KW » Kids cultural Centre KW » Liquor law reform » New small bar culture » Reinvigorate the fine grain spaces of the City Centre with business grants and new public art » Satisfaction with natural environment
	» Number of edgy activities that are thrill seeking but safe in secular community
8. City Hall & Infrastructure	
Internal	

201x Sub-Group	Composite
Leadership – staff	» Leadership Awards » Measure qualitative Capacity of Leadership performance » Award in the area of natural city » Green City Award » Institutional collaborations between departments and sectors » Integrated System of Public Participation » Advisory working groups influence decision making. » Local group participation, facilitation & reports » City uses Facebook group and public hearings. » Public participation is one of main pillars for city admin. » How often, in what forums does city hall engage with community » Number of Participants in Public participation monitored regularly
Leadership – elected	» Measure developmental capacity of Elected Leadership
Community Relationships/ Engagement	» Number of visitors to Parks » Attendance at the Citizen-City Particpation Breakfasts » Number participants engaging on topics ranging from capacity-building through culture to peak oil. » Number Sustainability Dialogues & audience numbers » Number of viewers of City-sponsored Info TV program as a significant engagement medium
Voter turnout	» Local democracy » Number of population participating in democratic process » Web forum » Children & youth forums.
Public safety	» Available security from Police, Fire, Ambulance services » For Youth - Available security from Police, Fire, Ambulance services
Research/ Learning	» What is city hall learning to improve, change, start, stop doing? » City annually reports progress against Sustainable City 205x. You can watch the progress report presentations or download a copy at http://www.city
Foresight	» MOUs with the State/Provincial Government to investigate and deliver Sustainable City 205x » Projects in areas including housing, public transport, and new civic spaces » Setting a vision for 30-year time horizon; imagining scenarios with possible constraints to set a direction for the city to develop strategic plans

201x Sub-Group	Composite
External	
Financial	» Financial satisfaction (infrastructure, social and financial capitals) » Number farmers quitting their jobs in order to work in their land » Number farmers integrated to local market » Number youth obtain a minimum wage
Noise	

Eco-Footprint / Energy Use	» The reduction of energy consumption of the Town Hall itself by x %.
	» Homes and facilities built within the municipality with the use of solar power for sanitary hot water (% of new buildings).
	» Buildings not to exceed an energy consumption of 105 kWh/m2/year, including energy produced as well as used or recovered. Various indicators incorporated (amongst others) included:
	  › efficient use of space
	  › efficient heating
	  › efficient electricity use
	  › total energy
	  › environmentally conscious materials
	  › low noise, adjustable ventilation
	  › day-lighting
	  › attractiveness and
	  › a green space factor.

Water System	» Measure water use per capita and total population » Water quality in all natural water sources › 201a BOD=x, SS=y compared to results 201g BOD=x, SS=y
Food System & Urban Farm	» Measure nutritional needs per capita and total population » Measure calorie use per capita and total population » Meeting nutritional requirements » Vegetable garden number m2 and number persons/yr. » Green Village – number households/yr.
Wet Waste System	» Measure solid waste per capita » Volume of Collection of used cooking oil

201x Sub-Group	Composite
Solid Waste Management System	» Measure solid waste per capita » Implementation of x number separation and recycling parks (number of Ecocitizens benefit). » Collection of old tires (every six months, number tons of old tires transformed). » Beginning of the implementation of the garbage recycling and processing industry (% of all the garbage collected in City Metropolitan Region).
Public Safety Capital investment in FFE	» Measure of FFE investment by public safety services
Public Safety Capital Investment in physical plant	» Measure of long term Capital investment by public safety services » Annual $ investment in maintaining and replacement building » City council follows a policy of following sustainability criteria in the public procurement as a way to boost environmental protection and energy efficiency in the society: all the tenders that are opened by the City Council have environmental protection and/or energy efficiency criteria in the evaluations process. » All wood derived products acquired by the City Council are certified to belong to controlled forests, » Performance indicators were included and a Quality Programme implemented which aimed to: 1) give developers a single basic standard to secure attractiveness and quality; 2) act as an operative instrument for City and developers; 3) secure an environmental profile; 4) incorporate innovative technology and services, and 5) high quality architectural conception and design. » The Quality Programme included a number of indicators to be met by the district and its buildings to qualify as a sustainable city district. Most requirements were qualitative, such as to incorporate the lifecycle perspective of building materials, however there were quantitative measurements as well, including targets for energy consumption and green space.
Transportation Auto	» Eco-mileage = number households » All city vehicles of the new waste management service use electric, natural gas or biofuels as a power source.

201x Sub-Group	Composite
Transportation Cycle	» Number km for Bicycle model school – number schools – % of total » Financial Commitment for x years committed to deliver a x km new separated cycleway network, supported by over x km of on-road cycling provision, and social change programs » Bicycle road: x km constructed (x km of outer beltway for bicycles)
Transportation – Transit	» Measure accessibility and mobility from one part of city to another; and from this city to other cities » installed in 201x on-line, real-time information of the traffic via internet and the installation of on-line information panels, Bluetooth system and/or BIDI systems at bus stops that provide the info of the actual arrival time of the public transport buses. » Transit measure is complemented by solar photovoltaic energy facilities on the bus shelters that provide the energy required for the system, a voice information service, a SMS information service that permit to access the bus arrival time to any stop from anywhere and an on-line web that provide the actual positions of the buses in the city. » The municipal WIFI network is also used by the City Council in new management actions such as the real time control of the status of the public bicycle bins (outdoor closed kiosks used as public bicycle parking), » Implementation of the first step of the Green Line (a complete avenue: mass transportation corridor, traffic lanes, cycling facilities, sidewalks and linear park). » The incorporation of low energy consumption and ecologic fuel operated vehicles to local public transportation. » Use of public transit by residents, youth » Measure availability and use of public transit by hours used /week » User Satisfaction rating monthly
Transportation – Air, Rail	» Use of air, rail to connect to other cities » An historic MOU with the state Government to investigate new light rail for City
Communication	» Accessibility of Phones, wired, wireless, cable, TV, radio, internet, postal services, couriers » Km of installed modes per capita » # households with communication modes installed » Smart City Model. developed the infrastructure for free internet access via WIFI at the parks, squares and streets of the city. The investment reaches x Currency Total.

201x Sub-Group	Composite
GHG & Emission Reduction	» CO_2 reduction » Tube-stations climatized by a clean system (the system doesn't harm the ozone layer). » Control of the carbon monoxide emissions (in x v tons' reduction of carbon monoxide emissions and, measure reduction of x tons per month). » Council has committed x Currency over the next x years for environmental initiatives across the entire property portfolio and has already achieved a x% greenhouse gas reduction (and at Town Hall House, our biggest energy user, reductions estimated at x% are being verified)
Energy Use	» $$ for people with low energy consumption » Electric Power Generation in x years as KwH measured as xmm pine trees or reduce CO_2 x kg » Coordinates a working group of the development of Smart Cities Technology in the Association of Energy Agencies. » Use of biofuel in the Green Line busses (x% less smoke and x% less carbon monoxide emissions). » The introduction of efficiency and energy saving criteria in municipal contracts for services / municipal works and in tender offers. » KwH per household and per business » kjoules per household and per business
Energy Distribution	» Develop a distributed energy (trigeneration & renewables) master plan, green infrastructure master plan, total water cycle plan and a business case for alternative waste treatment
Energy Conservation Production	» Energy produced by waste recycling; wind; water; solar production » City Sharing Power Plant No1 & 2 » Kw Capacity » Plottage » Power Generation » Waterside solar street light » Wind power » Subterranean Heat » A new trial of LED and other energy efficient lighting is underway in the City Centre, ready to be rolled out across metropolitan City

201x Sub-Group	Composite
Land Use, Parks & Water Parks	» Land use set out in official community plan (OCP) » Greening City Center » Area of green fields » Number Trees » Wall greening in xm^2 » Roof greening xm^2 » Reserved for future acquisition x ha. of land, which corresponds to x% of the total territory of City, » Within the reserved land x ha. has been acquired » x linear parks were implemented so far in recovered public land along creeks. » The parks are distributed in all four regions: Total area transformed into parks adds to x ha. and total extension of creeks is about x km. » Now x linear parks are under construction along x km of creeks or rivers. » Implantation of x new parks (+ xm^2 of green areas equipped). » Identification of x private areas with potential to become MNHPR (+ x million m^2 of remaining forests). » Identification of x public areas with potential to become Urban Biodiversity Conservancy Groves (+ x million m^2 of remaining forests). » Implementation of 3 MNHPR (+ x m^2 of protected green areas). » Urban water parks: x established
9. Environment Context	
Internal	
	» Satisfaction with living environment » Environmental commitment (infrastructure, technical and environmental capitals)
External	
	» x families shifted rural productive matrix (out of x000 in rural site) » x ha area being restored » x families supplied with potable water (out of x00 in critical situation) » x waterfronts protected
Climate	» Change in ambient air temperature; sea temperature; sea level
Earth	» Measures for soil productivity, resilience

201x Sub-Group	Composite
Water	» Measure and Report Water Quality Daily » Conclusion of all the studies for the River basin revitalization Project. » Waterway restoration: xkm restored; x% of the total length (xkm) » River water circulation: x,000 tons per day in River; x,000 tons per day in Y River
Air	
Biosphere Diversity	» Implementation of 1 Biodiversity Conservancy Grove (+ x,000 m2 of protected green areas). » Avifauna survey (x00 species identified). » Conservancy of the protected species » Increased diversity in the life forms in River » - x types of birds, x types of fish, x types of insects, x type of amphibian » - x types of invertebrate animals at river bottom » - Inhabitation of (level 2 extinction-risk animal) » - Inhabitation of corbiculas and marsh snails (found only in cleanest waters)
Urban Forest	» Native trees planting (+ x0,000 seedlings planted). Eradication of invading exotic plants (x,000 exotic plants eradicated). » Urban afforestation » - Green zone area: xm² (x00% increase) » - Number of trees: (x% increase) » - Wall-planting: wall space of xm² planted per year on average » - Rooftop-planting: rooftop space of xm² planted per year on average
Eco-Region Sustainability	» Take responsibility for the watershed in which located » Produces a Sustainability Report that measures progress made on the collaboratively determined action items from the Sustainability Summit. » This report measures progress made at a regional level in a number of key areas, including liquid and solid waste, culture, land use and housing.

APPENDIX H: QUALITIES OF AN INTEGRAL DESIGNER

These qualities of the **Integral Sustainable Designer** are taken from Mark DeKay's opus *Integral Sustainable Design* (DeKay, 2011) *with permission from Earthscan.*

[An Integral Sustainable Designer will]:

expand... awareness of Sustainable Design to include its behavioral, experiential, cultural, and systemic perspectives; be able to readily identify which of the four foundational perspectives embodied in a given sustainable design, intention, strategy or idea; understand some of the basic issues and strategies for:

1. designing for engendering rich human experiences of Sustainable Design
2. designing for maximizing performance of Sustainable Design
3. designing for fitness to the context of ecological systems
4. designing for manifesting cultural meaning in Sustainable Design. (p. 10)

[The] **Integral Sustainable Designer** can choose to inhabit and work from any worldview required by the situation. Traditional worldview: Eco-manager designer (Level 1)... Modern worldview: Eco-strategist designer (Level 2)... Post-modern worldview: Eco-pluralist designer (Level 3)... Integral worldview: Eco-integralist designer (Level 4). (pp. 241–242)

DeKay identifies six perceptual shifts needed by the mature **Integral Sustainable Designer** as:

1. From objects to relationships to subject-object relationships
2. From analysis to context to analysis-context-ground
3. From structure to process to unfolding
4. From materiality to configuration to pattern languages
5. From parts to wholes to holons
6. From hierarchies to networks to holarchies (p. 261)

For [DeKay], the value of looking at design through an integral lens has been that it has allowed me to glimpse areas of expertise that others have developed more than I have and to finally be able to honor them and include their valuable perspectives in my own work. As a result, it has also opened my eyes to the fact that the perspective that I have been generally steeped in for the last 25 years is also only partially true! Telling the whole story involves listening to and from others' perspectives: cultural, individual, ecological as well as technical. Then each viewpoint takes its valuable and appropriate place in a wider perspective where nothing is missing—rich human experiences, significant cultural meaning, high technological performance and true ecological sense merge into something much richer, truer and ultimately more aesthetically pleasing. Welcome to the future of design! (p. 129)

APPENDIX I: TEAM CHARTER FORM

Team Name: _____Date: _____

Team Members

Name	Location	Phone	email

Team Member Types

(select a typology system to describe individual preferences; e.g. Enneagram, MBTI, CRG)

Name	Typology

Team Member Skill Inventory

(areas individual members can contribute/want to develop)

Name	Skills

Team Goals

_____

_____

_____

What are potential barriers to these goals?

_____

_____

_____

Group Agreements/Ground Rules
(e.g. Meeting Schedules, locations, attendance, agenda, assignments, communication methods, etc.)

_____

_____

_____

Conflict Management
What are potential conflicts that might arise among/between members? How will team members deal with these and other conflicts?

_____

_____

_____

APPENDIX J: INTEGRAL CITY SCOPE OF WORK LOGIC MODEL

Opportunity Statement: Durant is growing quickly, through economic impact of gaming tourism and needs 4 voices of city to develop a city vision, master plan and action plans

Goal: IC Design, Develop, Coach and Curate Visioning Process to create a Vision of Durant's long term future, coordinating with Imagine Durant (Executive Board of Directors and ED) and 4 City Voices to produce a report with recommendations for a Master Community Plan and Strategy that is Place Caring and Place Making.

Resources/Inputs	Activities	Outputs	OUTCOMES Year 1	OUTCOMES Year 2	OUTCOMES Year 3
	Visioning Round 1				
Dialogue 1: Thought Leaders					
ED, IC	Plan Visioning Round 1				
ED, IC	Coach Location of Event TL Dialogue 1				
ED, Tforce	Coach Selection & Invitation				
Thought Leaders	20 TL letters				
ED	Advise re Organizing Catering				
ED	Support ED to Find, Invite, Train Event Team	Event Team Operations			
ED, IC, EBoD	Select Themes	Economy, Community			
ED, IC	Plan Agenda, Invite Local Speakers	Speakers: Economy, Community, Environment, Culture			
IC	Organize IC Team, Travel				
Train, Coordinate ED	Itineraries				
ED, IC	Support Assembly of Materials	Agendas, Meeting Handouts			
ED, IC	Support Selection of Scribe, Train				
ED, Durant Team, IC Team	Coordinate Set Up Event Space				
IC Facilitator, ED, IC Team, Durant Team, Thought Leaders	Facilitate Day 1	Evening Meal/Stories			
IC Facilitator, ED, IC Team, Durant Team, Thought Leaders	Facilitate Day 1	4 Scenario Exploration			
IC Facilitator, ED, IC Team, Durant Team, Thought Leaders	Facilitate Day 1	Summary of Learning			
ED, IC, Durant Team	Post Dialogue Debrief	Action Steps	Carry Forward to Plan Dialogue 2 for Public		
Scribe, IC	Review Draft Report, Edit Report	Draft Report			
Scribe, Editor, ED, ExBoD	Coach Publishing of Report	Final Report	Public learns TL Views		
of Economy & Community	Ex BoD Considers TL Report Recommendations for Economy & Community	Combine with all 3 Dialogue Rounds			

Assumptions:
1. 3 rounds of dialogue - each with Thought Leaders, Public, Policy Makers
2. Each round has a theme-pair. Round 1 is Economy & Community
3. ExBoD stewards the visioning process
4. ED coordinates local resources with IC coaching
5. Handouts and report publication coordinated by ED with local printers

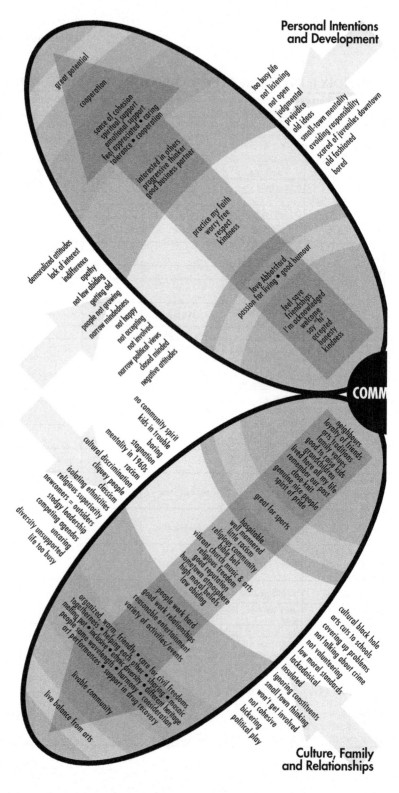

APPENDIX K: ABBOTSFORD VALUES FLOWER MAP

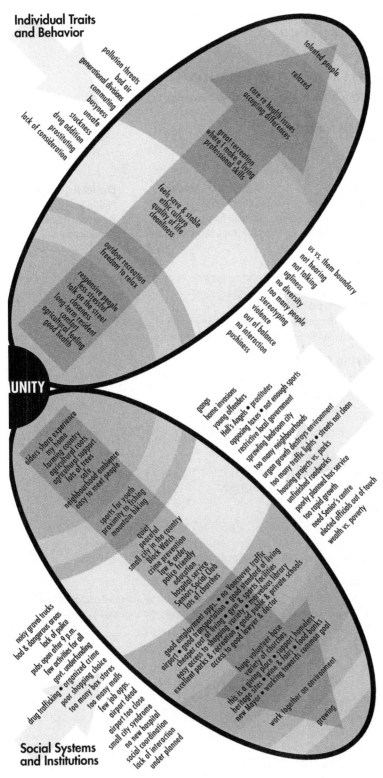

Individual Traits and Behavior

pollution threats
bad air
generational divisions
commuting
busyness
unsafe
stuckness
drug addiction
prostituting
lack of consideration

talented people
relaxed
care re health issues
accepting differences
great recreation
where I make a living
professional skills
feels save & stable
ethic culture
quality of life
cleanliness

outdoor recreation
freedom to relax
responsive people
less stressful
folk on the street
closeness
long-term resident
comfort
agricultural feeling
good health

us vs. them boundary
not hearing
not talking
ugliness
no diversity
too many people
stereotyping
violence
out of balance
no interaction
pushiness

UNITY

elders share experience
my home
farming country
agricultural roots
agricultural support
lots of trees
safe
neighbourhood ambience
easy to meet people

sports for youth
proximity to fishing
mountain biking

quiet
peaceful
small city in the country
Block Watch
crime prevention
law & order
police friendly
education
hospital service
Seniors Social Club
lots of churches

gangs
home invasions
young offenders
Hell's Angels • prostitutes
opposing taxes • not enough sports
restrictive local government
sprawling bedroom city
too many neighbourhoods
urban growth destroys environment
too many traffic lights • streets not clean
housing projects vs. parks
unfinished roadworks
poorly planned bus service
too rapid growth
need Senior's centre
elected officials out of touch
wealth vs. poverty

noisy gravel trucks
bad & dangerous areas
lack of police
pubs open after 9 p.m.
few activities for all
govt. underfunding
drug trafficking • organized crime
poor shopping choice
too many box stores
too many malls
few job opps.
airport dead
airport too close
small city syndrome
no new hospital
social coordination
lack of interaction
under planned

good employment opps. • no Vancouver traffic
airport • good transportation • good standard of living
cheaper cost of living • gym & sports facilities
easy access to shopping variety • marvelous library
excellent parks & recreation • good public & private schools
access to good lawyer & doctor

huge volunteer base
variety of churches
this is a giving place • support homeless
heritage sites • wine & fair • food banks
new Mayor • working towards common goal

work together on environment

growing

Social Systems and Institutions

Spiral Flower System Map of Abbotsford
© Marilyn Hamilton, 2003, 2006, 2016, TDG Holdings Inc. www. Integral

APPENDIX L: INTEGRATIVE DECISION-MAKING
(used with permission from HolacracyOne)

Governance Meetings

HOLACRACY®
v4.0

1

Check-in
One at a time. Call out distractions, get present, here and now.

2

Administrative Concerns
Account for time allotted, hard stops, breaks, etc.

3

Build Agenda
Build agenda of tensions in process. One or two words per item.

4

Present proposal – Proposer only, discussion to get to a proposal
This proposer can describe a tension and state a proposal to resolve it. Or the proposer can request discussion to help craft a proposal (not build consensus.)

Clarifying Questions – Anyone asks, proposer answers; repeat
Anyone can ask questions to better understand the proposal, not to convey opinions. The proposer can respond or say "not specified".

Reaction Round – One at a time, everyone speaks except proposer.
One at a time, each person reacts to the proposal as they see fit. No response.

Amend & Clarify – Only proposer speaks
The proposer can optionally clarify the intent of the proposal or amend it based on the reactions, if desired. No discussion allowed.

Objection Round – One at a time, everyone speaks including proposer.
The Facilitator asks: "Do you see any reasons why adopting this proposal would cause harm or move us backwards?" (an Objection"). Objections are stated, tested, and captured without discussion; the proposal is adopted if none surface.

Integration – Mostly objector & proposer speak; others can help.
Focus on each Objection one at a time. The goal is to craft an amended proposal that would not cause the Objection, but that would still address the proposer's tension. Once all are integrated, go back to the Objection Round.

5

Closing Round
Each person can share a closing reflection to improve next meetings. No discussion.

©2014 HolacracyOne, LLC   Version 4.0(b)   holacracy.org

REFERENCES

Abbotsford Team, W. I. C. W. P. (2009a). *Food for Thought, Summary Proposal, Demonstration Project.* Retrieved from SUCCESS, Abbotsford, BC:

Abbotsford Team, W. I. C. W. P. (2009b). *Values Mapping and Integral Vital Signs Monitor, Summary Proposal, Knowledge Development and Exchange Project.* Retrieved from Abbotsford:

Abrams, N. E., & Primack, J. R. (2006). *The View from the Centre of the Universe: Discovering our Extraordinary Place in the Cosmos.* New York: Riverhead Books, Penguin Group.

Adger, N., Aggarwal, P., Argawala, S., Alcamo, J., & etal. (2007). *Climate Change 2007: Impacts, Adaptation and Vulnerability, Summary for Policy Makers.* (2). IPCC Secretariat Retrieved from http://www.ipcc.ch/.

Adizes, I. (1999). *Managing Corporate Lifecycles.* Paramus, NJ: Prentice Hall Press.

Adizes, I. (2006). The Secrets of the Corporate Lifecycle. Retrieved from http://www.adizes.com/

Alley, R., Bernsten, T., Bindoff, N. L., Chen, Z., & etal. (2007). *Climate Change 2007: The Physical Science Basis, Summary for Policy Makers.* (1). IPCC Secretariat Retrieved from http://www.ipcc.ch/.

anon. Gross National Happiness Index. Retrieved May 23, 2016, from Wikipedia https://en.wikipedia.org/wiki/Gross_National_Happiness

anon. (2004). *Logic Model Development Guide: Using Logic Models to Bring Together Planning, Evaluation and Action*

anon. (2009). *40 Developmental Assets in Abbotsford (Grades 8–12)—2009 Survey (5384 Students).* Retrieved from Minneapolis, MN: http://www.search-institute.org/content/40-developmental-assets-adolescents-ages-12-18

anon. (2010). Canadian Institutes of Health Research, Natural Sciences and Engineering Research Council of Canada, and Social Sciences and Humanities Research Council of Canada TCPS2: Tri-Council policy statement: Ethical conduct for research involving humans. Retrieved May 16, 2016 http://www.ethics.gc.ca/pdf/eng/tcps2/TCPS_2_FINAL_Web.pdf

anon. (2013). *Mature Neighbourhood Strategy, Preliminary Consultation Program, Summary Report.* Retrieved from Strathcona County, Alberta, Canada:

anon. (2016a). Action Research. Retrieved May 16, 2016 https://en.wikipedia.org/wiki/Action_research

anon. (2016b). City of Character. Retrieved accessed August 19, 2016 from Abbotsford Youth Commission http://www.abbyyouth.com/uroc-awards/ accessed June 23, 2016

anon. (nd). *Logic Model Workbook*

Argyris, M., & Schön, D. (1974). *Theory in practice: Increasing professional effectiveness.* San Francisco: Jossey-Bass.

Barker, T., Bashmakov, I., Bernstein, L., Bogner, J., & etal. (2007). *Climate Change 2007: Mitigation of Climate Change, Summary for Policy Makers.* (3). IPCC Secretariat Retrieved from http://www.ipcc.ch/.

Beck, D. (2000a). *MeshWORKS™: A Second Tier Perspective & Process.* The Spiral Dynamics Group. Denton , TX.

Beck, D. (2000b). *Stages of Social Development: The Cultural Dynamics that Spark Violence, Spread Prosperity and Shape Globalization.* Paper presented at the State of the World Forum, New York.

Beck, D. (2001). *Human capacities in the integral age: How value systems shape organizational productivity, national prosperity & global transformation.* Paper presented at the International Productivity Conference, Singapore. http://www.integralworld.net/beck7.html

Beck, D. (2002a). *The Color of Constellations: A Spiral Dynamics Perspective on Human Drama.* Paper presented at the Bert Hellinger Constellation Conference, Germany.

Beck, D. (2002b). *Spiral Dynamics in the Integral Age*. Paper presented at the Spiral Dynamics integral, Level I, Vancouver, BC.

Beck, D. (2003, February). [private discussion].

Beck, D. (2004). *Natural Designs and MeshWORKS™: Creating our Region's Tomorrow through Second Tier Leadership, Organizational Foresight and Integral Alliances.* Paper presented at the Spiral Dynamics integral, Level 2, Natural Designs, Calgary, Alberta.

Beck, D. (2007a). The Meshworks Foundation: a New approach to Philanthropy. Retrieved from http://www.humanemergencemiddleeast.org/meshworks-foundation-philanthropy.html

Beck, D. (2007b, December 5, 2007). [Personal Communication re Meshweaving].

Beck, D. (2010). Natural Designs for Meshworking. Denton, Texas: Institute for Values & Culture.

Beck, D., & Cowan, C. (1996). *Spiral Dynamics: Mastering Values, Leadership and Change*. Malden, MA: Blackwell Publishers.

Beck, D., & Linscott, G. (2006). *The Crucible: Forging South Africa's Future* (hardcover ed.). Columbia, MD: Cherie Beck, Coera.us, Center for Human Emergence.

Benjamin, A., & McCullum, B. (2009). *A World Without Bees*. London, UK: Guardian Books.

Berg, B. L. (2004). *Qualitative Research Methods for the Social Sciences* (5th ed.). Boston: Pearson.

Bernstein, L., Bosch, P., Canziana, O., Chen, Z., & etal. (2007). *Climate Change 2007: Synthesis Report*. IPCC Secretariat Retrieved from http://www.ipcc.ch/publications_and_data/publications_ipcc_fourth_assessment_report_synthesis_report.htm.

Bets, J., Fourman, M., Merry, P., & Voorhoeve, A.-M. (2008). *Developing a Roadmap and Meshwork for Millennium Development Goal 5: Building a template for in-country implementation and a global collaborative network to accelerate achievement of MDG5.* Center for Human Emergence, Netherlands. The Hague. Retrieved from Gaiaspace, Meshworking, Private

Bjerga, A. (2007, June 30). Mysterious ailment kills millions of bees in U.S.; Disorder poses a $75billion threat to agriculture, Washington says. *Vancouver Sun*.

Bleys, R. L. A. W., Cowen, T., Groen, G. J., Hillen, B., & Ibrahim, N. B. N. (1996). Perivascular Nerves of the Human Basal Cerebral Arteries I. Topographical Distribution(16), 1034–1047. Retrieved from http://www.nature.com/jcbfm/index.html doi:10.1097/00004647-199609000-00029

Bloom, H. (2000). *The Global Brain: The Evolution of Mass Mind from the Big Bang to the 21st Century.* New York: John Wiley & Son Inc.

Bloom, H. (2010). *The Genius of the Beast: A Radical Revision of Capitalism.* Amherst, NY: Prometheus Books.

Bolan, K. (2009). Mission Abbotsford Highest Capita Homicide Rate. *Vancouver Sun.* Retrieved from http://www.vancouversun.com/entertainment/Abbotsford+Mission+highest+capita+homicide+rate +Canada/1812183/story.html

Burns, R. (2004) New York. Boston: PBS Home Video.

Bushe, G. (2001). *Clear Leadership.* Palo Alto, CA: Davies-Black Publishing.

Bushe, G. (nd). What is Appreciative Inquiry. Retrieved from http://www.gervasebushe.ca/appinq.htm

Capra, F. (1996). *The Web of Life: A New Scientific Understanding of Living Systems.* New York: Anchor Books, Doubleday.

Coghlan, D., & Brannick, T. (2007). *Doing Action Research in Your Own Organization* (2nd ed.). Thousand Oaks, CA: Sage Publications Ltd.

Constantine, D. (2006). They Look Alike, but There's a Little Matter of Size. *Science Times,* (August 15, 2016), F4. Retrieved from https://engineering.purdue.edu/ZhangLab/news/2006-poincare.pdf

Cook, D. (2005). *The Natural Step: Towards A Sustainable Society.* Totnes, Devon, UK: Green Books.

Cooperrider, D., & Whitney, D. (1999). *Appreciative Inquiry: Collaborating for Change.* San Francisco: Berrett-Koehler.

Creswell, J. (1998). *Qualitative Inquiry and Research Design: Choosing From Among Five Traditions.* Thousand Oaks, CA: Sage Publications Inc.

Cummins, R. A., Eckersley, R., Lo, S. K., Davern, M., Hunter, B., & Okerstrom, E. (2004). *The Australian Unity Well-being Index: An Update.* Paper presented at the Proceedings of the 5th Australian Conference on Quality of Life, Deakin University, Melbourne.

Dale, A. (2001). *At The Edge: Sustainable Development in the 21st Century.* Vancouver: UBC Press.

Dale, A., & Onyx, J. (Eds.). (2005). *A Dynamic Balance: Social Capital and Sustainable Community Development*. Vancouver: UBC Press.

De Landa, M. (1995). Homes: Meshwork or Hierarchy? http://www.media-matic.net/article-200.5956.html. Special: Home issue.

De Landa, M. (1997). *A Thousand Years of Nonlinear History*. New York: Zone Books.

De Landa, M. (2006). *A New Philosophy of Society: Assemblage Theory and Social Complexity*. London: Continuum.

DeKay, M. (2011). *Integral Sustainable Design: Transformative Perspectives*. London, UK: Earthscan.

Douglas, D. C., & Hamilton, M. (2013a). Knowing Cities: The Knowing Field and the Emergence of Integral City Intelligence. *The Knowing Field*(22), 25–32.

Douglas, D. C., & Hamilton, M. (2013b). The Knowing City: The Knowing Field and the Emergence of City Well-being. *Flying the Kites: Empowering Organizational and Societal Development Through a Systemic Perspective*. Amsterdam, Netherlands: Infosyon, Bert Hellinger Instituut, Nederland.

Eoyang, G., & Olson, E. (2001). *Facilitating Organization Change: Lessons from Complexity Science*. San Francisco: Jossey-Bass Pfeiffer.

Esbjörn-Hargens, S. (2015a, 2015). *Integral Theory Conference 2015*. Paper presented at the ITC 2105: Integral Impacts Using Integrative Metatheories to Catalyze Effective Change, Sonoma State University.

Esbjörn-Hargens, S. (2015b). *MetaIntegral Four Quadrant Impact Analysis*. Paper presented at the Integral Theory Conference 2015, Sonoma State University, California.

Esbjörn-Hargens, S., & Zimmerman, M. (2009). *Integral Ecology: Uniting Multiple Perspectives on the Natural World*. Boston: Shambhala Publications Inc.

Florida, R. (2008). *Who's Your City: How the Creative Economy is Making Where to Live the Most Important Decision of Your Life*. Toronto: Random House Canada.

Fourman, M., & Merry, P. (2009a). Case Study: Developing a roadmap and meshwork for reducing global CO_2 emissions by 80% by 2020. *in Slide Share*. Retrieved from http://www.slideshare.net/ website: http://www.slideshare.net/morelfourman/case-study-meshwork-2020-climate-leadership-campaign-final

Fourman, M., & Merry, P. (2009b). Meshworking—a support service for cross-cutting sustainability programs. *in Slide Share*. Retrieved from http://www.

slideshare.net/ website: http://www.slideshare.net/mvanmarrewijk/
meshworking-for-sustainability-090320-kopie?qid=cf93a0ba-2a70-40
e3-b442-33ece48cb2d5&v=&b=&from_search=1

Fourman, M., Reynolds, C., Firus, K., & D'Ulizia, A. (2008). *Online tools for developing Sustainability and Resilience: Methodology, experience and cost effective solutions from* MIDIR EU *Research Project*. Retrieved from London, UK:

Francis, P. (2015). *Encylical Letter Laudato Si: On Care for Our Common Home*. Rome: The Holy See.

Freire, P., & Horton, M. (1990). *We Make the Road by Walking*. Philadelphia: Temple Press.

Gasque, A. W., & Jackson, P. (Eds.). (2011). *Publication Manual of the American Psychological Association* (Sixth ed.): American Psychological Association.

Gladwell, M. (2002). *The Tipping Point: How Little Things Can Make a Big Difference*. New York: Back Bay Books.

Glesne, C. (1999). *Becoming Qualitative Researchers: An Introduction*. New York: Longman.

Graves, C. (1974). Human Nature Prepares for a Momentous Leap *The Futurist*, 8(2), 72–78.

Graves, C. (2003). *Levels of Human Existence: Transcription of a Seminar at Washington School of Psychiatry, Oct. 16, 1971*. Santa Barbara: Eclet Publishing.

Graves, C. (2005). *The Never Ending Quest: A Treatise on an Emergent Cyclical Conception of Adult Behavioral Systems and Their Development*. Santa Barbara, CA: ECLET Publishing.

Gunderson, L. C., & Holling, C. S. (Eds.). (2002). *Panarchy: Understanding Transformations in Human and Natural Systems* Washington, DC: Island Press.

Haidt, J. (2006). *The Happiness Hypothesis: Finding Modern Truth in Ancient Wisdom*. Cambridge, MA: Perseus Books Group.

Hameroff, S., Huston, T., & Pitney, J. (2010, April, 2010). Finiding Spirit in the Fabric of Space & Time: An Exploration of Quantum Consciousness. *EnlightenNext, Spring/Summer* 2010.

Hamilton, M. (1999). *The Berkana Community of Conversations: A Study of Leadership Skill Development and Organizational Leadership Practices in a Self-Organizing Online Microworld* Vol. PhD. *Thesis for Faculty of Administration and Management, Columbia Pacific University* (pp. 367). Retrieved from http://dissertation.

com/book.php?method=ISBN&book=1581123302 doi:http://www.
universal-publishers.com/book.php?method=ISBN&book=1581123302

Hamilton, M. (2003a). Abbotsford Values Systems Flower Map (Graphical Data). Retrieved July 24, 2008 http://www.integralcity.com/files/Spiral.flower.icity.pdf

Hamilton, M. (2003b). *Integral Community: Lenses, Values and Indicators for Maple Leaf Meme Maps.* manuscript. Abbotsford, BC.

Hamilton, M. (2007). Approaching Homelessness: An Integral Reframe. *World Futures: The Journal of General Evolution, Volume 63(2)*, 107–126.

Hamilton, M. (2008a). *Integral City: Evolutionary Intelligences for the Human Hive.* Gabriola Island BC: New Society Publishers.

Hamilton, M. (2008b). *Integral Methods from the Margins: Finding Myself in the Research—A Retrospective of Integral Leadership Development Methods Using Online Dialogue Analysis, a Competency Development Framework and Action Research.* Paper presented at the Conference—Integral Theory in Action: Serving Self, Community and Kosmos, John F. Kennedy University.

Hamilton, M. (2010a). *Mapping the Values of Abbotsford and Developing a Prototype for an Integral Vital Signs Monitor of City Well-being* Retrieved from Victoria, BC, Canada:

Hamilton, M. (2010b). *Meshworking Integral Intelligences for Resilient Environments; Enabling Order and Creativity in the Human Hive.* Paper presented at the Enacting an Integral Future Conference 2010, Pleasant Hill, CA.

Hamilton, M. (2012a). Integral Spirituality in the Human Hive: A Primer. *Trialog, 2010(4)*, 10–17.

Hamilton, M. (2012b). *Meshworking Evolutionary Intelligence for the Human Hive* Paper presented at the Buildings Sustainable Communities 5, Kelowna, BC.

Hamilton, M., & Dale, A. (2007). *Sustainable Infrastructure Development: A Learning Framework.* Unpublished Work.

Hamilton, M., Douglas, D. C., Aurami, A., Beck, C., Arnott, J., Verhoove, A.-M., . . . Van Dongen, E. (2015). *The Fruits of Deep Design: How Integral City Harvested Pomegranate Impact at ITC2015.* Paper presented at the ITC 2105: Integral Impacts Using Integrative Metatheories to Catalyze Effective Change, Sonoma State University.

Hamilton, M., Douglas, D. C., Beck, C., Aurami, A., & Arnott, J. (2016). We-space, Integral City and the Knowing Field. In M. Brabant & O.

Gunnlaugson (Eds.), *Cohering the We Space: Developing Theory and Practice for Engaging Collective Emergence, Wisdom and Healing in Groups* (pp. 131–154). San Francisco: Integral Publishing House.

Hamilton, M., & Sanders, B. (2013). Learning Lhabitat: City-Zen-tricity: A Fractal Non-Local Leap Toward Kosmocentricity Taken With Integral Kosmopolitans on an Evolutionary Mission. *Integral Theory Conference 2013*. San Francisco: Metaintegral.

Hammond, S. A. (1996). *The Thin Book of Appreciative Inquiry:* Kodiak Consulting.

Holling, C. S. (2001). Understanding the Complexity of Economic, Ecological, and Social Systems *Ecosystems, Vol.* 4, pp. 390–405.

IntegralLife (Producer). (2010, May 14, 2010). An Integral Look at Holosync. [Realplayer, Powerpoint] Retrieved from http://s3.amazonaws.com/integral-life-elearning/Holosync/player.html

Johnson, B. (1996). *Polarity Management: Identifying and Managing Unsolvable Problems,* . Amherst,: HRD Press,.

Kegan, R. (1994). *In Over Our Heads: The Mental Demands of Modern Life.* Cambridge, MA: Harvard University Press.

Lama, D., & Cutler, H. (1998). *The Art of Happiness: A Handbook for Living.* New York: Riverhead Books.

Laszlo, E. (2004). *Science and the Akashic Field: An Integral Theory of Everything* (2007 ed.). Rochester, Vermont: Inner Traditions.

Laszlo, E. (2006a). *The Chaos Point: The World at the Crossroads.* Charlottesville, VA: Hampton Roads Publishing.

Laszlo, E. (2006b). *Science and the Reenchantment of the Cosmos: The Rise of the Integral Vision of Reality* Rochester, VT: Inner Traditions • Bear & Company.

Laszlo, E. (2006c). Ten Benchmarks of an Evolved Consciousness *The Chaos Point: The World at the Crossroads* (pp. pp. 80–81). Charlottesville, VA: Hampton Roads Publishing.

Ling, C., Dale, A., & Hanna, K. (2007). *Integrated Community Sustainability Planning Tool.* Retrieved from Victoria, BC:

Lovelock, J. (2009). *The Vanishing Face of Gaia.* New York: Harmony Books.

McTaggart, L. (2001). *The Field: The Quest for the Secret Force of the Universe.* New York: Harper Perennial.

Merriam, S. (2002). *Qualitative Research in Practice: Examples for Discussion and Analysis.* San Francisco: Jossey-Bass.

Miller, J. G. (1978). *Living Systems.* New York: McGraw-Hill Book Company.

Mitchell, E., & Williams, D. (2001). *The Way of the Explorer: An Apollo Astronaut's Journey Through the Material and Mystical Worlds* (2nd ed.). Buenos Aires: Richter Artes Graficas.

Montgomery, C. (2014). *Happy City: Transforming Our Lives Through Urban Design.* New York: Farrar, Straus and Giroux.

Palys, T. (1997). *Research Decisions; Quantitative and Qualitative Perspectives.* Toronto: Harcourt Brace Canada.

Park, C., Purcell, M., & Purkis, J. (2009). *Integrated Community Sustainability Planning.* Ottawa: The Natural Step.

Patton, M. Q. (2013). Utilization-Focused Evaluation (U-FE) Checklist. Retrieved from https://www.wmich.edu/ website: https://www.wmich.edu/sites/default/files/attachments/u350/2014/UFE_checklist_2013.pdf

Robertson, B. (2016). Holacracy How It Works. Retrieved from http://www.holacracy.org/how-it-works/

Robertson, R. (2011, January, 2011). Dreams of an Eco-Spiritual Futurist: A Conversation with British Sustainability Strategist Hardin Tibbs.

S.M.A.R.T Goals. (2016). Retrieved May 5, 2016, from Wikipedia https://en.wikipedia.org/wiki/SMART_criteria

Sandercock, L. (2000). When Strangers Become Neighbours: Managing Cities of Difference. *Planning Theory and Practice, 1*(1), 13–30.

Sandercock, L., & Lyssiotis, P. (2003). *Cosmopolis II: Mongrel Cities of the 21st Century.* London: Continuum International Publishing Group.

Scharmer, C. O. (2009). *Theory U: Learning from the Future as It Emerges.* San Francisco: Berrett-Koehler Publishers.

Schlitz, M. M., Vieten, C., & Amorok, T. (2007). *Living Deeply: The Art & Science of Transformation in Everyday Life.* Oakland, CA: New Harbinger Publications Inc.

Scott, J., & Bromley, R. (2013). *Envisioning Sociology: Victor Branford, Patrick Geddes, and the Quest for Social Reconstruction.* Albany, NY: Suny.

Senge, P., Scharmer, C. O., Jaworski, J., & Flowers, B. S. (2004). *Presence: Exploring Profound Change in People, Organizations and Society.* New York: Currency Doubleday.

Sheldrake, R. (1988). *The Presence of the Past: Morphic Resonance and the Habits of Nature* (1995 ed.). Rochester, Vermont: Park Street Press.

Sheldrake, R. (1999). *Dogs That Know When Their Owners Are Coming Home: And Other Unexplained Powers of Animals*. New York: Three Rivers Press.

Sheldrake, R. (2003). *The Sense of Being Stared At: And Other Aspects of the Extended Mind*. New York: Three Rivers Press.

Sheldrake, R. (2012). *Science Set Free*. New York: Deepak Chopra Books, Crown Publishing Group, Division of Random House.

Smyre, R. (2012). Building and Connecting Communities for the Future. *World Future Society* (July-August).

Stevenson, B., & Hamilton, M. (2001). How Does Complexity Inform Community? How does Community Inform Complexity? *Emergence*, 3(No. 2), pp.57—77.

Stringer, E. T. (1999). *Action Research: Second Edition*. Thousand Oaks, CA: Sage Publications Inc.

Stringer, E. T. (2014). *Action Research: Fourth Edition*. Thousand Oaks, CA: Sage Publications Inc.

Taylor, M. (2009). *Summary Report on the National Values Assessment for Canada*. Retrieved from Victoria, BC.

Torbert, W., & Associates (Eds.). (2004). *Action Inquiry: The Secret of Timely and Transforming Leadership*. San Francisco: Berrett-Koehler Publishes Inc.

Torbert, W. R. (2015). *Kinds of Inquiry, Power and Love Required for Developmentally Transforming Practice*. Paper presented at the Integral Theory Conference, 2015, Sonoma State University, Rohnert Park.

Torbert, W. R., Livne-Tarandach, R., Herdman-Barker, E., Nicolaides, A., & McCallum, D. (2008). *Developmental Action Inquiry:A Distinct Integral Theory That Actually Integrates Developmental Theory, Practice, and Research*. Paper presented at the Conference—Integral Theory In Action: Serving Self, Community and Kosmos, John F Kennedy University, Pleasant Hill, CA.

Tuckman, B. W., & Jensen, M. A. C. (1977). Stages of small group development revisited. *Group and Organizational Studies*, 2, 419–427.

Watkins, J. M., & Mohr, B. J. (2001). *Appreciative Inquiry: Change at the Speed of Imagination*. San Francisco: Jossey-Bass/Pfeiffer.

Wheatley, M., & Frieze, D. (2006). Using Emergence to Take Social Innovation to Scale. Retrieved from www.margaretwheatley.com

Whitney, D., & Trosten-Bloom, A. (2010). *The Power of Appreciative Inquiry: A Practical Guide to Positive Change* (2nd rev. ed.). San Francisco, Calif.: Berrett-Koehler.

Wight, I. (2002). *Place, Placemaking and Planning*. Paper presented at the ACSP, Baltimore.

Wight, I. (2011, November 11–14, 2011). [Personal Communication].

Wight, I. (2016a). Elevating Placemaking as Transformative Innovation: Professing Anew, Integrally *Elevating Placemaking*: Unpublished Work.

Wight, I. (2016b). [Personal Communication re place, Place, PLACE in response to deKay critique].

Wight, I. (2016c). Programs in Earth Literacies: 4 Part Course presented and facilitated by Ian Wight. Victoria, BC: Wight, Ian.

Wilber, K. (1995). *Sex, Ecology and Spirituality: the spirit of evolution*. Boston: Shambhala Publications Inc.

Wilber, K. (1996). *A Brief History of Everything,* . Boston,: Shambhala Publications Inc.

Wilber, K. (2000a). *Integral Psychology*. Boston: Shambhala Publications Inc.

Wilber, K. (2000b). *A Theory of Everything*. Boston: Shambhala Publications Inc.

Wilber, K. (2001). *Marriage of Sense and Soul*. New York: Random House.

Wilber, K. (2006). *Integral Spirituality*. Boston: Shambhala Publications Inc.

Wilber, K. (2007). *The Integral Vision*. Boston: Shambhala Publications Inc.

Wilber, K., Patten, T., Leonard, A., & Morelli, M. (2008). *Integral Life Practice: A 21st Century Blueprint for Physcial Health, Emotional Balance, Mental Clarity and Spiritual Awakening* (1 ed.). Boston, MA: Integral Books.

Wills, E. H., Hamilton, M., & Islam, G. (2007a). *Subjective Well-being in Cities: Individual or Collective? A Cross Cultural Analysis*. Paper presented at the Well-being in International Development Conference, University of Bath.

Wills, E. H., Hamilton, M., & Islam, G. (2007b). *Subjective Well-being in Bogotá (B), Belo Horizonte (BH) and Toronto (T): A Subjective Indicator of Quality of Life for Cities*. Retrieved from Bogotá:

Wood, R. L., & Bruitzman, G. (2016). A Thrivability Scenario: Toward Thriving, Integrative Human Beings in a Thriving, Integrative, Global World. *Journal of Future Studies,* (20(3)), 55–78. Retrieved from http://jfsdigital. org/wp-content/uploads/2016/11/01_Articles04_Athriveability.pdf

INDEX

O

organ of reflection
  Gaia 240, 244–245

P

PAEI
  Adizes 93, 242, 246
Panarchy 47, 74, 124, 243, 332
perspectives 29–31, 35, 37–39, 90,
    101, 107, 114, 131, 155, 161, 173,
    176, 183, 196, 220, 233, 256,
    272, 313, 330, 359, 373–374
Placecaring xxviii, xxxviii, xxxix, 1,
    39, 56, 66, 85, 92, 99–100, 103,
    109, 118–119, 124, 127–128,
    132, 137, 141, 143, 146, 148–
    150, 154, 161–162, 191, 241,
    249, 256, 261, 283, 291, 294,
    299–301, 303–304, 306, 308,
    320, 322, 334
Placemaking xxviii, xxxviii–xxxix, 1,
    39, 56, 66, 85, 92, 99–101, 103,
    109, 118–119, 124, 127–128,
    132, 137, 141, 143, 146, 148–
    150, 154, 161–162, 191, 241,
    249, 256, 261, 283, 291, 294,
    299–301, 303–304, 306, 308,
    320, 322, 334
polarities 68, 70–71, 155, 170, 355
Polarities 71, 74, 83, 90
Policy Makers
  dialogues 167, 171, 174–175, 178,
    256
Pop-Up 190, 193–195, 204–209, 211,
    212–213, 313, 315, 317, 319
Practitioner
  Activator xxxii, xxxiv, xlii, 12, 23,
    40, 59, 77–78, 94, 120, 137, 162,
    183, 201–202, 212, 216, 234,
    263, 281, 295, 300, 313, 322

Producers
  Human Hive 45–46, 57, 109, 145,
    242, 246, 251, 279, 281, 320
prototype 18, 98, 118, 127, 131, 135,
    187, 206, 215–216, 218–220,
    222, 228, 231, 233–235, 258,
    301, 306, 307, 313, 315, 319, 359
prototyping 15, 17–18, 21–22, 189–
    192, 195, 202–205, 207, 209–
    213, 215–216, 219, 233–235,
    262, 286, 294, 313, 315, 317, 319
Public
  dialogues 166–167, 171, 174–179,
    256–257, 276
Purpose for the city 71

Q

Quadrants xxiv, xxxviii, 6, 81, 94,
    115, 146–148, 150, 194, 219,
    335–336
qualitative xl, 107–108, 111–112, 114,
    117, 124, 127, 232, 241, 271, 280,
    284, 289, 292, 294, 308, 355
Quality of Life 66, 69–70, 81, 83–85,
    94, 110, 113, 120, 170, 174, 196,
    309, 316
quantitative xl, 108, 112–114, 124, 127,
    241, 280, 289, 292, 294, 355

R

Reflective-Action xl
Resilience 146, 190, 333
Resilient City 2, 190, 302–304, 322,
    344
Resilient City Locator 344
Resource Allocators
  Human Hive 46, 51, 57, 109, 145,
    150, 159, 242, 246, 248, 251–
    252, 259, 279, 281, 320
Richard Florida 97, 305

CPSIA information can be obtained
at www.ICGtesting.com
Printed in the USA
BVOW10s0808300517

485397BV00013B/51/P